elBulli
2005
Catalogue

elBulli
2005
Catalogue

Ferran Adrià
Juli Soler
Albert Adrià

2005

Cocktails

1090 Margarita 2005

1091 Strawberry frozen air with raspberry crisp-LYO

1092 Peach/nitro-sangria.../...Watermelon/nitro-gin

1093 White sangria in suspension

1094 Liquid/vermouth

Snacks

1095 Spherical-I green olives

1096 Menthol watermelon-CRU

1097 Five pepper melon-CRU/melon-LYO with fresh herbs and green almonds

1098 'Tramuntana' peach paper

1099 Cantonese *músico*: mixed/pine nuts

1100 Nutmeg-flavoured popcorn with Reypenaer

1101 Marshmallow: Parmesan/pine nuts

1102 3Ds with ras-el-hanout spices and lemon basil sprouts

1103 Hazelnut meringues

1104 Mango and black olive discs

1105 Carrot ribbons with lemon verbena, ginger and liquorice

1106 Parmesan-LYO macaroon with lemon and wild strawberries-LYO

1107 Black olive Oreo with double cream

1108 Grilled sole skin, garlic flower and parsley

1109 Arlette *ibérica*

1110 Half-D cherries in yogurt

1111 Malt flour air-baguette with caramelised cinnamon caramel

1112 Virgin olive oil caramel spring

1113 Bitter almond, yogurt and elderflower quinoa crunch

1114 Light beetroot meringue with *kefir* and Fisherman's Friend

1115 'Tramuntana' passion fruit paper with Gorgonzola

1116 Roquefort-LYO tart with soursop

1117 Pumpkin oil sweet

1118 Thai nymph

1119 Coriander 'Chanquete'

1120 Garrapi-nitro pistachio

1121 Oyster with its pearl and ham cream

1122 Mandarin flower tempura

1123 Samphire tempura with saffron and oyster cream

1124 Belly of mackerel in batter, lemon air and *chuen-kai* with sesame

1125 Steamed brioche: mozzarella and mock tartufo/veal marrow and caviar/rose-scented mozzarella

1126 Melon with ham 2005

1127 Spherical-I mozzarella

1128 Malt flour and butter ravioli with sea urchin and lime zest

1129 Clams in Earl Grey tea, pink grapefruit and black sesame

Tapas

1130 Thaw 2005

1131 Earth 2005

1132 Almond kernels with elderflower, in egg yolk and lemon

1133 Pistachio-LYO with black truffle jellied consommé and mandarin air

1134 Carrot-LYO foam with hazelnut foam-air and Córdoba spices

1135 Jellied *tucupi* consommé with frozen passion fruit crumbs

1136 *Músico*

1137 Passion for olives

1138 Carrot-LYO desert

1139 Soy sauce nest with sesame, miso and wasabi sweets

1140 Dulse nest with sea urchins and lime caviar

1141 'Folie' salad

1142 Sprouting quinoa with *tucupi* and *kefir* chicken 'tripe'

1143 Green almond *empanadilla* with Szechuan button and cucumber balls in liquorice and yuzu

1144 Thai soup with coconut tofu

1145 Spherical-I yogurt nodules with ice plant, capers and black butter

1146 Peas and ham with creamy fresh mint and eucalyptus air ravioli

1147 Warm murex snails with *kikurage*, hot vinaigrette and basil-flavoured kombu

1148 Rock mussels with seaweed and fresh herbs

1149 Tender pine nut risotto in pine nut oil

1150 White asparagus with virgin olive oil capsules and lemon marshmallow

1151 Green almond and tamarillo crunch, in eucalyptus, with mangosteen

1152 Baby broad bean *albóndigas* in their juice with broad bean flowers

1153 Walnuts in their cream, hot yogurt jelly, apple velvet and mint aroma

1154 Green walnuts[3], smoked tea and wasabi

1155 Stewed walnuts with daisy buds, beurre noisette air-foam and mint aroma

1156 Warm spherical dashi cloud with fairy ring mushrooms flavoured with purple shiso, sesame and yuzu

1157 Sea tomatoes

1158 Warty venus clam with watermelon and yuzu in a saffron and kombu broth

1159 Earthy

1160 Monkfish liver fondue with ponzu and white sesame-flavoured kumquat

1161 Almonds/beans with small squid, daisy buds, mustard, bitter almond and fennel

1162 Sweetcorn snow egg with Mexican broth and *coquina* clams

1163 Creamy cannellone with Spanish bacon, anchovy caviar and black olive

1164 Macaroni with egg yolk, miso, sesame and green shiso

1165 Mock tartufo of Iberian pork and green olive

1166 Parmesan-LYO mini French toasts with onion-flavoured ham fat, egg yolk and coffee

1167 Pavé of St George's mushrooms with samphire and *kefir*

1168 Cep blocks with hot cep jelly, cat's claw and hazelnut cream

1169 Papillote of tomatoes in mastic, almond and tarragon oil and kumquat sorbet

1170 Baby snails in court-bouillon with crab escabeche and amaranth with fennel

1171 Belly of mackerel in chicken escabeche with onions and vinegar caviar

1172 Grilled oysters with pine jelly, oyster cream and borage shoots

1173 Langoustine with quinoa[3]

1174 Lobster curry with granadilla air-foam and cardamom

1175 Baby monkfish with lemon-scented egg yolk, daisy buds, pine nut oil and beurre noisette

1176 Sole with puffed amaranth, Córdoba air, coriander-flavoured amaranth/popcorn, Chinese garlic flowers and lemon

1177 Turtle dove with tuna medulla, enokis and samphire

1178 Tandoori chicken wings with borage shoots, oyster cream and frothy *mató* cheese

1179 Lamb's brains with sea urchin and sea grape

1180 Rack of Iberian pork with Thai aroma

1181 Red cabbage with *jamón ibérico* lentils

Pre desserts

1182 Tennessee infusion

1183 Peach liquid

1184 Spherical-I mozzarella/burrata with fir honey, fruit-CRU

1185 Hot passion fruit marshmallow, fresh mint coconut milk and chocolate pearls

1186 Coulant/soufflé of granadilla with cardamom toffee

Desserts

1187 Peach-CRU in amaretto with electric ice cream

1188 Mango-puzzle with frozen elderflower wedge and coconut foam

1189 Red variation

1190 Strawberries or roses?

1191 Mont Blanc

1192 Pea jelly with banana and lime ice cream

1193 Thai ice cream nigiri with lime marshmallow

1194 Figs with light rose and white chocolate meringue powder

1195 Light honey meringue with apple-CRU and rosemary and cinnamon ice cream

1196 Chocolate air-LYO with crisp raspberry sorbet and eucalyptus water ice

1197 Apricot palet with milk chocolate and passion fruit ice cream

1198 Frozen chocolate and hazelnut praline crumbs with passion fruit caramel

1199 Des/sert

Morphings

1200 Pineapple/fennel

1201 Spherical-I cherries with yogurt and elderflower

1202 Daiquiri, coffee and caramel nigiri

1203 Yogurt and raspberry/passion fruit and liquorice/coffee and soursop *mochi*

1204 Light coffee and chocolate meringue slice

1205 Honey Filipino biscuits

1206 Chestnut *ningyo-yaki*

1207 Passion fruit tree

1208 After Eight marshmallow

1209 Palet-croquant: passion fruit, chocolate and hazelnut/white chocolate and macadamia nut

1210 Strawberry iced lolly with eucalyptus Peta Zetas

1211 Frozen truffles: raspberry/passion fruit

1212 Chocolate coral

1213 Fruit crisp-LYO in chocolate

1214 Fruit-LYO in chocolate

Cocktails
1090–1094

1090   Margarita 2005

1091   Strawberry frozen air with raspberry crisp-LYO

1092   Peach/nitro-sangria …/… Watermelon/nitro-gin

1093   White sangria in suspension

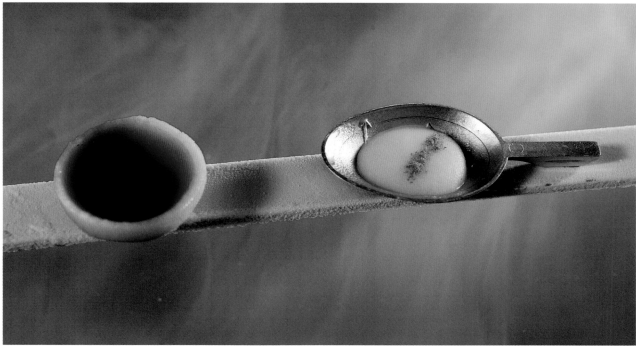

1094　Liquid/vermouth

Snacks

1095–1129

1095 Spherical-I green olives

1096   Menthol watermelon-CRU

1097   Five pepper melon-CRU/melon-LYO with fresh herbs and green almonds

1098   'Tramuntana' peach paper

1099 Cantonese *músico*: mixed/pine nuts

1100   Nutmeg-flavoured popcorn with Reypenaer

1101   Marshmallow: Parmesan/pine nuts

1102   3Ds with ras-el-hanout spices and lemon basil sprouts

1103 Hazelnut meringues

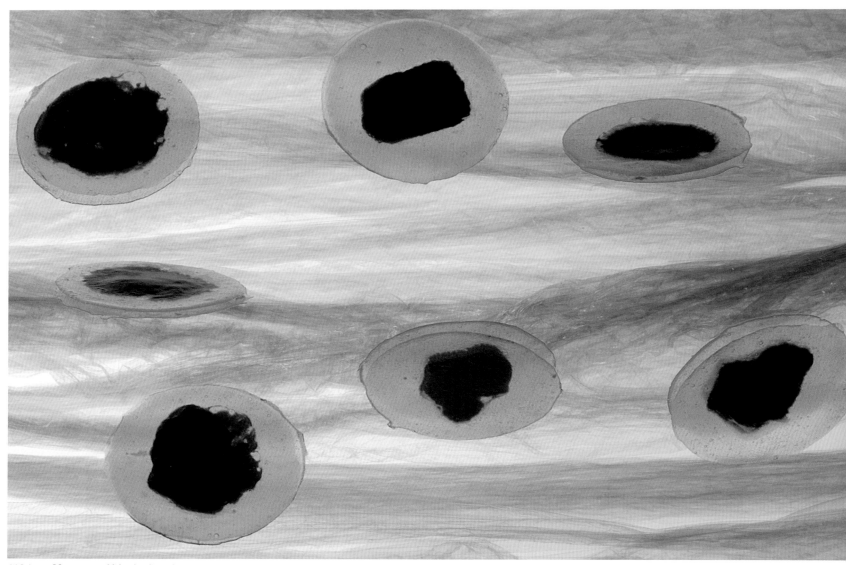

1104   Mango and black olive discs

1105 Carrot ribbons with lemon verbena, ginger and liquorice

1106   Parmesan-LYO macaroon with lemon and wild strawberries-LYO

1107   Black olive Oreo with double cream

1108　Grilled sole skin, garlic flower and parsley

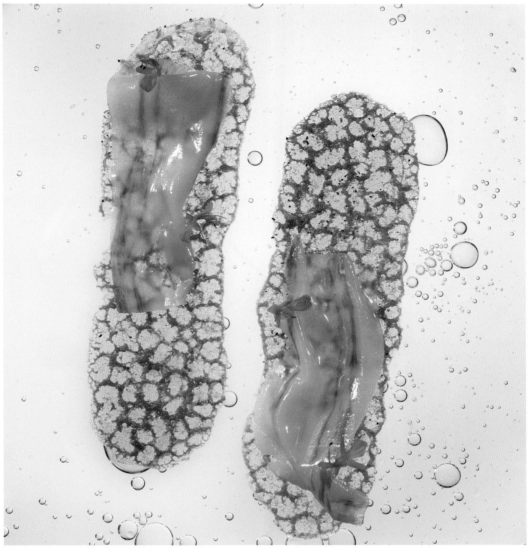

1109   Arlette *ibérica*

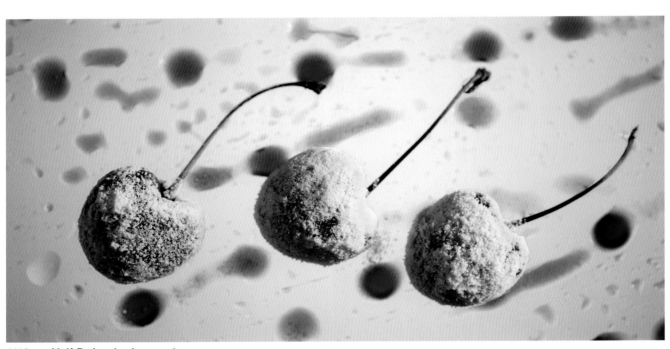

1110   Half-D cherries in yogurt

1111   **Malt flour air-baguette with caramelised cinnamon caramel**

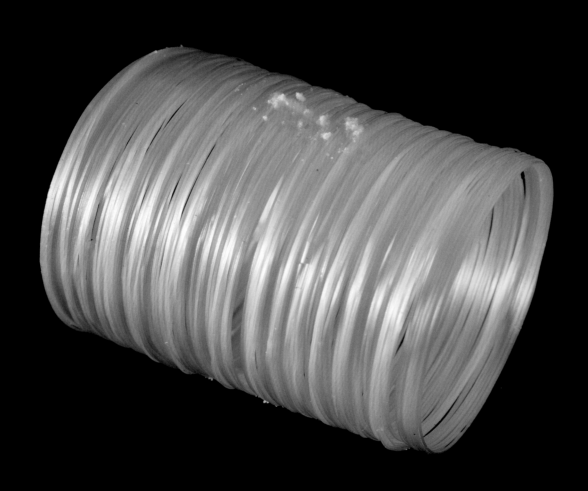

1112   Virgin olive oil caramel spring

1113   Bitter almond, yogurt and elderflower quinoa crunch

1114   Light beetroot meringue with *kefir* and Fisherman's Friend

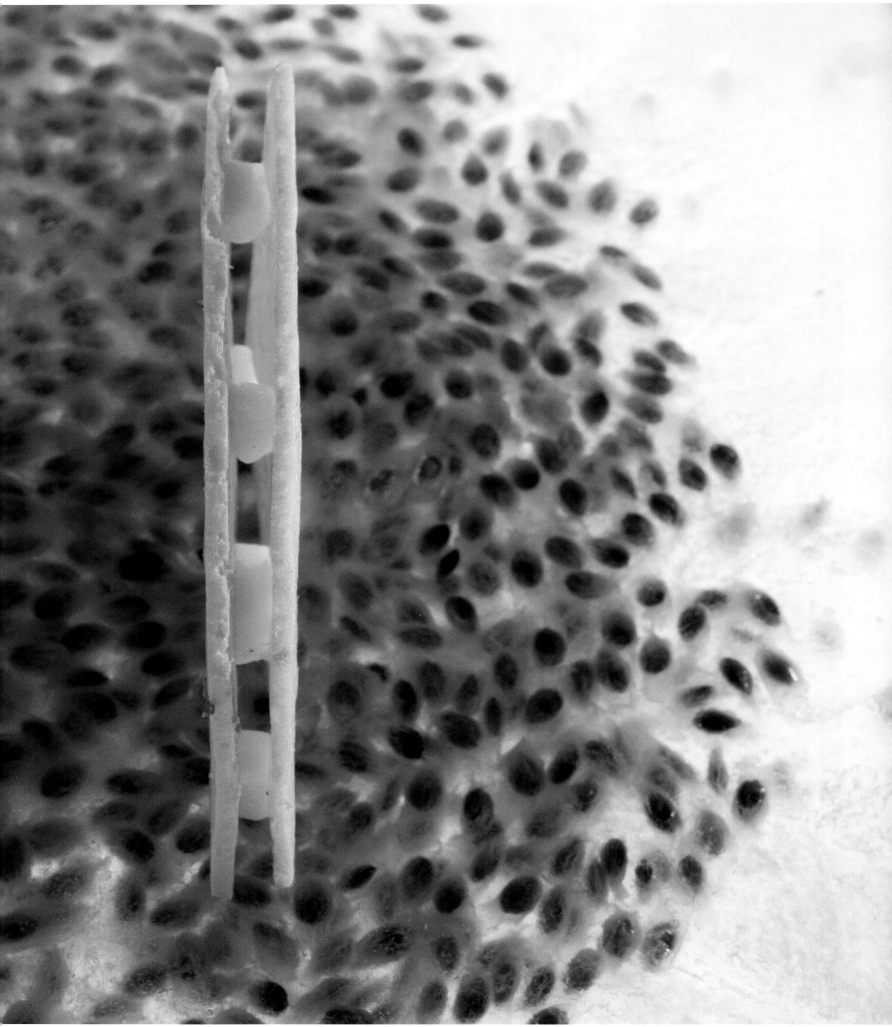

1115   'Tramuntana' passion fruit paper with Gorgonzola

1116   Roquefort-LYO tart with soursop

1117   Pumpkin oil sweet

1118   Thai nymph

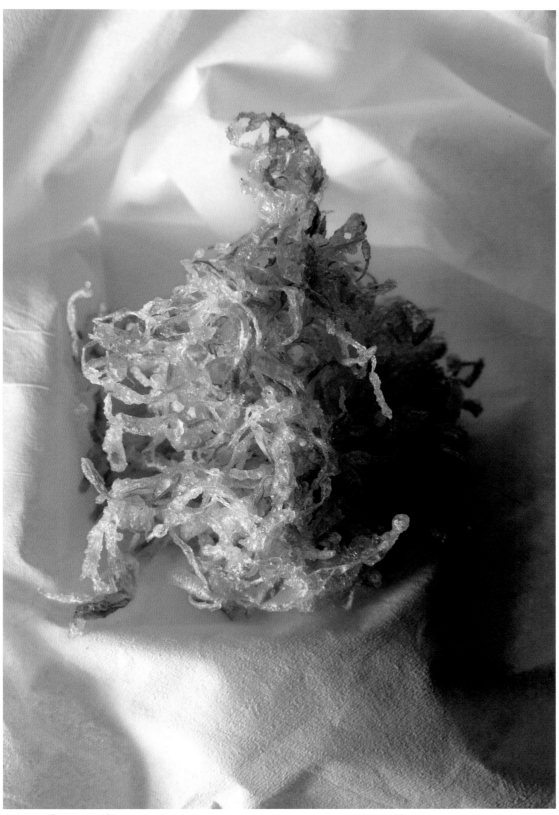

1119   Coriander 'Chanquete'

1120   Garrapi-nitro pistachio

1121   Oyster with its pearl and ham cream

1122   Mandarin flower tempura

1123   **Samphire tempura with saffron and oyster cream**

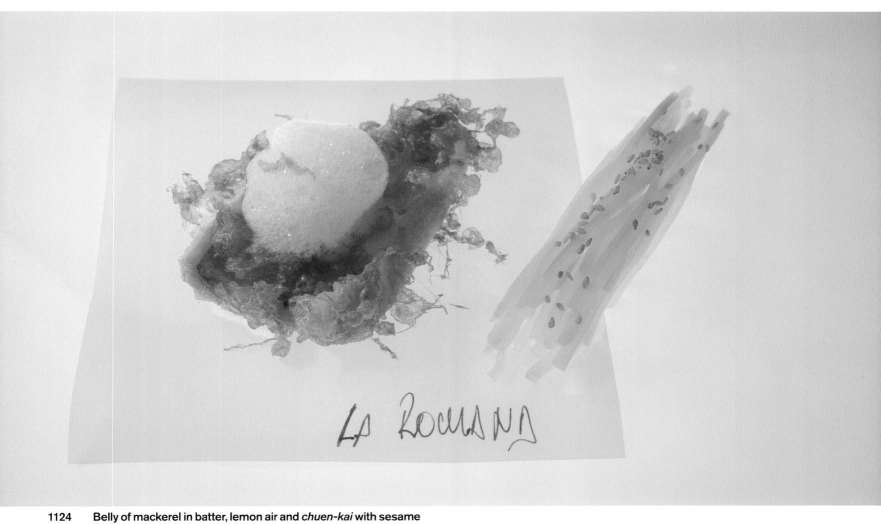

1124   Belly of mackerel in batter, lemon air and *chuen-kai* with sesame

1125   Steamed brioche: mozzarella and mock tartufo/veal marrow and caviar/rose-scented mozzarella

1126   Melon with ham 2005

1127   Spherical-I mozzarella

1128   Malt flour and butter ravioli with sea urchin and lime zest

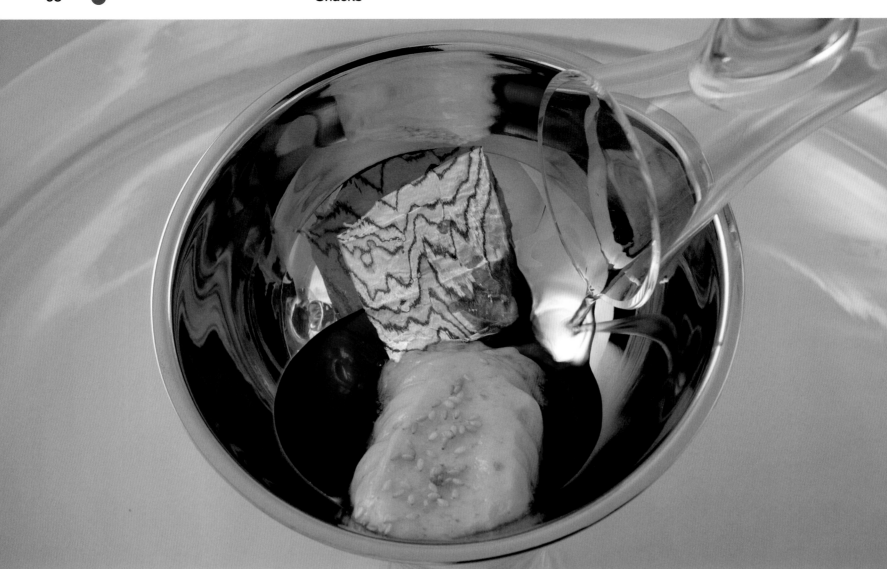

1129 Clams in Earl Grey tea, pink grapefruit and black sesame

Tapas
1130–1181

Tapas
1130–1181

1130   Thaw 2005

1131   Earth 2005

1132   Almond kernels with elderflower, in egg yolk and lemon

1133   Pistachio-LYO with black truffle jellied consommé and mandarin air

1134   Carrot-LYO foam with hazelnut foam-air and Córdoba spices

1135   Jellied *tucupi* consommé with frozen passion fruit crumbs

1136   *Músico*

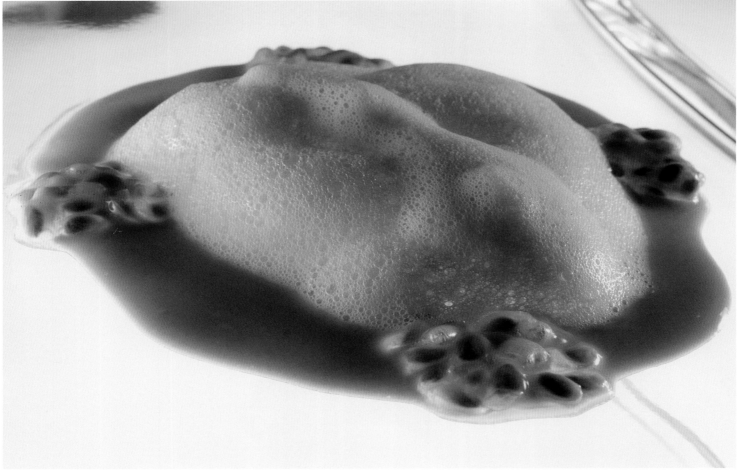

1137   Passion for olives

1138   Carrot-LYO desert

1139   Soy sauce nest with sesame, miso and wasabi sweets

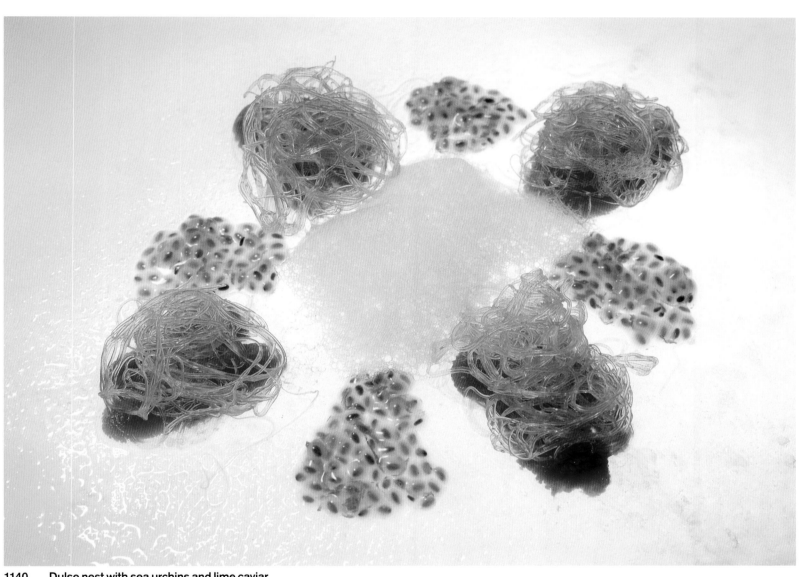

1140   Dulse nest with sea urchins and lime caviar

1141   'Folie' salad

1142   Sprouting quinoa with *tucupi* and *kefir* chicken 'tripe'

1143   Green almond *empanadilla* with Szechuan button and cucumber balls in liquorice and yuzu

1144   Thai soup with coconut tofu

1145   Spherical-I yogurt nodules with ice plant, capers and black butter

1146 Peas and ham with creamy fresh mint and eucalyptus air ravioli

1147 Warm murex snails with *kikurage*, hot vinaigrette and basil-flavoured kombu

1148   Rock mussels with seaweed and fresh herbs

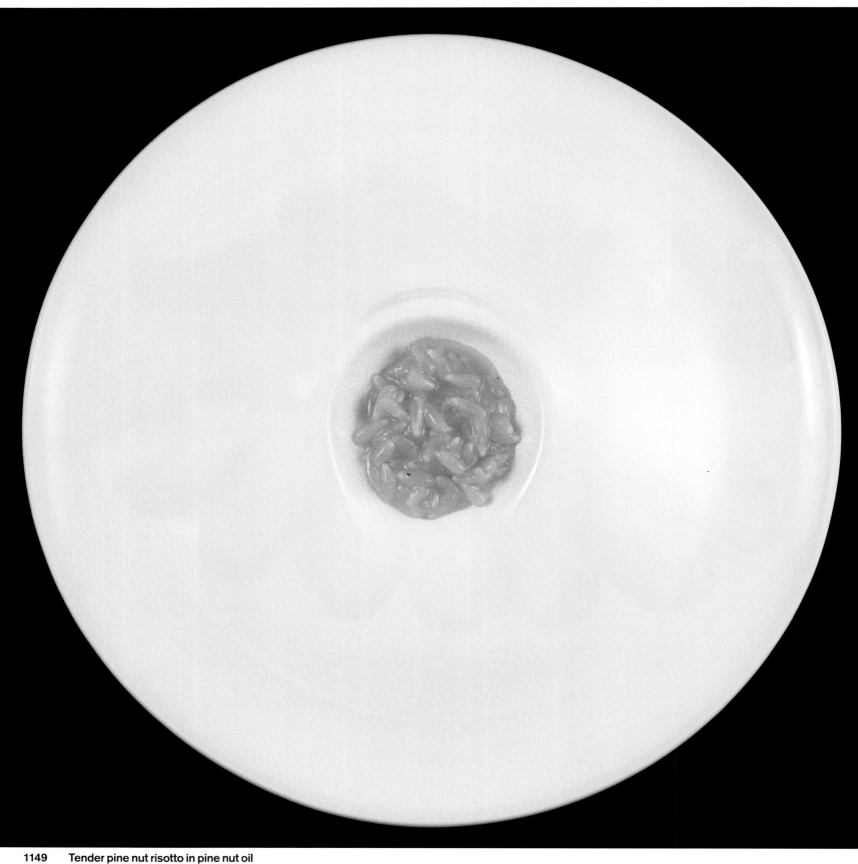

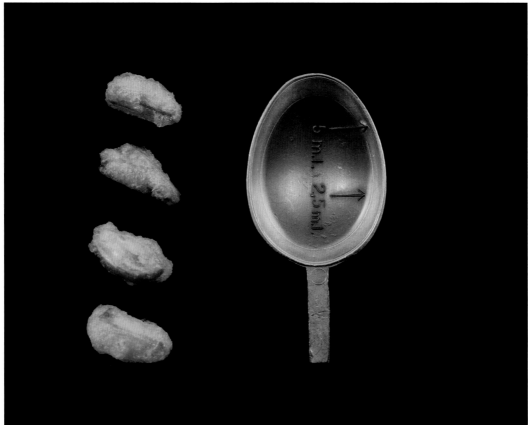

1150   White asparagus with virgin olive oil capsules and lemon marshmallow

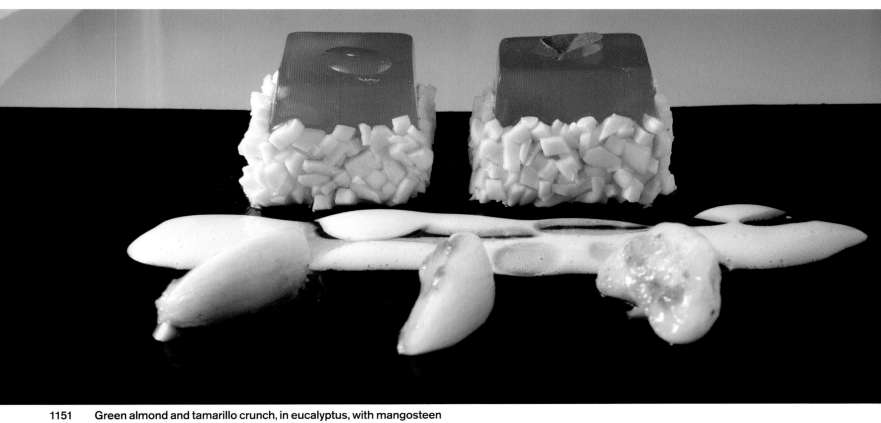

1151   Green almond and tamarillo crunch, in eucalyptus, with mangosteen

1152 Baby broad bean *albóndigas* in their juice with broad bean flowers

1153   Walnuts in their cream, hot yogurt jelly, apple velvet and mint aroma

1154   Green walnuts[3], smoked tea and wasabi

1155   Stewed walnuts with daisy buds, beurre noisette air-foam and mint aroma

1156 Warm spherical dashi cloud with fairy ring mushrooms flavoured with purple shiso, sesame and yuzu

GELATINA DE YUZU

NUBE SFERIFICA
D= DASHI

GEL...
S...

...TADO
...RGEN DE
...A NUBE)

TAJINE
...SOD NUBE)

1157   Sea tomatoes

1158   Warty venus clam with watermelon and yuzu in a saffron and kombu broth

1159 Earthy

1160   Monkfish liver fondue with ponzu and white sesame-flavoured kumquat

1161   Almonds/beans with small squid, daisy buds, mustard, bitter almond and fennel

1162　　Sweetcorn snow egg with Mexican broth and *coquina* clams

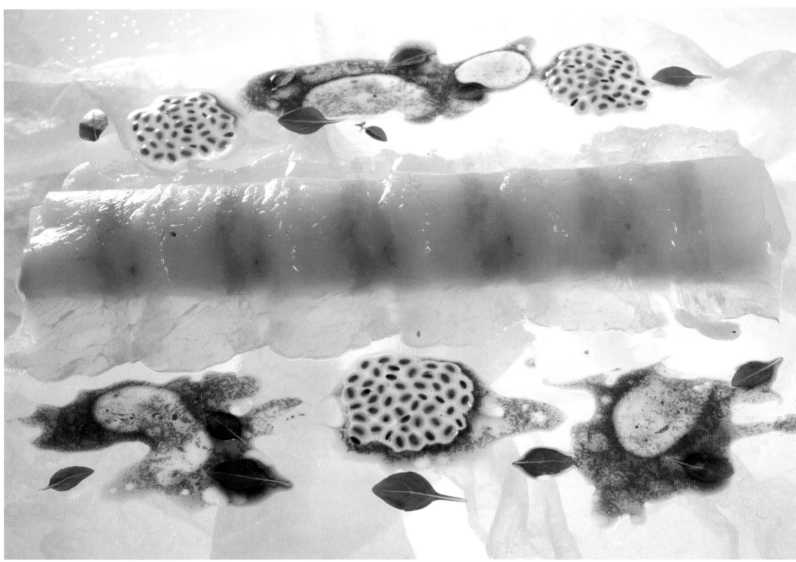

1163   Creamy cannellone with Spanish bacon, anchovy caviar and black olive

1164   Macaroni with egg yolk, miso, sesame and green shiso

1165   Mock tartufo of Iberian pork and green olive

1166   Parmesan-LYO mini French toasts with onion-flavoured ham fat, egg yolk and coffee

1167   Pavé of St George's mushrooms with samphire and *kefir*

1168   Cep blocks with hot cep jelly, cat's claw and hazelnut cream

1169   Papillote of tomatoes in mastic, almond and tarragon oil and kumquat sorbet

1170   Baby snails in court-bouillon with crab escabeche and amaranth with fennel

1171   Belly of mackerel in chicken escabeche with onions and vinegar caviar

1172   Grilled oysters with pine jelly, oyster cream and borage shoots

1173   Langoustine with quinoa[3]

1174 Lobster curry with granadilla air-foam and cardamom

1175   Baby monkfish with lemon-scented egg yolk, daisy buds, pine nut oil and beurre noisette

1176   Sole with puffed amaranth, Córdoba air, coriander-flavoured amaranth/popcorn, Chinese garlic flowers and lemon

1177   Turtle dove with tuna medulla, enokis and samphire

1178   Tandoori chicken wings with borage shoots, oyster cream and frothy *mató* cheese

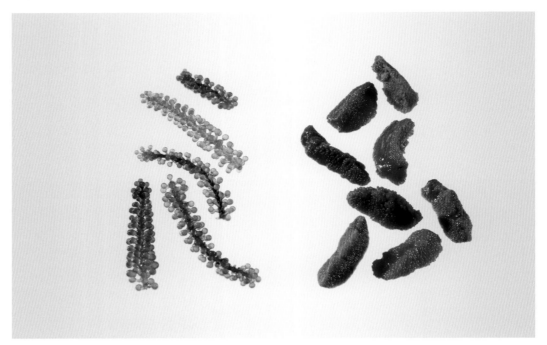

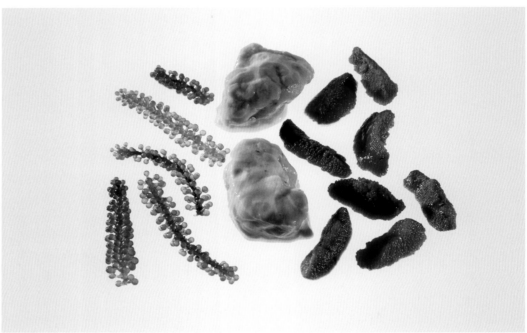

1179   Lamb's brains with sea urchin and sea grape

1180   Rack of Iberian pork with Thai aroma

1181   Red cabbage with *jamón ibérico* lentils

Pre desserts
1182–1186

1182   Tennessee infusion

1183   Peach liquid

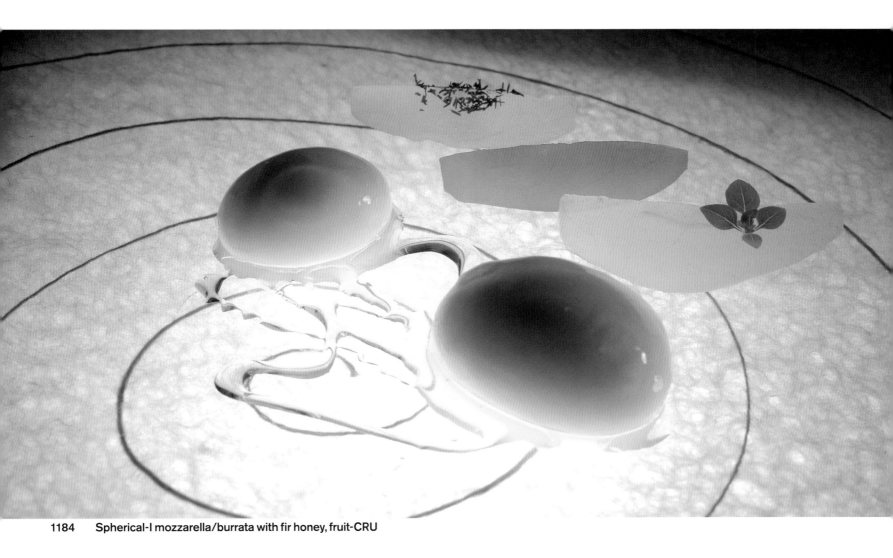

1184   Spherical-I mozzarella/burrata with fir honey, fruit-CRU

1185   Hot passion fruit marshmallow, fresh mint coconut milk and chocolate pearls

1186   Coulant/soufflé of granadilla with cardamom toffee

Desserts
1187–1199

1187   Peach-CRU in amaretto with electric ice cream

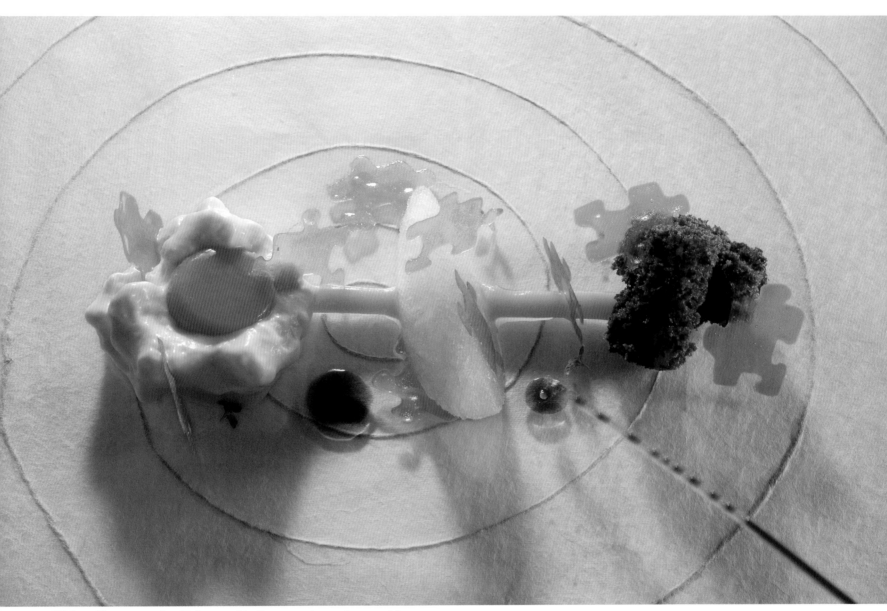

1188   Mango-puzzle with frozen elderflower wedge and coconut foam

1189　Red variation

1190   Strawberries or roses?

1191   Mont Blanc

1192   Pea jelly with banana and lime ice cream

1193 Thai ice cream nigiri with lime marshmallow

1194   Figs with light rose and white chocolate meringue powder

1195   Light honey meringue with apple-CRU and rosemary and cinnamon ice cream

1196   Chocolate air-LYO with crisp raspberry sorbet and eucalyptus water ice

1197   Apricot palet with milk chocolate and passion fruit ice cream

1198   Frozen chocolate and hazelnut praline crumbs with passion fruit caramel

1199   Des/sert

Morphings
1200–1214

1200   Pineapple/fennel

1201   Spherical-I cherries with yogurt and elderflower

1202   Daiquiri, coffee and caramel nigiri

1203   Yogurt and raspberry/passion fruit and liquorice/coffee and soursop *mochi*

1204   Light coffee and chocolate meringue slice

1205   Honey Filipino biscuits

1206   Chestnut *ningyo-yaki*

1207   Passion fruit tree

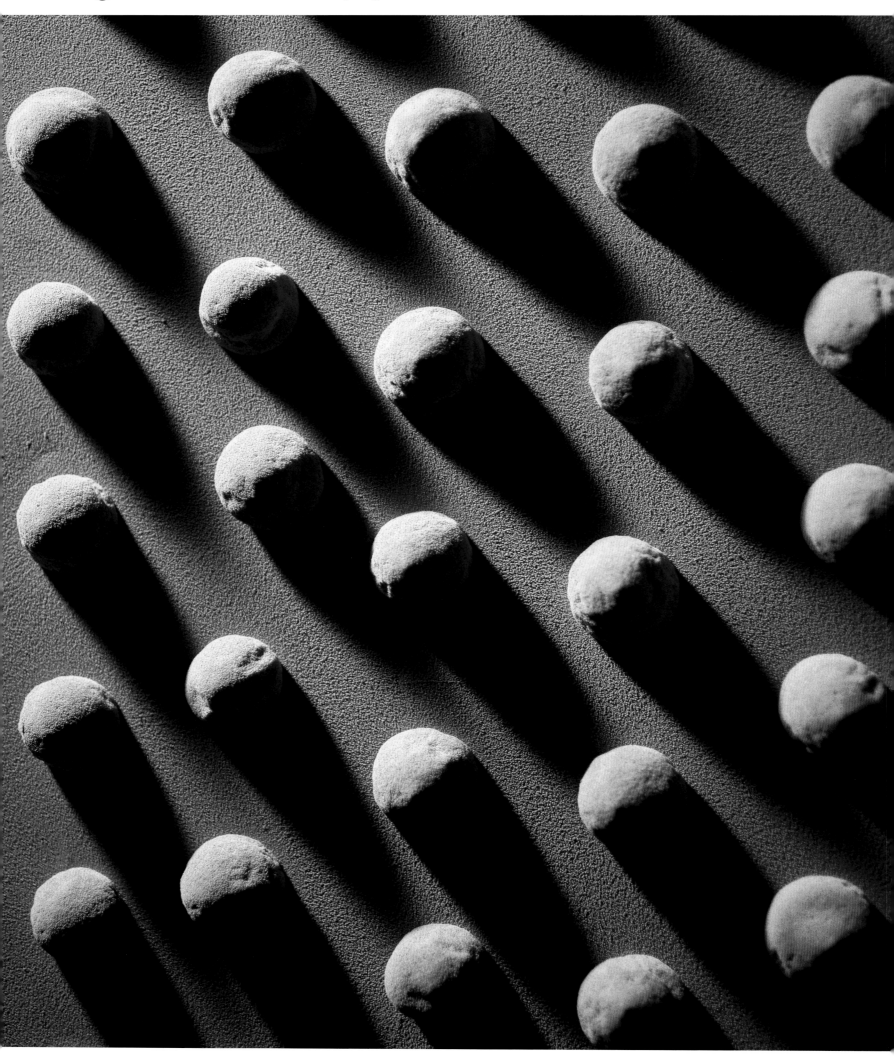

1208   After Eight marshmallow

1209   Palet-croquant: passion fruit, chocolate and hazelnut/white chocolate and macadamia nut

1210 Strawberry iced lolly with eucalyptus Peta Zetas

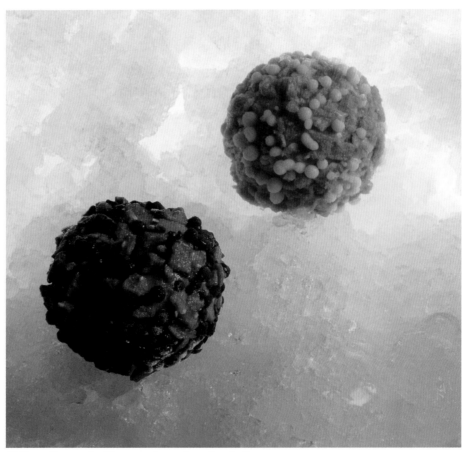

1211   Frozen truffles: raspberry/passion fruit

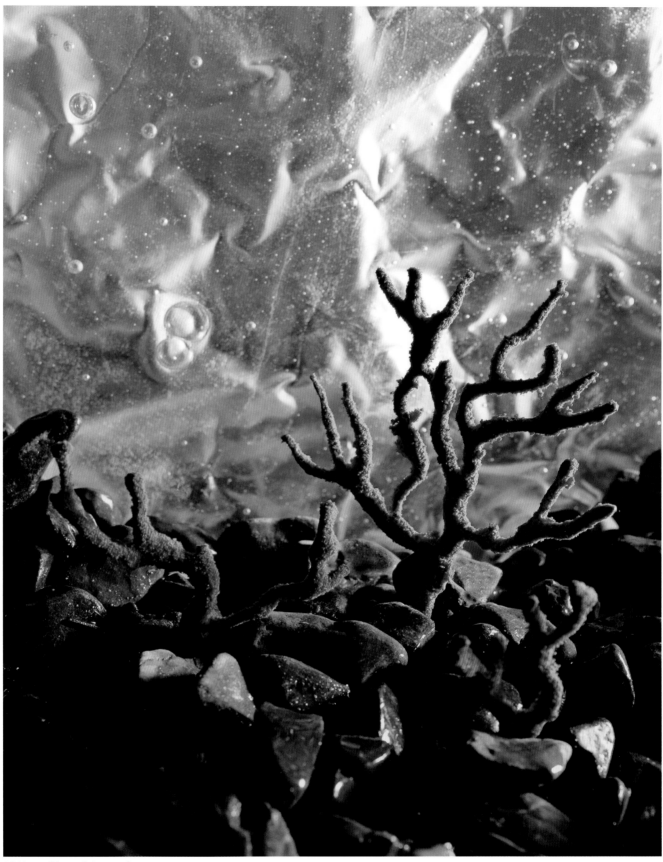

1212   Chocolate coral

1213   Fruit crisp-LYO in chocolate

1214   Fruit-LYO in chocolate

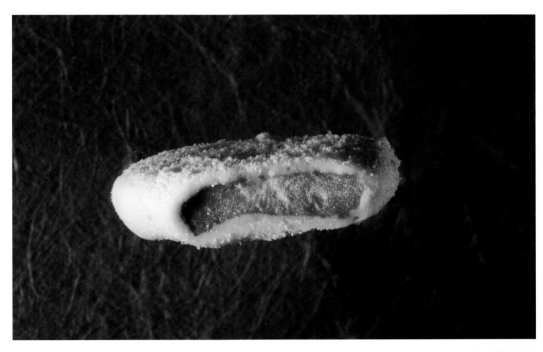

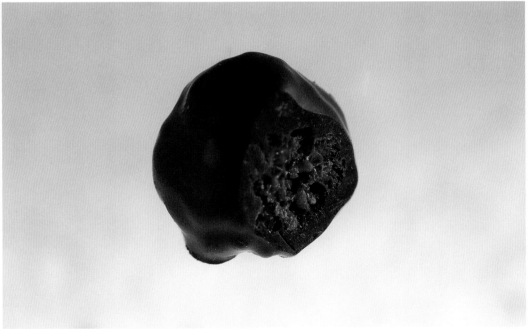

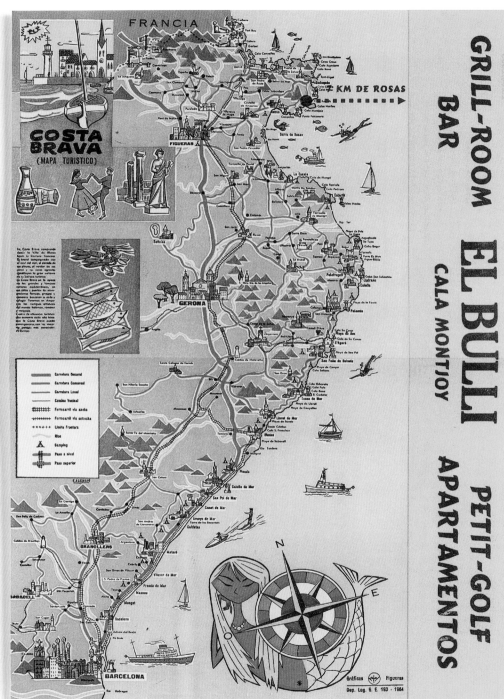

GRILL-ROOM
BAR

EL BULLI
CALA MONTJOY

PETIT-GOLF
APARTAMENTOS

Menu 04/08/2005

Margarita 2005

Spherical-I green olives

Pine nut marshmallow
3Ds with ras-el-hanout spices and lemon basil sprouts
Cantonese *músico*
Mango and black olive discs

Five pepper melon-CRU/melon-LYO with fresh herbs and green almonds

Pumpkin oil sweet
Thai nymph
Melon with ham 2005
Spherical-I mozzarella
Samphire tempura with saffron and oyster cream
Steamed brioche: mozzarella and mock tartufo

Thaw 2005
Carrot-LYO foam with hazelnut foam-air and Córdoba spices
'Folie' salad
Rock mussels with seaweed and fresh herbs
Baby snails in court-bouillon with crab escabeche and amaranth with fennel
Earthy
Monkfish liver fondue with ponzu and white sesame-flavoured kumquat
Belly of mackerel in chicken escabeche with onion and vinegar caviar
Langoustine with quinoa[3]
Tandoori chicken wings with borage shoots, oyster cream and frothy *mató* cheese

Coulant/soufflé of granadilla with cardamom toffee
Peach liquid
Chocolate air-LYO with crisp raspberry sorbet and eucalyptus water ice

Morphings

What could have been but wasn't

2005

Watermelon/nitro-sangria
Curuba cocktail frozen air
Elderberry suspension
Rum-LYO spheres
Elderberry cocktail with beer

Miraculín
Fresh palm heart carpaccio
Lobster roe with hazelnut cream
Mock tartufo *empanadilla* with anchovy and lemon

Fresh palm heart sorbet with acai berry
Lobster brains with lamb's brain cream
Unravelled fresh palm heart with butter gnocchi
Duck testicles with creamy cannellone
Omelette with fine herbs
Roasted palm heart purée with pistachio, lemon and sweetcorn germ juice
Wild asparagus with mini-asparagus *albóndigas*
Unravelled razor clams
Pistachio *empanadilla* with mandarin and yuzu soup
Foie-sion
Pine nut *pipas* with Himalayan crystal salt, served warm
Amaranth and yuzu bag with Peta Zetas
Chip spherical gnocchi
Meringue and croquant slice
Serla roe with seaweed/cold seaweed jelly with serla sweetbreads
Deep-fried serla sweetbreads with kombu and basil
Beetroot spiral with pink grapefruit
Egg with hot bacon jelly
Hibiscus/milk nitro-cloud macaroon
Egg with Parmesan methyl

What could have been but wasn't

2005

French toast with morels
Langoustine with three quinoa varieties
Flowering gherkin en papillote with green almond
Duck foie gras powder-LYO, black truffle cream and pistachio foam-air
Butter ravioli with kombu seaweed
Warm lobster carpaccio
Steamed lobster with Parmesan, yogurt butter and mint flower

Instant jelly
Peach water with *pu-erh* tea spherical marbles
Hot honey jelly with hot mastic cloud
Pineapple-LYO with cream and black olives
Citrus with olive oil and pâte de fruits
Leche merengada
Cotton ball with ice cream
Citrus crème brulée with milk skin
CUBE
Carrot cheese curls-LYO
Garrapi-nitro hazelnut, pine nut and macadamia nut with cocoa
Boca Bits with celery salt and green tomato
Wild strawberry-LYO with several peppers

Fried sweetcorn communion wafer
Hazelnut spherical *catanias* with cocoa
Gazpacho-LYO
Chestnut water
Hot pineapple soda
Lobster cocktail
Kikurage with razor clams and rack of Iberian pork ribs
Baby monkfish cheeks and liver
Lluell with its roe
Virgin olive oil and lemon caramel rings
Scallops with oil air and seaweed *gargouillou*
Chuen-kai with Iberian pork jus and fermented milk spaghetti
Oriental-style vegetables with fermented milk
Tuna medulla and enoki en papillote
Butter spherical gnocchi with samphire and oysters
Fairy ring mushroom, hot foam spheres with fairy ring mushrooms
Baby monkfish liver with oil air and hot bouillabaisse jelly
Peanut Bollycao
Baby monkfish with bouillabaisse air
Homemade *mató* cheese with dashi
Crystal almond risotto
Eucalyptus leaves with chocolate
Chocolate-coated raspberry linear croquant and crisps
Chocolate and raspberry crunch bar
Raspberry/yogurt biscuit

Cocktails
1090–1094

1090

Margarita 2005

Year
2005

Family
Cocktails

Temperature
Ambient/frozen

Season
All year round

Serves 10

For the 100% syrup

75 g water
75 g sugar

- Mix both ingredients and bring to the boil.
- Refrigerate.

For the margarita frappé

160 g lemon juice
150 g water
100 g 100% syrup (previously prepared)
120 g tequila
30 g Cointreau

- Mix all of the ingredients together and place in a container to a depth of 2 cm.
- Freeze the mixture.
- Once frozen, crush with a spoon until a granular, frappé-like texture is achieved.

For the ice moulds

2 kg ice cubes
1 x 8 cm square Perspex mould, 6 cm deep
1 x 5 cm diameter cylinder, 5 cm long

- Crush the ice and press it into the Perspex mould to a height of 4 cm.
- Place the cylinder in the middle and fill in the space around it with crushed ice.
- Remove the cylinder.
- Repeat this process to make 10 ice moulds with a cylindrical gap in the middle.

NB: Alternatively, the ice mould can be made simply filling a silicon mould with water and letting it freeze.

For the salt air mixture

2.5 kg water
345 g salt
9 g soya lecithin powder

- Mix all of the ingredients in a bowl and process with a stick blender.

Finishing and presentation

1 x 3 cm Himalayan salt crystal
1 Microplane grater

- Put 50 g Margarita frappé into the ice mould.
- Work the stick blender over the surface of the salt air mixture until it emulsifies and the air forms.
- Leave the air to stabilise for 1 minute to achieve a more compact texture. Then, put 2 dessertspoons of salt air over the Margarita frappé.
- The waiter should grate a little Himalayan crystal salt over the air in front of the diner with the Microplane grater.

NB: This dish, like the *Margarita spray/***827** and *Frozen margarita/***956** from 2003, is an adaptation of the classic Margarita cocktail.

Cutlery

- Tapas spoon.

NB: The tapas spoon is 14 cm long and 3 cm wide at its widest point.

How to eat

- From bottom to top, taking frappé and air at the same time.

1091

Strawberry frozen air with raspberry crisp-LYO

Year
2005

Family
Cocktails

Temperature
Frozen

Season
April, May, June, July, August, September

Serves 10

For the strawberry air base

600 g strawberries
450 g limes
300 g sugar
250 g cachaça
50 g water
6 g soya lecithin powder

- Use a paring knife to remove the cap and stem of the strawberries.
- Combine the strawberries with the water in a mixing bowl and process with a stick blender.
- Cut the limes into eighths and crush them with the sugar in another bowl.
- Combine both preparations and crush lightly.
- Add the cachaça, mix with a spatula and strain through a Superbag.
- Add the lecithin and refrigerate.

For the flower pots of frozen strawberry air

Strawberry air base (previously prepared)
10 silver flower pots

- Work the stick blender over the top of the mixture so it emulsifies and the air is obtained.
- Use a spoon to capture the air forming at the top of the mixture and fill the frozen silver flower pots with it one at a time.
- Freeze immediately at -20 °C.
- Cover with clingfilm when frozen.

For the bags of freeze-dried raspberry crisp

35 g freeze-dried raspberry crisp
10 elBulli snack bags

- Fill each of the bags with 3.5 g of freeze-dried raspberry crisp.
- Store in an airtight container in a cool, dry place.

For the sprigs of fresh basil

1 small-leaved basil plant growing in a pot

- Cut 10 small sprigs of basil, making sure that none of the leaves are withered.
- Refrigerate in a container covered with a damp paper towel.

Finishing and presentation

- Serve the flower pot of frozen strawberry air on a slate with a sprig of basil beside it.
- Place the bag of freeze-dried raspberry crisp on another slate with a pair of small scissors for the basil.

Cutlery

- Tapas spoon.

How to eat

- The waiter will cut a few leaves of fresh basil and sprinkle them over the strawberry air. Diners will add more leaves and raspberry crisp as they eat the frozen air.

1092

**Peach/nitro-sangria.../
...Watermelon/nitro-gin**

Year
2005

Family
Cocktails

Temperature
Frozen

Season
**April, May, June, July,
August, September**

Serves 10

Peach/Sangria

For the sangria

350 g fruity red wine
100 g sugar
20 g brandy
35 g Cointreau
rind of ½ orange
rind of ½ lemon
½ cinnamon stick

- Combine all the ingredients in a metal bowl while cold and stir well to dissolve the sugar.
- Refrigerate for 12 hours.

For the peach-CRU wedges with sangria

2 x 200 g vineyard peaches
Sangria (previously prepared)

- Cut 5 mm from each end of the peaches to remove their irregularities. Peel them.
- Use a pineapple corer to remove the stone.
- Slice each peach in half vertically.
- Cut each peach half into 4 x 5.5 cm wedges measuring 2.3 cm at their widest point.
- Vacuum seal the peach wedges with the sangria.
- Refrigerate for 24 hours before serving.

For the pressed mint juice

1 Green Star juice extractor
100 g fresh mint leaves

- Blanch the mint in boiling water for 20 seconds.
- Drain and chill in iced water.
- Drain the mint and introduce it into the juice extractor.
- Make 50 g of pressed mint juice.
- Refrigerate.

  NB: This preparation should be made immediately before finishing and presentation to prevent the mint from oxidising.

Watermelon/gin

For the cubes of watermelon-CRU with gin and sugar

1 x 500 g piece of seedless watermelon
75 g gin
20 g sugar

- Cut the watermelon into 10 x 3 cm cubes.
- Refrigerate.
- Dissolve the sugar in the gin.
- Place the watermelon cubes in a vacuum bag with the gin and sugar mixture.
- Vacuum seal and refrigerate for 3 hours before serving.

1092

**Peach/nitro-sangria.../
...Watermelon/nitro-gin**

Finishing and presentation

Peach/Sangria

5 g freshly ground cinnamon stick
500 g liquid nitrogen

- Open the vacuum bag containing the peach wedges in sangria and drain.
- Freeze the peach wedges by dipping them in liquid nitrogen for 25 seconds each.
- Arrange the peach wedges over a glass dish filled with crushed ice.
- Finish by sprinkling a little pressed mint juice and cinnamon powder over each frozen peach and sangria wedge.

Cutlery

- None.

How to eat

- One at a time, each one in two mouthfuls.

Watermelon/gin

15 juniper berries freshly chopped
2 lemons
500 g liquid nitrogen
1 Microplane grater

- Open the vacuum bag containing the watermelon cubes and drain.
- Freeze the watermelon cubes by dipping them in liquid nitrogen for 25 seconds each.
- Arrange them over a glass dish filled with crushed ice.
- Finish by topping each frozen watermelon and gin cube with a little chopped juniper berry and 3 drops of lemon juice. Use the Microplane to grate a little lemon rind over each cube.

Cutlery

- None.

How to eat

- One at a time, each one in two mouthfuls.

1093

White sangria in suspension

Year
2005

Family
Cocktails

Temperature
Cold/frozen

Season
All year round

Serves 10

For the 100% syrup

50 g sugar
50 g water

- Mix both ingredients in a small pan and bring to the boil.
- Refrigerate.

For the white sangria mixture

500 g Albariño wine
100 g Cointreau
100 g white rum
50 g 100% syrup
100 g ginger ale
1 lemon
1 orange

- Combine all the ingredients in a metal bowl.
- Add the well-squeezed rinds of 5 oranges and 5 lemons to the sangria and leave to stand for 1 hour.
- Strain and refrigerate.

For the cantaloupe melon juice

1 x 500 g cantaloupe melon

- Peel and de-seed the melon.
- Blend the melon pulp in a liquidiser.
- Strain the juice through a Superbag.
- Refrigerate.

For the freeze-dried wild strawberries

20 x 1.5 g wild strawberries

- Freeze dry the wild strawberries for 48 hours.
- When the freeze-drying process is complete, store the strawberries in an airtight container in a cool, dry place.

For the spherical cantaloupe melon caviar base

250 g cantaloupe melon juice (previously prepared)
2 g sodium alginate

- Mix the sodium alginate with a third of the melon juice.
- Process with a stick blender to obtain a smooth, lump-free mixture.
- Mix with the remaining two thirds of the juice. Strain and set aside at room temperature for 30 minutes.

For the calcium chloride mixture

500 g water
2.5 g calcium chloride

- Dissolve the calcium chloride in the water with a whisk, then set aside.

For the lime emerald

100 g lime juice
100 g water

- Mix the lime juice with the water.
- Freeze in rectangular ice trays.
- Once the ice is made, cut 30 x 1.5 cm squares.
- Store in the freezer.

For the white sangria and Xantana mixture

500 g white sangria mixture (previously prepared)
1.4 g Xantana

- Combine 200 g of sangria with the Xantana in a bowl and process with a stick blender. Pour in the remaining sangria.
- If necessary, strain the mixture and vacuum seal to remove the air bubbles trapped inside.

For the mango and Granny Smith apple cubes

1 mango
1 Granny Smith apple

- Peel the mango and cut it into 50 x 5 mm cubes.
- Peel the apple and cut it into 100 cubes of the same size.
- Place 5 mango cubes and 10 apple cubes together in 10 shot glasses

For the fresh herbs

20 small fresh lemon verbena leaves
20 fresh small-leaved basil leaves
20 small fresh mint leaves
20 small fresh peppermint leaves

- Separate 2 leaves of each fresh herb and place them in each of the shot glasses from the previous section.
- Refrigerate in an airtight container.

For the bags of freeze-dried raspberry crisp

15 g freeze-dried raspberry crisp
10 bags

- Weigh out 1.5 g of freeze-dried raspberry crisp and place in each of the 10 bags.
- Store in an airtight container in a cool, dry place.

1093

White sangria in suspension

Finishing and presentation

30 g lime juice
1 orange
1 lemon
1 Microplane grater
4 x 50 ml syringes with the outer diameter
of the opening measuring 5 mm
The seeds of 1 passion fruit

- Fill 4 syringes with the melon caviar mixture.
- Release the mixture from the syringe, one drop at a time, into the calcium chloride mixture. Cook for 3 minutes.
- Drain the melon caviar obtained, then wash in iced water. Drain the excess water off well.
- Place the lime emeralds in the lime juice to soften their shapes 30 seconds before serving the cocktail.
- Fill 10 cocktail glasses with 45 g of white sangria.
- Add the contents of 1 bag of raspberry crisp to each glass.
- Place 10 g of spherical melon caviar over the top.
- Add the contents of 1 shot glass of fruit, seeds and fresh herbs to each of the glasses.
- Place 3 lime juice emeralds in each glass.
- Use a small spatula to mix everything together homogeneously from the bottom to the top of each glass.
- Add a little grated lemon and orange rind.
- Finish by placing 2 freeze-dried wild strawberries on top of each glass. Serve very cold.

NB: All the ingredients should be mixed well and floating at different levels inside the sangria with Xantana, except for the strawberries, which should remain on the surface.

Cutlery

- None.

How to eat

- Drinking and chewing at the same time.

1094

Liquid/vermouth

Year
2005

Family
Cocktails

Temperature
Frozen/cold

Season
All year round

Serves 10

For the kumquat purée

20 x 30 g kumquats

- Clean the kumquats, cut into quarters and remove any seeds from inside.
- Liquidise the kumquat pulp and refrigerate.

For the cold kumquat purée jelly

100 g kumquat purée (previously prepared)
½ x 2 g gelatine leaf (previously rehydrated in cold water)

- Drain the gelatine and dissolve it in a third of the kumquat purée that was previously warmed to 45 °C.
- Add the remaining juice, mix and pour into a container to a thickness of 5 mm.
- Leave to set in the refrigerator for 2 hours.

For the freeze-dried cold kumquat purée jelly powder

Cold kumquat purée jelly (previously prepared)

- Introduce the kumquat purée jelly into the freeze-dryer and process for 72 hours.
- Once complete, break up to obtain a powder.
- Vacuum seal, then store in a cool, dry place.

For the vermouth liquid

100 g red Yzaguirre vermouth
100 g kumquat purée (previously prepared)
1 kg liquid nitrogen

- Dip a 5 ml hemispherical measuring spoon into the liquid nitrogen for 10 seconds to freeze.
- Fill the spoon with the vermouth and introduce it into the liquid nitrogen so that the surface is not in contact with the nitrogen and only the metal of the spoon freezes.
- When the inside edge of the spoon is frozen (about 8 seconds), dip the spoon in completely so the surface also freezes.
- Freeze for 8 more seconds. Remove from the nitrogen and hit the spoon so that the peach liqueur comes out of it as a hemispherical ice cube.
- Quickly dip in the kumquat purée, ensuring that no part remains uncovered; return it to the liquid nitrogen for 3 seconds.
- Remove from the nitrogen and store the liquids in the freezer at -20 °C.
- Make one liquid per person.

NB: Red Yzaguirre vermouth is made in El Morell, in the province of Tarragona. This vermouth is aged for 1 year using the solera process.

For the lemon purée

2 x 250 g thick-skinned lemons

- Clean the lemon and cut off the ends.
- Quarter the lemon, remove the seeds and liquidise.
- Refrigerate the purée.

For the 100% syrup

75 g water
75 g sugar

- Mix both ingredients and bring to the boil.
- Refrigerate.

For the cold lemon zest purée

75 g lemon zest
55 g 100% syrup (previously prepared)
30 g lemon juice
22.5 g butter

NB: This is the minimum recommended amount to ensure a good result.

- Blanch the lemon zest 3 times, starting with cold water each time.
- Drain the lemon zest and blend in the liquidiser with the lemon purée and the syrup to obtain a fine mixture.
- Emulsify with the butter to give the purée a creamy texture.
- Strain and refrigerate.

For the lemon purée and cold lemon zest purée mixture

60 g lemon purée (previously prepared)
10 g cold lemon zest purée (previously prepared)
5 g sugar

- Mix the ingredients to obtain a smooth mixture.
- Refrigerate.

1094

Liquid/vermouth

Finishing and presentation

5 g freshly ground cinnamon stick

- Fifteen minutes before serving, remove the liquid from the deep freezer (-20 °C) and put in a the freezer at -8 °C so that the vermouth inside becomes liquid.
- Half fill a medicine spoon with the lemon mixture and place it over one of the slots on a frozen rectangular slate with 2 holes.
- Sprinkle a pinch of freshly ground cinnamon over the lemon.
- Coat the vermouth liquid in cold kumquat juice jelly-LYO powder, place over the remaining slot and serve immediately.

NB: This cocktail is served with *Spherical-I green olives/***1095**, as it is typical for vermouth to be accompanied by olives as a pre-meal drink in Spain.

Cutlery

- None.

How to eat

- Eat the liquid first, followed by the spoon with the lemon and cinnamon.

Snacks
1095–1129

1095

Spherical-I green olives

Year
2005

Family
Snacks

Temperature
Ambient

Season
All year round

Serves 10

For the sodium alginate solution

1.5 kg water
7.5 g sodium alginate

- Mix the water and the sodium alginate with a stick blender until the mixture is lump-free.
- Leave it to stand in the refrigerator for 48 hours until the air bubbles disappear and the sodium alginate is completely rehydrated.

For the green olive juice

500 g green Verdial olives

- Pit the olives.
- Blend the olives in a liquidiser.
- Strain the purée through a Superbag, pressing the mixture through.
- Refrigerate the juice.

For the spherical-I green olive base

200 g green olive juice (previously prepared)
0.75 g Xantana
1.25 g calcium chloride

- Add the calcium chloride to the juice and leave for 1 minute to hydrate well.
- Mix with a whisk and sprinkle the Xantana over the surface.
- Mix with a stick blender at medium speed.
- Refrigerate for 24 hours.

For the aromatised olive oil

4 cloves of garlic
500 g extra virgin olive oil
Zest of 4 lemons
Zest of 4 oranges
4 sprigs of fresh thyme
4 springs of fresh rosemary
12 black peppercorns

- Lightly crush the garlic cloves and fry them in 100 g of olive oil without allowing them to brown.
- Add the remaining oil and wait for it to heat up before adding the rest of the ingredients.
- Store the oil in an airtight container in a cool, dry place.

For the spherical-I green olives

Spherical-I green olives base
(previously prepared)
Sodium alginate solution (previously prepared)
Aromatised olive oil (previously prepared)

- Fill a 5 ml measuring spoon with the spherical-I green olive mixture.
- Drop the contents of the spoon into the sodium alginate solution to form spherical olives. Make 2 olives per person. Do not allow the olives to touch one another, as they may stick.
- Leave the olives in the sodium alginate solution for 2 minutes.
- Remove the olives from the sodium alginate solution using a slotted spoon and dip them in cold water to rinse them.
- Carefully strain the olives and place them in the aromatised oil without letting them touch one another.
- Refrigerate for 12 hours.

Finishing and presentation

2 glass jars for the olives

- Put 1 piece of lemon zest, 1 piece of orange zest, 1 sprig of thyme, 1 sprig of rosemary and 4 black peppercorns into each jar.
- Divide the 20 spherical olives between the 2 jars.
- Cover with the aromatised oil.
- Serve each jar on a slate accompanied by one slotted spoon per jar and as many medicine spoons as there are guests.

Cutlery

- Medicine spoon.

How to eat

- In a single mouthful.

1096

Menthol watermelon-CRU

Year
2005

Family
Snacks

Temperature
Cold

Season
June, July, August

Serves 10

For the 30% syrup base

500 g water
150 g sugar

- Mix both ingredients and bring to the boil.
- Refrigerate.

For the 30% syrup and menthol infusion

500 g 30% syrup (previously prepared)
0.7 g menthol crystals

- Heat the syrup and dissolve the menthol in it with a whisk.
- Refrigerate in an airtight container.

For the menthol watermelon-CRU cubes

½ seedless watermelon
400 g 30% syrup with menthol

- Peel the watermelon with a knife.
- Cut 20 x 2.5 cm cubes.
- Vacuum seal the watermelon cubes with the syrup for 2 hours before use.
- Refrigerate.

For the peppermint sprigs

1 peppermint growing in a pot

- Cut 10 x 4 cm sprigs of peppermint.
- Refrigerate in a bowl covered with a damp paper towel.

For the silver flower pots with ice

5 silver flower pots
2 kg ice cubes

- Crush the ice with an ice crusher.
- Fill the five flower pots with crushed ice and store in the freezer.

Finishing and presentation

5 pepper blend

- Open the vacuum bag and drain the contents through a strainer.
- Arrange 4 pieces of watermelon and 2 sprigs of peppermint in each flower pot.
- When serving, grind a generous amount of the 5 pepper blend over each piece of watermelon.
- Place each flower pot on a slate. Place 2 sets of silver tweezers beside each one so that diners can help themselves to the ingredients, then serve.

Cutlery

- Silver tweezers.

How to eat

- Alternate the peppermint leaves with the watermelon-CRU cubes.

1097

Five pepper melon-CRU/melon-LYO with fresh herbs and green almonds

Year
2005

Family
Snacks

Temperature
Cold

Season
June, July, August, September

Serves 10

For the 30% syrup base

500 g water
150 g sugar

- Mix both ingredients and bring to the boil.
- Refrigerate.

For the freeze-dried cantaloupe melon cubes

½ cantaloupe melon

- Remove the seeds from the melon half with a spoon.
- Cut the melon into 6 slices.
- Remove the skin from each slice with a paring knife.
- Cut the ends off each slice to obtain 2 x 2 cm cubes from each.
- Make 10 cantaloupe melon cubes.
- Place in the freeze dryer.
- Once the freeze-drying process is complete, store the cubes in an airtight container in a cool, dry place.

For the cantaloupe melon cubes

½ ripe cantaloupe melon

- Remove the seeds from the melon half with a spoon.
- Cut one half of the melon into 6 slices.
- Remove the skin from each slice with a paring knife.
- Cut the ends off each slice to make 2 cubes from each.
- Make 10 x 2 cm cantaloupe melon cubes.
- Refrigerate in an airtight container.

For the *piel de sapo* (toad skin) melon cubes

½ *piel de sapo* melon

- Remove the seeds from the melon half with a spoon and cut into 2 cm slices.
- Remove the skin from each slice with a paring knife.
- Cut 3 x 2 cm cubes.
- Cut 3 x 2.5 cm equilateral triangles.
- Cut 4 x 2.5 cm diamond shapes.
- Refrigerate.

For the mint and basil melon-CRU

10 cantaloupe melon cubes (previously prepared)
10 *piel de sapo* melon cubes (previously prepared)
10 fresh mint leaves
10 fresh basil leaves
500 g 30% syrup (previously prepared)

- Place all of the ingredients in a vacuum bag.
- Vacuum seal the contents so that the syrup will soak into the fruit and herbs.
- Chill in the freezer but do not allow to freeze.

For the peeled green almonds

20 green almonds

- Peel the green almonds and store in an airtight container in the refrigerator.

For the silver flowerpots with ice

5 silver flowerpots
2 kg ice cubes

- Crush ice with an ice crusher.
- Fill the 5 flower pots with crushed ice and store in the freezer.

1097

Five pepper melon-CRU/melon-LYO with fresh herbs and green almonds

Finishing and presentation

5 types of peppercorn in a pepper grinder

- Open the vacuum bag and drain the contents through a strainer.
- Arrange 2 pieces of cantaloupe melon-CRU, 2 pieces of *piel de sapo* melon-CRU, 2 basil leaves, 2 mint leaves and 4 green almonds in each flowerpot.
- When serving, grind a generous amount of the 5 pepper blend over each piece of the 2 kinds of melon.
- Place each flower pot on a slate. Place 2 sets of silver tweezers beside each one so that diners can help themselves to the ingredients.
- Finish by placing 2 pieces of freeze-dried cantaloupe melon on each flower pot, then serve.

Cutlery

- Silver tweezers.

How to eat

- Alternate the different ingredients.

1098

'Tramuntana' peach paper

Year
2005

Family
Snacks

Temperature
Ambient

Season
All year round

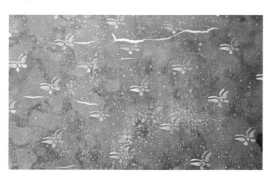

Serves 10

For the red peach water

500 g Garnier red vineyard peach purée

- Defrost the red peach purée in a fine strainer lined with paper towel to extract the liquid.
- Keep the pulp left in the strainer for other dishes.
- Strain the liquid through a Superbag to obtain crystal clear red peach water.
- Refrigerate.

For the peach paper

250 g red peach water (previously prepared)
3 g methylcellulose
3½ x 2 g gelatine leaves (previously rehydrated in cold water)

- Use a stick blender to mix the methylcellulose with 200 g of red peach water until there are no lumps.
- Place the mixture in the freezer to reduce the temperature quickly to 3 °C.
- Dissolve the drained gelatine leaves in 50 g of preheated red peach water. Keep at 39 °C.
- Once the methylcellulose mixture has reached 3 °C, remove it from the freezer and leave it out until the temperature rises to 14 °C.
- Put the solution into a mixer and begin beating at medium speed.
- When foam starts to form, add the peach water with gelatine that has been set aside at 39 °C.
- Beat for about 7 minutes until the mixture forms peaks like beaten egg whites.
- Spread out the peach methyl cloud to a thickness of 3 mm in 2 40 x 20 cm baking trays lined with Silpats.
- Dry in the oven at 80 °C to obtain a dry peach paper sheet.
- Remove the paper from the oven, place a sheet of parchment paper over it and flatten the surface with a rolling pin to obtain a final paper thickness of 1 mm.
- Quickly store in an airtight container in a cool, dry place.

For the prune kernel oil

50 g prune kernel oil
25 g olive oil

- Combine the oils and set aside.

Finishing and presentation

500 g Tennessee whiskey barrel wood
1 Japanese ink stamp

- Heat the Japanese ink stamp with a blow torch and mark the surface of the paper, leaving a space of 3 cm between each design.
- Lay the papers on baking trays lined with parchment paper and heat under the salamander grill for 1 second to make them crisp.
- Brush the papers with the prune kernel oil.
- Line the box bases with barrel wood, cover with Japanese paper and place the papers in the boxes.
- Close the boxes and serve immediately.

  NB: This dish is given the name 'Tramuntana' because the optimal atmospheric humidity required to eat this snack should be less than 45%, which only occurs at elBulli when the Tramuntana wind blows.

Cutlery

- None.

How to eat

- Open the box, smell the paper to appreciate the aroma of the wood, break the paper into large pieces and eat quickly, appreciating its texture.

1099

Cantonese *músico*: mixed/pine nuts

Year
2005

Family
Snacks

Temperature
Ambient

Season
All year round

Serves 10

Mixed Cantonese *músico*

For the honey confit walnuts

20 x 2 cm walnut halves, shelled
300 g water
225 g sugar
450 g rosemary honey

- Divide the water, honey and sugar equally between the 3 pans, so that each pan contains a third of the water, a third of the sugar and a third of the rosemary honey.
- Place the walnuts into 1 of the pans and slowly bring to the boil, skimming off the froth. Remove the nuts and put them in next pan.
- Repeat the same operation, place the nuts in the final pan and repeat again.
- Keep the walnuts covered with the cooking liquid in a container and refrigerate for 24 hours.

For the honey confit green pistachios

60 green pistachios, shelled
300 g water
225 g sugar
450 g rosemary honey

- Divide the water, honey and sugar equally between the 3 pans, so that each pan contains a third of the water, a third of the sugar and a third of the rosemary honey.
- Place the pistachios into 1 of the pans and slowly bring to the boil, skimming off the froth. Remove the nuts and put them in next pan.
- Repeat the same operation, place the nuts in the final pan and repeat again.
- Keep the pistachios covered with the cooking liquid in a container and refrigerate for 24 hours.

For the honey confit wild pine nuts

80 wild pine nuts
300 g water
225 g sugar
450 g rosemary honey

- Divide the water, honey and sugar equally between the 3 pans, so that each pan contains a third of the water, a third of the sugar and a third of the rosemary honey.
- Place the pine nuts into one of the pans and slowly bring to the boil, skimming off the froth. Remove the nuts and put them in next pan.
- Repeat the same operation, place the nuts in the final pan and repeat again.
- Keep the pine nuts covered with the cooking liquid in a container and refrigerate for 24 hours.

For the spice powder

12 g Szechuan pepper
12 g star anise
16 g coriander seeds

- Grind the spices to a fine powder.
- Store the oil in an airtight container in a cool, dry place.

Pine nut Cantonese *músico*

For the honey confit wild pine nuts

120 wild pine nuts
300 g water
225 g sugar
450 g rosemary honey

- Divide the water, honey and sugar equally between the 3 pans, so that each pan contains a third of the water, a third of the sugar and a third of the rosemary honey.
- Place the pine nuts into one of the pans and slowly bring to the boil, skimming off the froth. Remove the nuts and put them in next pan.
- Repeat the same operation, place the nuts in the final pan and repeat again.
- Keep the pine nuts covered with the cooking liquid in a container and refrigerate for 24 hours.

For the green pine cone infusion

480 g green pine cones
600 g water
75 g sugar
0.6 g ascorbic acid

- Soak the green pine cones in hot water for 1 minute to clean.
- Coarsely chop the green pine cones into 2 cm chunks.
- Bring the water and sugar to the boil, add the pine cone chunks and remove from the heat.
- Add the ascorbic acid and refrigerate for 24 hours.
- Strain through a Superbag and refrigerate.

NB: Ascorbic acid (vitamin C) is used as an antioxidant.

1099

Cantonese *músico*: mixed/pine nuts

For the freeze-dried green pine cone infusion reduction

175 g green pine cone infusion (previously prepared)

- Freeze dry the green pine cone infusion for 48 hours.
- It will have a texture similar to that of honey.

For the spice powder

12 g Szechuan pepper
12 g star anise
16 g coriander seeds

- Grind the spices to a fine powder.
- Store the oil in an airtight container in a cool, dry place.

Finishing and presentation

Mixed cantonese *músico*

1 kg sunflower oil
Salt

- Drain the 3 types of nuts from the syrup and fry them separately in sunflower oil at 165 °C until caramelised.
- Remove from the oil and dust lightly with salt and spices. Allow to cool on a tray lined with parchment paper so that the sugar crystallises and a crunchy coating develops.
- Arrange nuts on a black slate.

Cutlery

- None.

How to eat

- Eat one at a time and alternate the nut variety.

Pine nut cantonese *músico*

1 kg sunflower oil
Salt

- Drain the pine nuts from the syrup and fry them in sunflower oil at 165°C until caramelised.
- Remove from the oil and dust lightly with salt and spices. Allow to cool on a tray lined with parchment paper so that the sugar crystallises and a crunchy coating develops.
- Arrange the honey pine nuts over a black slate.

Cutlery

- None.

How to eat

- Eat half of the pine nuts one by one, followed by the freeze-dried green pine cone infusion reduction to impregnate the palate with flavour before finishing the pine nuts.

1100

Nutmeg-flavoured popcorn with Reypenaer

Year
2005

Family
Snacks

Temperature
Warm

Season
All year round

Serves 10

For the Reypenaer cheese crunch

100 g Reypenaer cheese
1 Microplane grater

NB: Reypenaer is an aged Gouda cheese
with very particular characteristics.

- Use the Microplane grater to grate the cheese
  into long strings. Form 10 x 6 cm discs with
  the cheese on a Silpat, avoiding excess piling.
- Place in the oven at 210 °C and bake for 3 minutes
  until the cheese becomes crunchy.
- Remove the cheese crunches from the Silpat
  with a spatula so as not to break them.
- Store in an airtight container in a cool, dry place.

For the popcorn

1 bag of microwave popcorn

- Heat the bag of popcorn for 3 minutes
  in the microwave at full power.
- Open the bag and take out the kernels that have
  not popped. Discard them.
- Store the popcorn in an airtight container in a cool,
  dry place.

NB: Make the popcorn immediately before use.

Finishing and presentation

Freshly ground Moluccan nutmeg

- Arrange 20 groups of 2 pieces of popcorn
  on a tray lined with a Silpat.
- Place one half of a cheese crunch over each
  group to cover the popcorn.
- Heat under the salamander grill for 10 seconds
  to melt the cheese and so that it takes the shape
  of the popcorn.
- Remove from the salamander and quickly finish
  moulding the cheese onto the popcorn with
  your fingers.
- Place the popcorn with the cheese on grid trays
  and finish by seasoning the cheese with a pinch
  of freshly ground nutmeg.

Cutlery

- None.

How to eat

- One at a time. It is important to eat it warm.

1101

Marshmallow: Parmesan/pine nuts

Year
2005

Family
Snacks

Temperature
Cold

Season
All year round

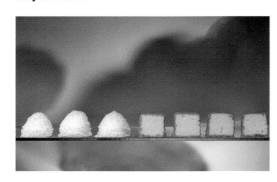

Serves 10

For the Parmesan marshmallow

500 g milk
9 x 2 g gelatine leaves (previously rehydrated
in cold water)
250 g grated Parmesan
40 g virgin pine nut oil
Salt

- Place 400 g milk in the freezer until it cools to 3 °C.
- Meanwhile, mix the gelatine with the remaining
milk in a pan.
- Dissolve the gelatine at 40 °C and pour into
a mixing bowl.
- Start to whip the mixture. After 30 seconds,
add all the cooled milk in one go.
- Continue to whip for 3 minutes. Add the virgin
pine nut oil and fill a 14 inch piping bag.
- Pipe 20 milk marshmallow balls onto a
transparent sheet.
- Lightly salt and sprinkle the Parmesan cheese
over them.
- Refrigerate for 2 hours.
- Then store in an airtight container and return
to the refrigerator.

For the pine nut oil marshmallow

500 g milk
9 x 2 g gelatine leaves (previously rehydrated
in cold water)
40 g virgin pine nut oil
75 g toasted pine nut powder
Salt

- Place 400 g milk in the freezer until it cools to 3 °C.
- Meanwhile, mix the gelatine with the remaining
milk in a pan.
- Dissolve the gelatine at 40 °C and pour into
a mixing bowl.
- Start to whip the mixture. After 30 seconds,
add all the cooled milk in one go.
- Continue to whip for 3 minutes. Add the pine
nut oil.
- Keep whipping for another 30 seconds and
spread out over a transparent sheet to a thickness
of 2.5 cm.
- Refrigerate for 2 hours.
- Then cut into 2.5 cm cubes.
- Refrigerate in an airtight container.
- Immediately before serving, lightly salt the cubes
and coat 4 sides with toasted pine nut powder,
leaving 2 uncoated sides.

Finishing and presentation

- Serve 2 pieces per person on a blue glass tray.

Cutlery

- None.

How to eat

- In a single mouthful.

1102

3Ds with ras-el-hanout spices and lemon basil sprouts

Year
2005

Family
Snacks

Temperature
Warm

Season
All year round

Serves 10

For the fried 3Ds

20 raw 3Ds
500 g olive oil
10 g Fatéma Hal's ras-el-hanout
Salt

- Heat the oil to 180 °C.
- Deep-fry the 3Ds until they puff up and turn a light golden colour.
- Take them out with a slotted spoon and drain the excess oil on a paper towel.
- Season with salt and ras-el-hanout.

NB: Fry the 3Ds immediately before finishing and presentation, and only fill those with a well-defined opening.

For the filling

100 g double cream
60 lemon basil shoots

- Put the cream into a piping bag and refrigerate.
- Trim the lemon basil shoots to a length of 3 cm.

Finishing and presentation

10 g Fatéma Hal's ras-el-hanout

- Fill each 3D with cream.
- Place 3 lemon basil shoots in each cream-filled 3D.
- Finish by sprinkling a little of the ras-el-hanout over the 3Ds. Take care not to stain the lemon basil shoots.

NB: elBulli's collaboration with snack manufacturer Lays has made the use of 3Ds possible.

Cutlery

- None.

How to eat

- Eat each 3D separately and in a single mouthful.

1103

Hazelnut meringues

Year
2005

Family
Snacks

Temperature
Ambient

Season
All year round

Serves 10

For the hazelnut meringues

110 g egg white
1.5 g salt
40 g toasted hazelnut paste
10 x 1.2 g toasted hazelnuts

- Combine the egg white with the salt in the mixing bowl.
- Beat in the mixer until it is close to forming peaks.
- Drizzle in 35 g of the toasted hazelnut paste while folding into the mixture with a spatula.
- Make 10 small mounds of meringue 1.5 cm thick and 3.5 cm in diameter on a baking tray lined with a Silpat.
- Make a well in the middle of each meringue. Fill it with 0.4 g of hazelnut paste and place a whole toasted hazelnut on top.
- Bake at 130 °C for 45 minutes.
- Remove them from the oven and store in an airtight container in a cool, dry place.

Finishing and presentation

Prune kernel oil
Toasted hazelnut paste
1 g powdered citric acid

- Spread 0.4 g of hazelnut paste around the hazelnut meringue.
- Finish with 2 drops of prune kernel oil and a pinch of powdered citric acid.
- Serve.

Cutlery

- None.

How to eat

- In a single mouthful.

1104

Mango and black olive discs

Year
2005

Family
Snacks

Temperature
Ambient

Season
All year round

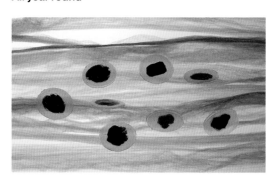

Serves 10

For the mango crisp base

150 g Garnier mango purée
45 g icing sugar
25 g Isomalt
5 g glucose

- Blend the mango purée, Isomalt, glucose and half the icing sugar in a Thermomix at 80 °C for 5 minutes.
- Strain the mixture and add the rest of the sugar, stirring with a whisk.
- Store in an airtight container.

For the dehydrated mango discs

150 g mango crisp base (previously prepared)
1 transparent sheet the same size as the dehydrator disc with 20 x 2.5 cm diameter circles cut out
1 Silpat the same diameter as the dehydrator disc

- Place the transparent sheet over the Silpat and spread the mango crisp mixture evenly over the circular holes to a depth of 1 mm.
- Dry out in a dehydrator for 48 hours at 55 °C.
- Once completely dried, store the mango discs in an airtight container in a cool, dry place.

For the black olive water and oil

400 g black Aragón olives

- Pit the olives and purée them in a liquidiser.
- Squeeze the purée through a Superbag to obtain as much liquid as possible.
- Pour all the liquid into a measuring cup and store in a cool, dry place.
- After 12 hours, the fat will have risen to the top. Separate the fat from the liquid.
- Refrigerate both parts.

For the black olive emulsion

50 g black olive water (previously prepared)
½ x 2 g gelatine leaf (previously rehydrated in cold water)
0.5 g sucrose ester
50 g black olive 'fat' (previously prepared)
0.5 g monoglyceride

- Dissolve the gelatine with a third of the black olive water over a medium heat, then add the remaining water.
- Add the sucrose ester and process with a stick blender.
- At the same time, dissolve the monoglyceride with the black olive 'fat' at around 50 °C.
- Gradually add the fat to the black olive water while processing with the stick blender.
- Refrigerate for 2 hours.
- Once it has set, make 10 x 2 mg portions.

Finishing and presentation

- Fold 3 small sushi rolling mats.
- Arrange the mats on a slate.
- Place 10 mango discs on the mats and put 0.2 g of olive emulsion on top of each disc.
- Place another mango disc on top of each one and serve.

Cutlery

- None.

How to eat

- In a single mouthful.

1105

Carrot ribbons with lemon verbena, ginger and liquorice

Year
2005

Family
Snacks

Temperature
Ambient

Season
All year round

Serves 10

For the carrot crisp base

5 x 70 g carrots
20 g icing sugar
25 g Isomalt
5 g glucose

- Peel the carrots.
- Chop them up and boil from cold.
- Drain once cooked.
- Weigh out 150 g of cooked carrots.
- Combine 150 g of carrot purée with the remaining ingredients in a Thermomix and blend at 80 °C at medium speed to obtain a smooth, even mixture.
- Set aside.

For the carrot crisp ribbons

150 g carrot crisp base (previously prepared)
1 PVC mould, 30 x 1 cm

- On a baking tray lined with a Silpat spread 10 x 1 mm thick strips of carrot crisp base the size of the mould.
- Dehydrate in the oven at 120 °C for 10 minutes.
- Turn the tray around as the part that is closer to the back of the oven tends to be a little hotter, and dehydrate for 10 more minutes.
- Give the ribbons the desired shape while still hot.
- It is important to wait until each ribbon has cooled slightly so it will hold its shape when released.
- Store in an airtight container in a cool, dry place until use.

For the reconstituted egg white

5 g powdered egg white
10 g water

- Mix both ingredients to obtain a smooth mixture.
- Refrigerate.

For the glazed ginger slices

1 piece of glazed ginger

- Cut the ginger into 10 1 cm x 2 mm slices.
- Store in an airtight container.

Finishing and presentation

10 x 2 cm leaves of fresh lemon verbena
5 g powdered liquorice

- Use a fine paintbrush to make 3 spots of reconstituted egg white on each of the carrot ribbons.
- Place a piece of glazed ginger on one spot, a lemon verbena leaf on another and a little powdered liquorice on the other.
- Store them in quail egg boxes so that they keep their shape.
- Put in the dehydrator for 3 hours before serving.

Cutlery

- None.

How to eat

- In a single mouthful.

1106

Parmesan-LYO macaroon with lemon and wild strawberries-LYO

Year
2005

Family
Snacks

Temperature
Ambient

Season
All year round

Serves 10

For the Parmesan water

500 g grated Parmesan cheese
800 g water

- Bring the water to the boil in a pot and add the grated Parmesan cheese.
- Stir until it forms an elastic paste.
- Remove from the heat and leave to infuse for 1 hour.
- Strain through a Superbag and refrigerate.
- After 10 hours, skim off the fat (reserve for use in another dish) from the surface of the cheese water.

For the cold Parmesan water jelly

150 g Parmesan water
(previously prepared)
0.7 g powdered agar-agar
20 x 30 ml plastic shot glasses

- Mix the cheese water with the agar-agar in a pan and bring to the boil, stirring constantly.
- Introduce 5 ml of the cold Parmesan water jelly mixture into each shot glass.
- Leave it to set at room temperature, then refrigerate.

For the freeze-dried Parmesan water jelly discs

20 shot glasses of cold Parmesan water jelly (previously prepared)

- Place in the freeze-dryer for 48 hours.
- Once the freeze-drying process is complete, store in an airtight container in a cool, dry place.

For the freeze-dried wild strawberries

30 x 1 g wild strawberries

- Freeze dry the wild strawberries for 48 hours.
- When the freeze-drying process is complete, store in an airtight container in a cool, dry place.

For the 100% syrup

75 g water
75 g sugar

- Mix both ingredients and bring to the boil.
- Refrigerate.

For the cold lemon rind purée

75 g lemon zest
55 g 100% syrup (previously prepared)
30 g lemon juice
22.5 g butter

- Blanch the lemon zest 3 times, starting with cold water each time.
- Drain the lemon zest and blend in the liquidiser with the lemon juice and the syrup to obtain a fine purée.
- Emulsify with the butter to give the purée a creamy texture.
- Strain, put in a piping bag and refrigerate.

Finishing and presentation

- Pipe 4 g of cold lemon zest purée over the 10 freeze-dried Parmesan water jelly discs.
- Cover each one with another disc to form a macaroon.
- Pipe 0.2 g of lemon purée on top of each macaroon.
- Arrange 3 freeze-dried wild strawberries over the purée.
- Serve.

Cutlery

- None.

How to eat

- In one or two mouthfuls.

1107

Black olive Oreo with double cream

Year
2005

Family
Snacks

Temperature
Ambient/cold

Season
All year round

Serves 10

For the dehydrated black olive purée

1 x 220 g jar black olive purée

- Leave the olive purée in a fine strainer for 30 minutes to drain off the excess oil.
- Spread the olive purée over parchment paper and dry in the oven for 10 hours at 70 °C.
- Store in an airtight container in a cool, dry place.

For the black olive Oreo dough

170 g dehydrated black olive purée (previously prepared)
210 g plain flour
190 g butter
180 g egg
3.4 g salt

- Leave the eggs at room temperature for 30 minutes before use.
- At the same time, cut the butter into cubes and soften in a metal mixing bowl.
- Combine the flour and black olive in a liquidiser and blend.
- Add half the egg and half the flour and black olive mixture to the softened butter.
- Fold with a rubber spatula and add the rest of the ingredients.
- Mix together with the spatula until smooth, then spread out to a thickness of 2 mm between 2 sheets of parchment paper.
- Refrigerate for 2 days.
- Freeze the dough to make subsequent handling easier.

For the black olive Oreo biscuits

Black olive Oreo dough (previously prepared)

- Cut out 20 x 4 cm discs and lay them out on a baking tray lined with a Silpat.
- Bake at 170 °C for 7 minutes. Turn them over and cook for 7 more minutes.
- Leave to cool down at room temperature and store in an airtight container in a cool, dry place.

Finishing and presentation

1 piping bag with 60 g double cream
1 piping bag with 20 g of black olive purée

- Pipe 5.5 g of double cream over 1 biscuit. Repeat the operation with 9 more biscuits.
- Pipe 1 g of black olive purée at the centre of each.
- Cover with the other 10 biscuits and serve.

  NB: Freeze-dried black olive purée can also be used instead of black olive purée.

Cutlery

- None.

How to eat

- In two mouthfuls.

1108

**Grilled sole skin, garlic flower
and parsley**

Year
2005

Family
Snacks

Temperature
Warm

Season
All year round

Serves 10

For the sole skins

5 x 15 cm soles
50 g extra virgin olive oil
Sea water
20 sheets of parchment paper, 7 x 18 cm

- Gently scrape the scales from the soles without breaking the skin. Ensure that the skin is completely free of scales.
- Peel off the skin in one piece from each side of the fish.
- Save the fish for another dish.
- Remove any traces of flesh that may be sticking to the skin.
- Wash the skins in seawater to ensure that there are no scales left on them.
- Dry the skins over paper towel.
- Pour a teaspoonful of extra virgin olive oil on a sheet of parchment paper. Lay 1 dry sole skin over it, spreading well.
- Cover the sole skin with another piece of parchment paper. Repeat this operation with all the skins.
- Refrigerate.

For the fried garlic oil

40 g garlic
75 g extra virgin olive oil

- Peel and finely slice the garlic.
- Fry in 40 g of oil.
- When they have browned, remove from the heat and add the remaining 35 g of oil.
- Leave to cool down at ambient temperature.
- Strain the oil and fill a squeeze bottle with it.

Finishing and presentation

- Introduce the sole skins inside the parchment paper into a hot sandwich maker (200 °C) and close quickly.
- Cook for 1 minute.
- Take the skins out of the machine and remove the paper, taking care not to break the skins. They should be very crisp.
- Season with salt if required.
- Sauté the garlic flowers in a little olive oil and salt to taste.
- Drizzle 3 drops of garlic oil over each sole skin and arrange 3 sautéed wild garlic flowers and 3 parsley flowers on top.
- Serve on a black slate.

Cutlery

- None.

How to eat

- In several mouthfuls.

1109

Arlette *ibérica*

Year
2005

Family
Snacks

Temperature
Warm

Season
All year round

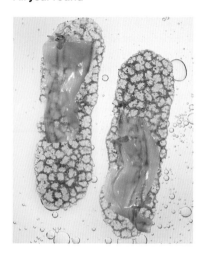

Serves 10

For the boiled pig's trotter

1 x 500 g pig's trotter
Water
Salt

- Cut the pig's trotter in half and cover with iced water for 24 hours to drain off any remaining blood.
- Place the blood-free pig's trotter in a pot, cover it with water and blanch.
- Change the water, season with salt and boil on a medium heat until well cooked (some 2 hours).
- Once cooked, drain and bone while hot.

For the *jamón ibérico* lard

100 g *jamón ibérico* fat

- Remove any lean or rancid bits from the fat.
- Simmer until the solid fat is fully rendered into lard.
- Strain the liquid lard and set aside.

For the arlette base

40 g boiled pig's trotter (previously prepared)
23 g water
20 g *jamón ibérico* lard (previously prepared)
1.2 g plain flour
Salt

- Heat the pig's trotter meat lightly in the microwave and process with a stick blender with the water to obtain a grainy mixture.
- Add the lard and mix until it forms a sticky paste.
- Add the flour and mix to obtain a lump-free mixture. Season with salt.
- Refrigerate.

For the smoked streaky Spanish bacon slices

50 g smoked streaky Spanish bacon

- Remove the pork belly rind and any rancid parts.
- Square off the edges of the bacon to form a 2.8 x 6 cm rectangular block.
- Freeze.
- Once frozen, cut 10 x 1.5 mm thin slices with a meat slicer.

Finishing and presentation

40 fresh thyme flowers
Freshly ground black pepper

- Warm the arlette base in the microwave for 10 seconds until it is runny.
- Use a spoon to form 7 x 2 cm strips of the arlette base with rounded edges in a non-stick frying pan.
- Cook until the arlettes are golden and crisp.
- Use a turner to remove the arlette gently from the frying pan without breaking. Drain the excess oil on paper towel.
- Place the arlettes under the salamander grill to finish toasting and crisping.
- Season the arlettes with freshly ground black pepper and place a slice of smoked streaky Spanish bacon over each.
- Finish by arranging 4 fresh thyme flowers on top of each bacon slice.
- Serve.

  NB: If fresh thyme flowers are not available, substitute with fresh rosemary flowers or similar.

  NB: An arlette is a petit four made from pastry and sugar. A forerunner of the Arlette *ibérica* at elBulli was *Pork scratching arlettes/**226***, from 1993, in turn inspired by the traditional coca de llardons (coca bread with pork scratchings).

Cutlery

- None.

How to eat

- In two mouthfuls.

1110

Half-D cherries in yogurt

Year
2005

Family
Snacks

Temperature
Ambient

Season
May, June, July

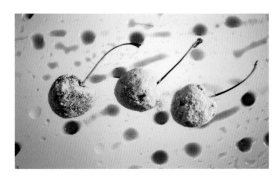

Serves 10

For the yogurt sugar

20 g Pral yogurt powder
12 g dextrose
1.6 g citric acid

- Grind the citric acid in a mortar and mix the resulting powder with the dextrose and yogurt powder.
- Store in an airtight container in a cool, dry place.

For the pitted cherries with bitter almonds

10 x 8.5 g cherries
2 bitter almonds

- Pit the cherries, taking care not to break them.
- Chop the bitter almonds roughly into 5 mm pieces.
- Insert a piece of bitter almond into each cherry.

For the semi-dehydrated cherries in yogurt

10 cherries with bitter almonds (previously prepared)
50 g gin
Yogurt sugar (previously prepared)

- Place the cherries in the dehydrator at 55 °C for 2½ hours.
- Immerse the cherries in the gin one by one and coat them in the yogurt sugar.
- Return them to the dehydrator for 1 more hour at 55 °C

Finishing and presentation

- Serve each cherry on a black glass dish with holes that allow the cherries to stand upright.

Cutlery

- None.

How to eat

- In a single mouthful.

1111

Malt flour air-baguette with caramelised cinnamon caramel

Year
2005

Family
Snacks

Temperature
Ambient

Season
All year round

Serves 10

For the malt flour miniair-baguette dough

140 g plain flour
60 g malt flour
110 g cold milk
2 g fresh pressed yeast
6 g salt

- Mix all the ingredients (except the salt) in a mixer with a dough hook.
- Knead for 4 minutes on a medium speed.
- Add the salt and knead for 2 more minutes.
- Knead manually for 1 minute and keep in a bowl, well covered up, in the refrigerator.
- Leave to rise for 4 hours.

For the miniair-baguettes

200 g malt flour miniair-baguette dough
(previously prepared)

- Roll the dough out through a rolling machine at maximum thickness.
- Leave the dough to stand for approximately 1 minute, covered with a damp cloth.
- Roll the dough out twice more to 5 mm.
- Cut into 10 22.5 x 3 cm ovals.
- Bake at 240 °C for 2 minutes. Turn over and bake for another minute until the dough has risen well and is golden brown.
- Take out of the oven, leave to cool and keep in an airtight container in a cool, dry place.

For the caramelized cinnamon powder

50 g sugar
2½ cinnamon sticks

- Cut each of the cinnamon sticks into 4 pieces.
- Put the sugar in a dry pan and caramelise.
- When it has caramelised well, add the cinnamon stick pieces and mix with a spatula to stop the cinnamon from burning.
- When it is all well caramelised, spread it out over a sheet of parchment paper and leave it to cool down in a cool, dry place.
- Blend the cinnamon and sugar in a liquidiser and store in an airtight container.

For the caramelised cinnamon caramel

60 g caramelised cinnamon powder
(previously prepared)
140 g Isomalt
100 g glucose

- Heat the glucose.
- When it is half melted, add the Isomalt.
- Raise the temperature to 160 °C and remove from the heat (the remaining 5 °C will be reached by its own heat).
- Add the caramelised cinnamon and sugar powder and mix with a spatula until smooth.
- Spread over parchment paper and slice into 4 cm squares before it cools.
- Store in an airtight container in a cool, dry place.

For the caramelised cinnamon caramel powder

Caramelised cinnamon caramel
(previously prepared)

- Blend in a liquidiser to obtain a caramelised cinnamon caramel powder.
- Store in an airtight container in a cool, dry place.

1111

Malt flour air-baguette with caramelised cinnamon caramel

For the spice blend

5 g speculoos biscuit powder
1.8 g powdered star anise
1 g freshly ground black pepper

- Mix the ingredients in a bowl and store in an airtight container in a cool, dry place.

For the miniair-baguettes with caramelised cinnamon caramel

10 miniair-baguettes (previously prepared)
Caramelised cinnamon caramel powder (previously prepared)
Salt

- Sprinkle the caramelised cinnamon caramel powder through a sieve onto a baking tray lined with a Silpat.
- Heat in the oven at 175 °C for 2 minutes, then remove. Place a sheet of parchment paper over it and roll over the surface with a rolling pin to obtain a more subtle and even thickness.
- Season the caramel with salt while it is hot and begin to wrap the miniair-baguettes one by one with the same croquant.
- It is important that the caramel layer should not be even, as this would turn out to be an excessive amount.
- Store in an airtight container in a cool, dry place.

Finishing and presentation

- Arrange on top of a black slate with a vertical groove at the centre.
- Finish by sprinkling a little spice powder over the miniair-baguettes.

Cutlery

- None.

How to eat

- In several mouthfuls.

1112

Virgin olive oil caramel spring

Year
2005

Family
Snacks

Temperature
Ambient

Season
All year round

Serves 10

For the virgin olive oil caramel

100 g Isomalt
25 g glucose
1.5 g sucrose ester
45 g extra virgin olive oil
1.5 g monoglyceride

- Mix the Isomalt, glucose and sucrose ester and heat to 160 °C (the remaining 5 °C will be reached by its own heat).
- While the caramel is cooking, dissolve the monoglyceride with the virgin olive oil at 50 °C.
- When the caramel reaches 160 °C, remove from the heat and drizzle in the oil while stirring with a spatula to bind it.
- Once the caramel has absorbed all the oil, spread it out over a sheet of parchment paper.
- Use a knife to mark out 5 cm squares.
- Store in an airtight container in a cool, dry place.

For the virgin olive oil caramel springs

125 g virgin olive oil caramel (previously prepared)
1 nylon cylinder, 28 x 10 cm, for coupling to a drill

- Heat the caramel in a sugar heating lamp.
- When it melts, pull a string of caramel and roll it using the drill and nylon mould.
- Repeat the operation to make 10 x 3.7 cm springs.
- Store in an airtight container in a cool, dry place.

For the powdered salt

20 g salt

- Grind into a powder in a salt mill.
- Store in an airtight container in a cool, dry place.

Finishing and presentation

1 Misto sprayer filled with virgin olive oil
10 x 7 cm square jewellery boxes
250 g coarse salt

- Use the Misto sprayer to spray a little olive oil over each spring.
- Fill each box with a little coarse salt on which the olive oil caramel spring will rest.
- Sprinkle a little powdered salt over the springs and place one in each of the jewellery boxes.

Cutlery

- None.

How to eat

- Pick up a spring by inserting your finger inside it. Eat it straight away. Allow the caramel to melt in your mouth so you can appreciate the taste of the oil.

1113

Bitter almond, yogurt and elderflower quinoa crunch

Year
2005

Family
Snacks

Temperature
Frozen/cold

Season
May, June, July

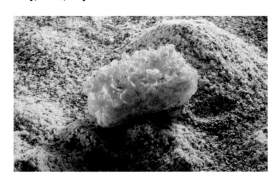

Serves 10

For the puffed quinoa

100 g quinoa
Water
500 g olive oil
Salt

- Boil the quinoa for 25 minutes in plenty of water.
- Drain, rinse in cold water to stop the cooking process, then drain well.
- Spray the cooked quinoa out over trays lined with parchment paper; ensure the grains are not overlapping.
- Leave the quinoa in a warm place for 24 hours until it is completely dry.
- Once dry, puff the quinoa in oil at 180 °C.
- Drain, soak up the excess oil on paper towel and season with salt while still hot.

For the cold elderflower jelly

100 g water
30 g elderflower
10 g Hafi elderflower drink concentrate
1 x 2 g gelatine leaf (previously rehydrated in cold water)

- Bring the water to the boil and add the elderflower.
- Remove from the heat and leave to infuse for 1 minute.
- Strain and dissolve the well-drained gelatine leaf in it.
- Add the elderflower drink concentrate, mix and transfer to a shallow container to a depth of 3 mm.
- Leave to set in the refrigerator for 2 hours.
- Once it has set, cut the jelly into 10 rectangles, 1 x 2.5 cm.

For the prune kernel oil

7.5 g prune kernel oil
2.5 g olive oil

- Mix the oils and set aside.

For the puffed quinoa crunch with prune kernel oil

30 g puffed quinoa (previously prepared)
10 g prune kernel oil (previously prepared)
10 sheets of potato starch paper
1 Flexipan rectangular mould, 2 x 4 x 1.5 cm

- Season the puffed quinoa with the prune kernel oil.
- Line each of the Flexipan moulds with a sheet of potato starch paper. Fill the moulds with 4 g of puffed quinoa with prune kernel oil.
- Wrap the puffed quinoa with the potato starch paper to make 10 rectangular packets of puffed quinoa.
- Store at room temperature inside the Flexipan moulds so that the packages keep their shape.

For the yogurt

30 g plain yogurt

- Beat the yogurt and fill a squeeze bottle with it.

Finishing and presentation

10 g elderflower petals
2 g citric acid granules
1 kg liquid nitrogen

- Dip each crunch into the liquid nitrogen for 10 seconds.
- Then remove from the nitrogen and coat the top of each crunch with 2 g of plain yogurt.
- Place an elderflower rectangle over the yogurt and cover it with elderflower petals.
- Finish by placing 4 grains of citric acid on top of each crunch.
- Serve on a frozen slate.

Cutlery

- None.

How to eat

- In two mouthfuls. To be eaten quickly.

1114

Light beetroot meringue with *kefir* and Fisherman's Friend

Year
2005

Family
Snacks

Temperature
Ambient/cold

Season
All year round

Serves 10

For the beetroot juice

2 x 120 g beetroots

- Peel and chop the beetroots.
- Liquidise and strain the juice.
- Pour it into a pan and bring to a simmer.
- Remove from the heat and skim off any impurities.
- Refrigerate.

For the light beetroot meringue base

150 g beetroot juice (previously prepared)
10.6 g powdered egg white

- Mix both ingredients and process with a stick blender until a lump-free mixture is obtained.
- Rehydrate the egg white in the refrigerator for 12 hours.

For the light beetroot meringue rocks

Light beetroot meringue base (previously prepared)

- Whip the meringue base with a hand-held blender to obtain a compact texture.
- Place a spoon of meringue at a time on a Silpat to make 2 x 4 cm irregular rock shapes. Make 10 pieces.
- Dry them in the oven at 100 °C for 1½ hours.
- Store in an airtight container in a cool, dry place.

For the hollow light beetroot meringue rocks

Light beetroot meringue rocks
(previously prepared)

- Use a 5 mm diameter rod to make a hole in each meringue, which will be filled later.
- It is important that the opening seen from the outside is as small as possible.

Finishing and presentation

80 g fresh goat's milk *kefir*
10 shoots of fresh basil
1 Fisherman's Friend lozenge
1 Microplane grater

- Use a syringe to fill the 10 hollow light beetroot meringue rocks with *kefir*.
- Grate plenty of Fisherman's Friend over the meringue rocks.
- Finish by placing a fresh basil sprig in the opening on each of the meringues.

Cutlery

- None.

How to eat

- Pick up the meringue carefully so as not to break it and eat it in a single mouthful.

1115

'Tramuntana' passion fruit paper
with Gorgonzola

Year
2005

Family
Snacks

Temperature
Ambient

Season
All year round

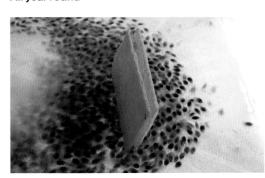

Serves 10

For the passion fruit purée methyl cloud

250 g Garnier passion fruit purée
3.5 g methylcellulose
3½ x 2 g gelatine leaves (previously rehydrated
in cold water)

- Combine 200 g of passion fruit purée
  with the methylcellulose in a bowl.
- Process with a stick blender until
  it is lump-free.
- Place in the freezer and leave there until
  a temperature of 3 °C is reached. Mix with
  a whisk every 3 minutes.
- When it has reached 3 C, leave at room
  temperature until it rises to 14 °C.
- Meanwhile, dissolve the gelatine leaves in
  the remaining 50 g of passion fruit purée in a pan.
- The passion fruit pulp and methylcellulose mixture
  should reach 14 °C at the same time as
  the passion fruit pulp and gelatine mixture
  is at 39 °C.
- Whip the methylcellulose mixture in the mixer
  while gradually pouring in the gelatine mixture.
- Whip at medium speed for 7 minutes until
  the mixture forms peaks like beaten egg whites.

For the passion fruit purée methyl cloud paper

Passion fruit purée methyl cloud
(previously prepared)

- Spread out the methyl cloud on a Silpat
  to a thickness of 2 mm.
- Dry in the oven at 85 °C for 2 hours.
- Once dry and crisp, cut out 20 rectangles,
  sized 5 x 8.5 cm.
- Store in an airtight container in a cool, dry place.

For the Gorgonzola cheese cubes

1 x 70 g piece of Gorgonzola cheese

- Cut the cheese into 60 cubes, 4 mm in size.
- Store at room temperature.

Finishing and presentation

- Arrange 6 Gorgonzola cubes per sheet on
  10 sheets of passion fruit paper.
- Cover them with another sheet of passion
  fruit paper making sure the edges meet to form
  a 'sandwich'.
- Serve immediately.

  NB: This dish is given the name 'Tramuntana'
  because the optimal atmospheric humidity
  required to eat this snack should be less than
  45%, which only occurs at elBulli when the
  Tramuntana wind blows.

Cutlery

- None.

How to eat

- Pick up a sheet of paper gently so as not
  to break it and eat it quickly in three mouthfuls
  so that it does not become moist.

1116

Roquefort-LYO tart with soursop

Year
2005

Family
Snacks

Temperature
Ambient/cold

Season
All year round

Serves 10

For the cold Roquefort foam

150 g Roquefort cheese
200 g water
2 x 2 g gelatine leaves (previously rehydrated in cold water)
1 x 0.5 litre ISI siphon
1 N₂O cartridge

- Chop the Roquefort and place the pieces in a liquidiser.
- Add the boiling water and blend to obtain a smooth mixture.
- Add the gelatine leaves. Dissolve them well and strain.
- Refrigerate and fill the siphon with it.
- Close and load.
- Refrigerate for 12 hours.

For the freeze-dried cold Roquefort foam

Cold Roquefort foam (previously prepared)
10 glasses, 5.5 cm diameter, 2.5 cm height

- Fill the glasses with cold Roquefort foam and place them in the freeze-dryer.
- Freeze dry for 48 hours.
- Once the freeze-drying process is complete, store in an airtight container in a cool, dry place.

For the freeze-dried Roquefort foam tart bases

10 glasses of freeze-dried cold Roquefort foam
10 PVC moulds, 18 x 2.7 cm

- Remove the Roquefort foam from the glasses.
- Trim the smaller side to obtain 10 x 1.5 cm discs and wrap each tart base in the PVC, closing with a little adhesive tape.
- Keep in the dehydrator at a temperature of 55 °C until it is ready to serve.

For the 60% syrup

100 g water
60 g sugar

- Mix both ingredients and bring to the boil.
- Set aside.

For the cold soursop foam

300 g Jugolandia soursop pulp (previously drained)
75 g 60% syrup (previously prepared)
125 g 35% fat single cream
2 x 2 g gelatine leaves (previously rehydrated in cold water)
1 x 0.5 litre ISI siphon
1 N₂O cartridge

- Dissolve the gelatine in the 60% syrup in a pan.
- Add the cream and soursop pulp.
- Mix, strain and fill the siphon.
- Close and load.
- Refrigerate for 4 hours.

NB: The soursop fruit comes from the custard apple family and has a very similar taste and texture. elBulli uses frozen soursop pulp because the ripeness and flavour are more reliable.

Finishing and presentation

- Fill each Roquefort tart base with soursop foam.
- Use a spatula to level the foam filling to the height of the PVC mould.
- Carefully remove the moulds and serve the tarts on a black slate.

NB: This snack can also be served as a pre dessert.

Cutlery

- None.

How to eat

- Pick up the tart gently by the base and eat it quickly in two mouthfuls so that the freeze-dried base does not become moist.

1117

Pumpkin oil sweet

Year
2005

Family
Snacks

Temperature
Ambient

Season
All year round

Serves 10

For the pumpkin oil sweets

250 g Isomalt
75 g Familie Engl pumpkin seed oil
1 x 2.5 cm metal pastry cutter
1 x 18 g hemispherical measuring spoon

- Melt the Isomalt in a pan over a medium heat until the temperature reaches 120 °C.
- Place 4 g of pumpkin oil in each hemispherical measuring spoon.
- Dip the sharp edge of the pastry cutter in the melted Isomalt caramel and remove it slowly so that a fine film forms across the base of the cutter.
- Quickly pour the pumpkin seed oil from the spoon through the still-hot film on the cutter. In this way, the oil will be coated in a thin layer of caramel.
- With scissors, cut the sugar thread that forms on top of the sweet to a length of 4 cm.
- Repeat the operation to make 10 sweets.
- Keep the pumpkin oil sweets in an airtight container in a cool, dry place.

NB: It is important to maintain the Isomalt caramel at 120 °C to give the sweets a fine, even coating.

Finishing and presentation

1 sheet of gold leaf, 5 x 5 cm
Salt

- Put a pinch of salt on each sweet and apply a piece of gold leaf with a fine brush.
- Serve on a black slate with holes.

Cutlery

- None.

How to eat

- Pick up a sweet carefully with your fingers and place in your mouth. Without chewing it, let the sugar melt and the pumpkin seed oil flow out.

1118

Thai nymph

Year
2005

Family
Snacks

Temperature
Ambient

Season
All year round

Serves 10

For the cucumber batons

1 x 300 g cucumber

- Peel and halve the cucumber lengthways.
- Remove the seeds with a spoon.
- Cut the cucumber into 10 batons each measuring 5 x 1 x 1 cm.
- Refrigerate.

For the Thai filling

20 g coriander shoots
20 x 1 cm fresh basil leaves
50 fresh coriander leaves
10 toasted peanuts, shelled
4 g red curry paste
4 g Madras curry powder
6 g toasted white sesame seeds
5 g tamarind paste

- Clean the coriander shoots and remove any seeds.
- Lay out the coriander shoots on parchment paper and form 10 small 2 x 5 cm rectangular piles.
- Place a spot of red curry paste on each of the peanut halves and place 2 on top of each coriander shoot pile.
- Arrange 5 coriander leaves and 2 basil leaves on top of each shoot pile.
- Dust each pile with Madras curry powder and the toasted white sesame seeds.
- Keep at room temperature so that they do not become moist.
- Put the tamarind paste in a piping bag.

Finishing and presentation

10 g coconut milk powder
50 g sugar

- Put 8 g of sugar into a candyfloss machine and collect the floss to make 10 cm strips.
- Place the candyfloss strips on a tray lined with parchment paper.
- Sprinkle the coconut milk powder over the candyfloss strips and place a coriander shoot salad on each one, leaving a 6 cm space.
- Place a cucumber baton on top of each salad pile and pipe two spots of tamarind paste on each one.
- Fold the candyfloss strips over each salad to cover the salad completely and cut with a dry knife to produce a candyfloss tube with the salad inside.
- Remove any excess candyfloss from the edges.
- Serve immediately on a black slate.

NB: This snack is only served when the atmospheric humidity is below 65%.

Cutlery

- None.

How to eat

- Pick up the Thai nymph and eat in two mouthfuls. It must be eaten quickly so that the candy floss does not collapse.

1119

Coriander 'Chanquete'

Year
2005

Family
Snacks

Temperature
Hot

Season
All year round

Serves 10

For the tempura batter

50 g glutinous rice flour
80 g water

- Mix the ingredients with a whisk and refrigerate.

For the coriander shoots

50 g x 5 cm coriander shoots

- Clean the coriander shoots and remove any roots or seeds.
- Refrigerate.

For the coriander seed salt

5 g coriander seeds
3 g salt

- Grind the coriander seeds into a powder in a spice mill.
- Mix the powder with the salt and set aside.

Finishing and presentation

1 kg olive oil

- Heat the oil to 150 °C.
- Dip the coriander shoots in the tempura batter and drain off the excess so that the shoots are completely coated with a fine layer of batter.
- Put them into the oil without pilling and fry quickly for 3 seconds. Take them out with a spider skimmer and drain.
- Soak up the excess oil on paper towel.
- Season with coriander seed salt and serve.

Cutlery

- None.

How to eat

- Eat small amounts each time without breaking it up so you can appreciate the texture.

1120

Garrapi-nitro pistachio

Year
2005

Family
Snacks

Temperature
Frozen

Season
All year round

Serves 10

For the toasted pistachio savoury praline

100 g whole pistachios, shelled and toasted
15 g olive oil
Salt

- Blend the pistachios with the oil in the liquidiser until they form a fine, lump-free cream.
- Strain and season with salt.
- Store at room temperature.

For the garrapi-nitro pistachios

100 g toasted pistachio savoury praline (previously prepared)
40 shelled and toasted whole pistachios
1 kg liquid nitrogen

- Dip the whole pistachios into the pistachio praline and then dip them into the liquid nitrogen for 5 seconds to freeze the praline so that the pistachios are completely coated with it.
- Remove from the nitrogen and keep the pistachios at -10 °C.

Finishing and presentation

- Dip the garrapi-nitro pistachios into the liquid nitrogen for 2 seconds to chill and serve immediately on a frozen stone (4 pistachios per person).

Cutlery

- None.

How to eat

- One by one so as to appreciate their crisp texture.

1121

Oyster with its pearl and ham cream

Year
2005

Family
Snacks

Temperature
Cold

Season
All year round

Serves 10

For the cleared oysters and their shells

10 x 200 g Napoleon oysters

- Open the oysters with an oyster knife. Retain the liquor.
- Cut through the muscle holding the oyster to the shell and remove the oyster.
- De-beard the oysters with a pair of scissors.
- Strain the liquor through a Superbag and add the oysters. Refrigerate.
- Clean the lower (concave) shells thoroughly. They will be used to serve the snack.

For the *jamón ibérico* stock

50 g *jamón ibérico*
100 g water

- Cut the ham into 1 cm pieces and cover with the water.
- Boil on medium heat for 15 minutes, skimming continuously.
- Strain, discard the excess fat and set aside.

For the *jamón ibérico* lard

50 g *jamón ibérico* fat

- Remove any lean or rancid bits from the fat.
- Simmer the prepared fat until the solid fat is fully rendered into lard.
- Strain the liquid lard and set aside.

For the *jamón ibérico* cream

50 *jamón ibérico* stock (previously prepared)
30 g *jamón ibérico* lard (previously prepared)
0.2 g Xantana

- Mix all 3 ingredients and emulsify with a stick blender to obtain a smooth, lump-free cream.
- Strain and refrigerate.

For the smoked water

200 g water
100 g dried pine needles

- Start up the smoking machine using the pine needles as fuel.
- Once smoke is released, smoke the water for 10 minutes.
- Vacuum seal the water to prevent it from losing its aroma, and set aside.

For the sodium alginate solution

100 g water
2 g sodium alginate

- Blend the ingredients together in a liquidiser until lump-free and the sodium alginate is completely dissolved in the water.
- Refrigerate.

For the spherical pearl base

100 g smoked water (previously prepared)
34 g sodium alginate solution (previously prepared)
3 g silver powder

- Mix the ingredients with a whisk.

For the calcium chloride mixture

500 g water
3.25 g calcium chloride

- Dissolve the calcium chloride in the water with a whisk.

1121

Oyster with its pearl and ham cream

For the sphericised pearls

100 g spherical pearl base (previously prepared)
500 g calcium chloride mixture
(previously prepared)
1 cm hemispherical measuring spoon

- Fill the hemispherical spoon with the spherical pearl base and drop into the calcium chloride mixture to form spheres. Make 1 pearl per person.
- Leave to 'cook' in the calcium chloride mixture for 3 minutes.
- Use a slotted spoon to remove the spherical pearls from the calcium chloride mixture. Immerse the pearls in cold water to clean.

NB: This should be done just before serving the snack.

For the powdered salt

10 g salt

- Grind into a powder in a salt mill.
- Set aside.

Finishing and presentation

1 kg crushed ice

- Place 6 g of ham cream at the base of each oyster shell.
- Place 1 cleaned oyster over it.
- Place 1 spherical pearl dusted with a pinch of powdered salt on top of the oyster.
- Serve the oyster on a tray covered with crushed ice.

Cutlery

- Tapas cutlery.

NB: Tapas cutlery consists of a 14 x 3 cm spoon and fork.

How to eat

- Eat the pearl first, followed by the oyster and the ham cream last of all.

1122

Mandarin flower tempura

Year
2005

Family
Snacks

Temperature
Hot/ambient

Season
March, April

Serves 10

For the mandarin essence

185 g mandarin juice
33 g mandarin flowers
2 mandarin leaves
4 g olive oil
5 g sunflower oil

- Reduce 160 g of orange juice to 35 g of orange juice reduction.
- Emulsify mandarin juice reduction while still hot with the 2 oils. Then add the mandarin flowers and broken up mandarin leaves. Remove from the heat and leave to infuse for 20 minutes.
- Press well to release all the juice and add the remaining 25 g of fresh mandarin juice.
- Refrigerate.

  NB: This is the minimum recommended amount to ensure a good result.

For the tempura batter

50 g glutinous rice flour
80 g water

- Mix the ingredients with a whisk and refrigerate.

Finishing and presentation

40 mandarin flowers
1 kg olive oil
1 mandarin
1 Microplane grater

- Heat the oil to 170 °C.
- Lightly coat the mandarin flowers in the tempura batter and fry them in the oil until they are very crisp.
- Drain the fried mandarin flowers and lay them on paper towel to soak up the excess oil.
- Grate the mandarin zest and sprinkle the grated zest over each battered mandarin flower.
- Arrange 8 fried mandarin flowers on each of 5 slates with 2 holes. Fill the holes with mandarin essence and serve.

Cutlery

- Silver tweezers.

How to eat

- Pick up a flower with the tweezers and dip it lightly in the mandarin essence. Eat one by one.

1123

Samphire tempura with saffron and oyster cream

Year
2005

Family
Snacks

Temperature
Hot/cold

Season
**May, June,
July, August**

Serves 10

For the cleaned oysters

3 x 200 g Napoleon oysters

- Open the oysters with an oyster knife. Reserve the liquor.
- Cut through the muscle holding the oyster to the shell and remove the oyster.
- De-beard the oysters with a pair of scissors.
- Strain the liquor through a Superbag and add the oysters. Refrigerate.

For the smoked streaky Spanish bacon fat

50 g smoked streaky Spanish bacon

- Slice the bacon into 2 cm pieces and put them in a small pan over a low heat to sweat and release the fat. Do not let them fry.
- Strain off the fat and set it aside.

For the oyster cream and smoked streaky Spanish bacon fat

25 g cleaned oysters (previously prepared)
30 g oyster liquor (previously prepared)
8 g melted smoked streaky Spanish bacon fat (previously prepared)

- Blend the oysters with the oyster liquor.
- Emulsify the resulting liquid with the melted bacon fat at room temperature.
- Strain and refrigerate.

For the tempura batter

50 g glutinous rice flour
80 g water

- Mix the ingredients with a stick blender and refrigerate.

For the toasted saffron powder

3 g saffron threads

- Toast the saffron threads in a frying pan.
- Break up the toasted saffron threads to make a coarse powder.

For the samphire shoots

120 g fresh samphire shoots, 4 cm long

- Select the best samphire and weigh out 10 x 10 g servings.
- Refrigerate.

NB: The samphire variety used, purple glasswort, *Salicornia ramosissima*, is an annual herb from the Chenopodiaceae family that grows in saline soils. The branches have a number of nodes and are fleshy and green, except towards the end of its cycle when the plant turns a reddish colour. It grows in places close to the sea or in marshy areas occasionally flooded with sea water.

Finishing and presentation

1 kg olive oil

- Heat the oil to 175 °C.
- Dip the samphire briefly in the tempura batter and fry in the oil. Do not let the tempura shoots touch, or they will stick together.
- Once the tempura is fried, drain off any excess oil on paper towel.
- Arrange them on 10 rectangular slates and lightly dust with toasted saffron powder.
- Serve 6 g of oyster cream per person in individual bowls.

Cutlery

- None.

How to eat

- Pick up the samphire tempura and dip in the oyster cream.

1124

**Belly of mackerel in batter,
lemon air and *chuen-kai*
with sesame**

Year
2005

Family
Snacks

Temperature
Hot/cold

Season
**March, April,
May, June**

Serves 10

For the mackerel bellies

10 x 250 g mackerel

- Use a knife to remove the mackerel bellies, taking care not to break the guts.
- Remove any bones from the bellies and use a sheet of paper to clean the meat of any membrane.
- Refrigerate.

For the *chuen-kai* julienne

2 x 6 cm diameter tender stalks of *chuen-kai*

- Peel and cut the *chuen-kai* stalks into 8 cm lengths.
- Cut the *chuen-kai* into a 1.5 mm julienne.
- Set the aside in iced water until finishing and presentation.

NB: *Chuen-kai* is a Chinese vegetable. Its stalk (almost the entire plant) is green and tender, resembling a lettuce stalk.

For the lemon air base

200 g lemon juice
100 g water
0.05 g lemon essence
0.6 g soya lecithin powder

- Mix all the liquids in a deep 25 cm diameter container.
- Add the lecithin powder and use a stick blender to dilute it in the liquid.
- Set aside until finishing and presentation.

Finishing and presentation

30 g raw sesame oil
10 g toasted white sesame seeds
15 g rice vinegar
1 kg olive oil
5 beaten eggs
250 g plain flour
Salt
1 lemon
1 Microplane grater

- Work a stick blender over the surface of the lemon air base until it emulsifies and the air forms.
- Heat the oil to 180 °C.
- Lightly flour the mackerel bellies and coat them in beaten egg. Quickly immerse the bellies in the hot oil so that strings of beaten egg form around them.
- Once fried, drain and lay them on paper towel to soak up the excess oil. Season with salt.
- Remove the *chuen-kai* julienne from the iced water and dry on paper towel.
- Place the mackerel belly in batter on a stone covered with absorbent paper.
- Place a spoon of lemon air over each mackerel belly and sprinkle with grated lemon zest.
- Next to the mackerel belly place a 20 g pile of *chuen-kai* julienne seasoned with the sesame oil, toasted white sesame seeds and rice vinegar.

NB: If *chuen-kai* is not available, substitute with lettuce stalks.

Cutlery

- None.

How to eat

- Pick up the mackerel belly with the paper and eat in two mouthfuls. Eat the *chuen-kai* julienne last.

1125

Steamed brioche: mozzarella and mock tartufo/veal marrow and caviar/rose-scented mozzarella

Year
2005

Family
Snacks

Temperature
Mozzarella and mock tartufo: Hot
Veal marrow and caviar: Hot/cold
Rose-scented mozzarella: Hot/ambient

Season
Mozzarella and mock tartufo: June, July, August
Veal marrow and caviar/ rose-scented mozzarella: All year round

Serves 10

Mozzarella and mock tartufo

For the brioche dough

375 g plain flour
100 g sourdough starter
67.5 g cold milk
32.5 g sugar
6.5 g fresh pressed yeast
140 g beaten eggs
115 g butter
Salt

- Place the flour and sourdough starter in the bowl of the mixer.
- Start the mixer at three quarters of the full speed with dough hook attached.
- Dissolve the sugar and yeast in the milk and add to the mixer.
- Wait for 1 minute before adding the beaten eggs.
- Knead until the dough is smooth.
- Add the salt and knead for 1 more minute.
- Add the butter in chunks and knead until the brioche dough comes away from the sides of the mixing bowl and the butter is fully incorporated.
- Keep refrigerated in a covered bowl for 12 hours.

For the fermented brioches

200 g brioche dough (previously prepared)

- Knead the brioche dough into a long strip.
- Cut into 10 x 12 g pieces.
- Shape into balls.
- Place the 10 brioche balls on parchment paper.
- Keep at room temperature for 30 minutes, then ferment at 32 °C for 3 hours.
- Cover well to prevent them from drying out and keep at room temperature until needed.

For the crumbled mozzarella

2 x 150 g fresh buffalo mozzarella balls

- Remove the outer layer of the mozzarella balls (set this aside for another dish).
- Break up the creamy interior of the mozzarella by hand.
- Refrigerate.

For the mock tartufo slices

2 x 30 g summer truffles
20 g white truffle oil
Salt

- Brush the truffle off under a little water to get rid of all the soil.
- Peel the truffle with a paring knife.
- In the slicer cut the truffle into 0.5 mm slices. Slice 4 g of sliced truffle per person.
- Season the slices of summer truffle with salt and white truffle oil and before finishing and presentation.

Veal marrow and caviar

For the brioche dough

375 g plain flour
100 g sourdough starter
67.5 g milk
32.5 g sugar
6.5 g fresh pressed yeast
140 g beaten eggs
115 g butter
Salt

- Place the flour and sourdough starter in the bowl of the mixer.
- Start mixer at three quarters of the full speed with dough hook attached.
- Dissolve the sugar and yeast in the milk and add to the mixer.
- Wait for 1 minute before adding the beaten eggs.
- Knead until the dough is smooth.
- Add the salt and knead for 1 more minute.
- Add the butter in chunks and knead until the brioche dough comes away from the sides of the mixing bowl and the butter is fully incorporated.
- Keep refrigerated in a covered bowl for 12 hours.

For the fermented brioches

200 g brioche dough (previously prepared)

- Knead the brioche dough into a long strip.
- Cut into 10 x 12 g pieces.
- Shape into balls.
- Place the 10 brioche balls on parchment paper.
- Keep at room temperature for 30 minutes, then ferment at 32 °C for 3 hours.
- Cover well to prevent them from drying out and keep at room temperature until needed.

For the blanched veal marrow slices

3 x 1 kg veal marrowbones

- Leave the bones at room temperature for at least 4 hours.
- Carefully split open the bone with a meat cleaver without breaking the marrow. Scrape the marrow out with a round-bladed knife.
- Bleed the marrow for at least 24 hours in water in the refrigerator.
- Slowly blanch the marrow until the water comes to the boil.
- Remove from the heat and leave to cool in the pan in its cooking water.
- When it is cold, remove from the water and cut into 10 4 x 2 cm slices.
- Refrigerate.

Rose-scented mozzarella

For the brioche dough

375 g plain flour
100 g sourdough starter
67.5 g milk
32.5 g sugar
6.5 g fresh pressed yeast
140 g beaten egg
115 g butter
Salt

- Place the flour and sourdough starter in the bowl of the mixer.
- Start the mixer at three quarters of the full speed with dough hook attached.
- Dissolve the sugar and yeast in the milk and add to the mixer.
- Wait for 1 minute before adding the beaten eggs.
- Knead until the dough is smooth.
- Add the salt and knead for 1 more minute.
- Add the butter in chunks and knead until the brioche dough comes away from the sides of the mixing bowl and the butter is fully incorporated.
- Keep refrigerated in a covered bowl for 12 hours.

For the fermented brioches

200 g brioche dough
(previously prepared)

- Knead the brioche dough into a long strip.
- Cut into 10 x 12 g pieces.
- Shape into balls.
- Place the 10 brioche balls on parchment paper.
- Keep at room temperature for 30 minutes, then ferment at 32 °C for 3 hours.
- Cover well to prevent them from drying out and keep at room temperature until needed.

For the crumbled mozzarella

2 x 150 g fresh buffalo mozzarellas balls

- Remove the outer layer of the mozzarella balls (set this aside for another dish).
- Break up the creamy interior of the mozzarella by hand.
- Refrigerate.

For the rose air base

500 g milk
4 drops rose essence
2.5 g soya lecithin powder

- Mix all 3 ingredients in a 25 cm deep container.

1125

Steamed brioche: mozzarella and mock tartufo/veal marrow and caviar/rose-scented mozzarella

Mozzarella and mock tartufo

Finishing and presentation	• Steam the balls of brioche dough for 16 minutes. • Once the brioches are cooked, cut open the top with scissors and put 7.5 g crumbled mozzarella into each one. • Heat the mozzarella brioches under the salamander grill for 30 seconds and remove. Place the mock tartufo slices on top of them. • Reheat under the salamander grill for 10 seconds and serve on a black slate with satin paper.
Cutlery	• None.
How to eat	• Hold the brioche by the base and eat in two mouthfuls.

Veal marrow and caviar

Finishing and presentation	• Steam the balls of brioche dough for 16 minutes. • Heat the marrow slices under the salamander grill until hot. • Once the brioches are cooked, cut the top open with scissors and set the veal marrow slices on top. • Heat up the plate again for 30 seconds. • Finish by placing 8 g of caviar over the marrow. • Serve on a black slate with satin paper. NB: Another version of this dish was made without the caviar and with a reduced wine and shallot sauce and seaweed salt over the marrow.
Cutlery	• None.
How to eat	• Hold the brioche by the base and eat in two mouthfuls.

Rose-scented mozzarella

Finishing and presentation	• Work a stick blender over the surface of the rose air mixture until it emulsifies and the air forms. • Steam the balls of brioche dough for 16 minutes. • Once the brioches are cooked, cut open the top with scissors and put 7.5 g crumbled mozzarella into each one. • Heat the mozzarella brioches under the salamander grill for 30 seconds. Remove and place a spoon of rose air on top of each brioche. • Serve on a black slate with satin paper.
Cutlery	• None.
How to eat	• Hold the brioche by the base and eat in two mouthfuls.

1126

Melon with ham 2005

Year
2005

Family
Snacks

Temperature
Cold

Season
All year round

Serves 10

For the *jamón ibérico* consommé

250 g *jamón ibérico* off-cuts
500 g water

- Remove the excess fat from the ham and cut it into uneven pieces of roughly 1 cm in size.
- Cover the ham with the water and simmer, skimming continuously to remove the fat and scum for 15 minutes.
- Strain through a Superbag. Do not allow the stock to become cloudy or remove any more fat.
- Refrigerate.

For the *jamón ibérico* consommé with Xantana

250 g *jamón ibérico* consommé
(previously prepared)
0.6 g Xantana

- Mix the Xantana with the ham consommé with a stick blender until no lumps remain.
- Refrigerate.

For the cantaloupe melon juice

500 g cantaloupe melon

- Peel the melon and remove the seeds.
- Blend the melon flesh in a liquidiser and strain through a Superbag to produce melon juice.

For the spherical melon caviar base

250 g melon juice (previously prepared)
2 g sodium alginate

- While cold, mix the sodium alginate with a third of the juice and process with a stick blender to dissolve the sodium alginate completely.
- Mix in the rest of the juice.
- Strain and set aside at room temperature.

For the calcium chloride mixture

500 g water
2.5 g calcium chloride

- Dissolve the calcium chloride in the water with a whisk and set aside.

Finishing and presentation

Freshly ground black pepper

- Fill 4 syringes with the melon juice.
- Drip the melon juice into the water and calcium solution one drop at a time and leave to 'cook' for 3 minutes.
- Strain, then wash the caviar in cold water. Drain.
- Pour 25 g of cold ham consommé with Xantana into each champagne flute.
- Put 10 g spherical melon caviar into each glass and stir to mix it through with the ham consommé.
- Finish with a little freshly ground black pepper.

  NB: This dish, like *Melon with ham/234* from 1994, is a variation on the traditional dish of cured ham with melon.

Cutlery

- None.

How to eat

- Drink a little *jamón ibérico* consommé and caviar at a time.

1127

Spherical-I mozzarella

Year
2005

Family
Snacks

Temperature
Cold

Season
All year round

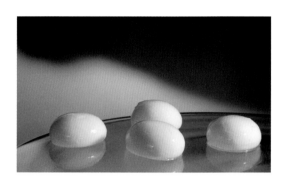

Serves 10

For the mozzarella water

4 balls fresh buffalo mozzarella in 500 g tubs

- Open the tubs without breaking the lids (they will be used later as a serving dish). Remove the mozzarella balls and reserve the water from the tubs.

For the mozarella base

220 g buffalo mozzarella
150 g mozzarella water (previously prepared)
70 g 35% fat single cream
20 g double cream
4 g salt

- Blend the mozzarella with the mozzarella water in the liquidiser until a slightly grainy cream forms.
- Bring the single cream to the boil and add the mozzarella cream and the double cream. Blend in the liquidiser for 10 seconds.
- Add the salt, stir and refrigerate.

For the sodium alginate solution

5 g sodium alginate
1 kg water

- Blend the sodium alginate with the water in the liquidiser until it is lump-free.
- Pour into a container to a thickness of 6 cm.

For the spherical-I mozzarella

200 g mozzarella base (previously prepared)
1 kg sodium alginate solution
(previously prepared)
1 x 15 g hemispherical measuring spoon

- Fill the spoons with the mozzarella base and drop into the sodium alginate solution to form spheres.
- Leave the mozzarella spheres to 'cook' in the sodium alginate solution for 12 minutes.
- Remove the mozzarella spheres with a slotted spoon. Rinse them, then keep them submerged in the mozzarella water.
- Refrigerate.

Finishing and presentation

- Put the spherical mozzarella balls in the mozzarella water in the tubs they came in. Present the tubs on a stone with spoons. The waiter opens the tub and serves the mozzarella to the guests.

  NB: A different version of this snack has been created by injecting cold fresh basil water jelly into the centre of the mozzarella spheres.

  NB: The spherical-I mozzarella has sometimes been accompanied by a freeze-dried mozzarella ball filled with basil oil.

Cutlery

- Soup spoon.

How to eat

- In a single mouthful. Break it up inside your mouth to release the liquid inside.

1128

Malt flour and butter ravioli with sea urchin and lime zest

Year
2005

Family
Snacks

Temperature
Hot

Season
January, February, March, April, May, June

Serves 10

For the fresh malt flour pasta

200 g plain flour
55 g malt flour
12 g olive oil
2 x 65 g eggs

- Mix both types of flour and add the eggs one at a time while kneading.
- Add the olive oil and continue to knead to obtain a smooth dough.
- Stand in the refrigerator for 1 hour covered with a damp cloth.

For the salted butter balls

250 g salted butter

- Use a 1.2 cm melon baller to make 20 butter balls.
- Refrigerate them immediately.

For the fresh malt flour pasta and salted butter ravioli

250 fresh malt flour pasta (previously prepared)
20 salted butter balls (previously prepared)
1 beaten egg
100 g fine wheat semolina
1 x 2 cm metal pastry cutter

- Use a dough rolling machine to roll out 7 cm bands of fresh pasta to a thickness of 1 mm.
- Once the dough has been rolled out, cut it into 4 x 7 cm rectangles. Press the middle down lightly to form a base and place a butter ball at the centre.
- Lightly brush around the butter with beaten egg.
- Form ravioli by folding up the dough leaving the butter in the middle and pressing around with your fingers to seal the pasta well and remove as much air as possible.
- Use the pastry cutter to make semicircular ravioli with a 2 cm diameter.
- Place the ravioli in a container and sprinkle with plenty of fine semolina. Refrigerate.

For the sea urchin roe

6 x 70 g sea urchins

- Kill the sea urchins by scalding them in boiling water for 10 seconds.
- Cut along the bottom of the sea urchins with a pair of scissors, making a 2 cm diameter circle.
- Remove the roe from inside the sea urchins and place each one in the sea urchin liquor previously strained through a Superbag.
- Choose the 20 largest pieces of roe.
- Refrigerate.

Finishing and presentation

1 lime
Water
1 Microplane grater

- Bring 2 kg of water to the boil.
- Cook the ravioli in the boiling water for 30 seconds and drain them with a spider skimmer, taking care not to break them.
- Arrange 2 butter ravioli on a black slate and 1 piece of sea urchin roe on top of each.
- Heat the ravioli and sea urchin roe under the salamander grill and finish by sprinkling a little grated lime zest over the top.

Cutlery

- Tapas cutlery.

  NB: Tapas cutlery consists of a 14 x 3 cm spoon and fork.

How to eat

- Take the ravioli one at a time without breaking and eat as a single mouthful together with the sea urchin roe.

1129

Clams in Earl Grey tea, pink grapefruit and black sesame

Year
2005

Family
Snacks

Temperature
Hot

Season
All year round

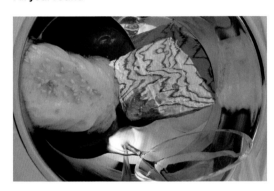

Serves 10

For the shelled clams

10 x 40 g grooved carpet shell clams
1 kg sea water

- Plunge the clams into boiling water for 6 seconds.
- Remove them from the water and leave them to cool at room temperature.
- Use a paring knife to slice off the muscle joining the clam to the shell.
- Carefully remove the clams from their shells without breaking them.
- Strain the clam liquor through a Superbag, cover the clams with it and refrigerate.

For the hot pink grapefruit foam

250 g pink grapefruit juice
2.5 g methylcellulose
1 x 0.5 litre ISI siphon
1 N$_2$O cartridge

- Mix the grapefruit juice with the methylcellulose and process with a stick blender until it is lump-free.
- Cool the mixture to 3 °C and process again with the stick blender.
- Strain and fill the siphon.
- Close it, insert the gas cartridge and set aside in a bain-marie at 45 °C.

For the oboro kombu sheets

2 sheets oboro kombu

- Cut the sheets of oboro kombu with a pair of scissors to obtain 10 4 x 3 cm rectangles.

  NB: Oboro kombu is the name for pressed sheets of kombu hearts previously soaked in rice vinegar and dried.

For the toasted black sesame savoury praline

60 g black sesame seeds
10 g sunflower oil
Salt

- Toast the black sesame in a frying pan.
- Grind the toasted black sesame with the oil to obtain a fine cream.
- Strain, season with salt and fill 10 pipettes with the praline.

For the Earl Grey tea

5.4 g Excelsior Earl Grey tea
300 g water

- Place the tea in a ball infuser and then in a teapot.
- Boil the water and pour it into the teapot.
- Leave to infuse for 2 minutes.

  NB: This preparation should be made immediately before finishing and presentation.

1129

Clams in Earl Grey tea, pink grapefruit and black sesame

Finishing and presentation

20 g toasted Japanese white sesame seeds

- Lightly warm the clams, covered in their liquor to keep them moist, under the salamander grill.
- Place a clam at the bottom of a preheated bowl.
- Cover the clam with a piece of oboro kombu, ensuring that it does not stick to the clam too much.
- Squirt a little hot grapefruit foam over the clam and smooth it slightly with a small spatula.
- Sprinkle a pinch of toasted Japanese white sesame over the foam.
- Serve the pipette of black sesame savoury praline separately. Do the same with the teapot so that the tea can be served in front of the diner.

Cutlery

- Tapas cutlery.

  NB: Tapas cutlery consists of a 14 x 3 cm spoon and fork.

How to eat

- 20 g of tea will be served in front of diners without touching the grapefruit foam. The tea should be taken together with the hot grapefruit foam. Then 1 drop of black sesame praline will be placed on the clam and eaten in one mouthful.

Tapas
1130–1181

Tapas
1130–1181

1130

Thaw 2005

Year
2005

Family
Tapas

Temperature
Frozen/ambient

Season
May, June

Serves 4

For the green pine cone infusion

480 g green pine cones
600 g water
75 g sugar
0.6 g ascorbic acid

- Soak the green pine cones in hot water for 1 minute to clean them.
- Coarsely chop the pine cones into 2 cm chunks.
- Bring the water to the boil with the sugar and add the chopped green pine cones.
- Add the ascorbic acid and refrigerate for 24 hours.
- Strain through a Superbag and refrigerate.

  NB: Ascorbic acid (vitamin C) is used as an antioxidant.

For the frozen green pine cone powder

200 g green pine infusion (previously prepared)
Pacojet

- Put the green pine cone infusion into a Pacojet beaker and freeze at -20 °C.
- Process the frozen green pine cone infusion in the Pacojet for each individual serving until a frozen powder with snow-like texture is achieved.
- Store the frozen powder at -20 °C.

For the wild pine nut milk

200 g peeled wild pine nuts
240 g water

- Process the pine nuts with the water using a stick blender until they are well broken up.
- Stand in the refrigerator for 12 hours.
- Blend the water and pine nut mixture in a liquidiser until it forms a cream.
- Squeeze firmly through a Superbag to release all the liquid and create a thick pine nut milk.
- Strain and refrigerate.

For the wild pine nut milk sorbet

250 g wild pine nut milk (previously prepared)
¼ x 2 g gelatine leaf (previously rehydrated in cold water)
Pacojet
Salt

- Lightly salt the pine nut milk.
- Heat a quarter of the pine nut milk at 45 °C and dissolve a gelatine leaf in it. Once it has dissolved, add the rest of the milk and mix well.
- Put the pine nut sorbet mixture in a Pacojet beaker and freeze at -20 °C.
- Five minutes before finishing and presentation, process the sorbet with the Pacojet twice and store at -8 °C.

For the toasted wild pine nut savoury praline

50 g toasted wild pine nuts
10 g olive oil
Salt

- Blend the pine nuts with the oil in the liquidiser until they form a fine, lump-free cream.
- Strain and season with salt.

For the garrapi-nitro pine nuts

12 toasted wild pine nuts
50 g wild pine nut savoury praline (previously prepared)
500 g liquid nitrogen

- Dip the whole pine nuts into the pine nut praline and then dip them into the liquid nitrogen for 5 seconds to freeze the praline so that the pine nuts are completely coated with it.
- Remove from the liquid nitrogen and keep the garrapi-nitro pine nuts at -10 °C.

For the liquorice paste light meringue powder

125 g water
125 g pasteurised liquid egg white
7.5 g powdered egg white
25 g sugar
35 g liquorice paste

- Mix all the ingredients together while cold and beat in the electric mixer for 5 minutes.
- Leave to stand for 2 minutes with the mixer switched off.
- Beat for 10 more minutes and spread over a baking tray lined with a Silpat to a depth of 1 cm.
- Dry in the oven at 100 °C for 40 minutes.
- Raise the oven temperature to 120°C and leave for a further 40 minutes.
- When dry, place in a bag and crush to a powder.
- Store in an airtight container in a cool, dry place.

1130

Thaw 2005

For the rocks and green pine cone light infusion meringue powder

125 g green pine cone infusion (previously prepared)
125 g pasteurised liquid egg white
7.5 g powdered egg white
25 g sugar

- Mix all the cold ingredients together and beat in the electric mixer for 10 minutes.
- Spread the meringue mixture over a baking tray lined with a Silpat to a depth of 1 cm.
- Dry in the oven at 90 °C for 1 hour and 40 minutes.
- Cut the light meringue into 8 x 1.5 cm rocks.
- Put the remaining meringue in a bag and crush to a powder.
- Store in an airtight container in a cool, dry place.

For the green pine cone jelly

200 g green pine cone infusion (previously prepared)
1 x 2 g gelatine leaf (previously rehydrated in cold water)

- Dissolve the gelatine in a quarter of the green pine cone infusion before mixing with the rest of it.
- Pour into a container to a depth of 1 cm and refrigerate for 2 hours to set.

For the freeze-dried green pine cone jelly

Green pine cone jelly (previously prepared)

- Freeze-dry for 72 hours, then keep in a vacuum-pack bag in a cool, dry place.

For the plain caramel slices

100 g fondant
50 g glucose
50 g Isomalt

- Dissolve the fondant and glucose in a pan and boil. Stir until everything has thoroughly dissolved, then add the Isomalt.
- Keep on a medium heat until the temperature reaches 160 °C (the temperature will increase by another 5 °C).
- Remove from the heat and spread out on parchment paper to a thickness of 1 cm.
- When the correct temperature is reached, cut into 5 x 5 cm pieces.
- Store in an airtight container in a cool, dry place.
- Put a caramel square between 2 Silpats and heat in the oven until the caramel melts.
- Remove and quickly roll out into a 1 mm thick caramel sheet.
- Store the caramel sheets in an airtight container in a cool, dry place.

Finishing and presentation

5 g freshly ground coffee
4 purple shiso shoots
4 green shiso shoots
4 g fresh basil shoots
4 borage shoots
4 borage flowers

NB: Shiso is a kind of Asian herb similar to basil and mint. There are two varieties, purple and green.

NB: If borage flowers are not available, substitute with cucumber flowers.

- Place half a spoonful of pine nut sorbet in the middle of a soup plate.
- Cover the pine nut sorbet with the frozen green pine cone powder. The surface should be rough.
- Make a bunch with 1 shoot of green shiso, 1 of purple shiso, 1 of borage and 1 of fresh basil and place it upright beside the pine nut sorbet.
- Place a borage flower beside the shoots.
- Imagining the dish as a clock face, put 1 g of ground coffee at 11 o'clock to the frozen powder.
- Place a 2 cm piece of freeze-dried green pine cone infusion at 1 o'clock.
- Stand a 2 cm piece of plain caramel sheet at 3 o'clock.
- Place 2 rocks made from the light green pine cone infusion meringue and half a teaspoon of light green pine cone infusion meringue powder at 6 o'clock.
- Place a teaspoonful of light liquorice meringue powder at 9 o'clock.
- Finish by arranging 3 garrapi-nitro pine nuts over the frozen powder.

Cutlery

- Tapas cutlery.

NB: Tapas cutlery consists of a 14 x 3 cm spoon and fork.

How to eat

NB: This dish is a variation on the theme of *Thaw /1059* from 2004.

- Start with a spoonful of powder and alternate with the different components without mixing them. It is important not to break the structure of the dish so as not to mix flavours.

1131

Earth 2005

Year
2005

Family
Tapas

Temperature
Frozen/ambient

Season
All year round

Serves 4

For the chicken and veal stock

500 g chicken
1.5 kg chicken carcasses
500 g veal knucklebones
50 g veal shank
20 g carrot
20 g leek
20 g onion
2.5 kg water

- Brown the veal knucklebones in the oven.
- Clean the chicken carcasses of any traces of fat and entrails. Brown in the oven.
- Chop up the veal shank.
- Clean the chicken of fat and entrails but keep whole.
- Peel and slice the onions. Brown them in a frying pan.
- Peel the carrot and clean the leek.
- Put all the ingredients in a pot and cover with water.
- Simmer for 8 hours.
- Strain. There should be about 1.5 kg remaining.

For the chicken and veal consommé

750 g chicken and veal stock (previously prepared)
20 g carrot
10 g leek
50 g ripe tomato
75 g minced veal
100 g egg white
15 g crushed ice

- Bring the stock to the boil. When it breaks into a boil, reduce the heat so it stays warm but does not evaporate.
- To prepare the egg white clarifying mixture, grate the tomato and leave it to drain in a colander. Next, chop the carrot and leek into small dice. Mix the chopped vegetables with the tomato and minced meat. Finally, add the egg whites and beat.
- Mix with the crushed ice.
- Stir the stock to create a swirl and gradually incorporate the egg white mixture.
- Gradually turn up the heat until the liquid breaks into a boil.
- Remove from the heat. Stand for 15 minutes, then make a small hole in the egg white mixture with a spoon so that you can take the consommé out with a ladle. As you take the consommé out of the pot, strain it through a Superbag.
- Refrigerate.

For the jellied black truffle juice consommé

50 g chicken and veal consommé (previously prepared)
20 g unsalted black truffle juice
Salt

- Check the texture of the jellied consommé and correct with gelatine leaves if required.
- Melt the consommé and mix with the truffle juice.
- Season with salt and pour into a container to a thickness of 1 cm.
- Leave to set in the refrigerator for 3 hours.

For the duck foie gras cream

100 g duck foie gras
100 g water
Salt

- Cut the duck foie gras into 3 cm pieces.
- Place the duck foie gras in the Thermomix and add the boiling water.
- Blend at 60 °C for 5 minutes to obtain a smooth, even cream.
- Strain and season with salt.

For the frozen duck foie gras air rocks

175 g duck foie gras cream (previously prepared)

- Raise the duck foie gras cream to room temperature in a deep 25 cm diameter container and work a stick blender over the surface until it emulsifies and the air forms.
- Leave the air to stand for 1 minute.
- Collect the foie gras air with a spoon, taking care not to damage the texture, and place it in a container to a thickness of 3 cm.
- Quickly freeze the foie gras air at -20 °C.
- Once frozen, cut 8 x 2 cm dice of foie gras air.
- Store at -20 °C.

1131

Earth 2005

For the frozen duck foie gras powder

250 g duck foie gras
125 g water
Salt
Pacojet

- Devein the duck foie gras, cut it into 2 cm chunks and place them in the liquidiser.
- Add the boiling water and blend to obtain a fine cream.
- Season with salt and strain.
- Transfer to a Pacojet beaker and freeze at -20 °C.
- Process a batch in the Pacojet and store the resulting powder in the freezer at -20 °C.
- Repeat the operation until 160 g of frozen duck foie gras powder is obtained.

For the liquidised sweetcorn juice

4 x 400 g tins of sweetcorn

- Open the tins and blend the contents (including the water) 3 times in a liquidiser.
- Strain and refrigerate.

For the tinned sweetcorn sorbet

150 g sweetcorn juice (previously prepared)
12 g liquid glucose
0.2 g sorbet stabiliser
Salt

- Combine 75 g of liquidised sweetcorn juice with the glucose and stabiliser and heat to 85 °C.
- Remove from the heat and when the mixture cools to 60 °C, add the rest of the sweetcorn juice and season with salt.
- Mix and then allow to stand in the refrigerator for 8 hours.
- Process in the sorbet maker immediately before finishing and presentation.
- Keep at -8 °C.

For the red peach powder

250 g Garnier red vineyard peach purée

- Spread out the red peach purée over a 60 x 40 cm tray lined with parchment paper.
- Dry out in the oven at 70 °C until it has a slightly solid texture.
- Place in the dehydrator and leave for 6 hours at 60 °C.
- Once the purée is completely dehydrated and crisp, blend in a liquidiser to obtain red peach powder.
- It is essential that the peach powder is kept immediately in an airtight bag; it absorbs moisture very easily.
- Store in a cool, dry place.

For the fried crushed almond

25 g crushed almond
100 g olive oil
Salt

- Mix the almond with the olive oil and fry on a medium heat while stirring constantly.
- Once fried, drain and lay on paper towel to soak up the excess oil.
- Season with salt while still hot.

For the puffed quinoa

50 g quinoa
Water
500 g olive oil
1 orange
1 Microplane grater
Salt

- Boil the quinoa for 25 minutes in plenty of water.
- Drain, rinse in cold water to stop the cooking process, then drain again thoroughly.
- Spray the cooked quinoa out over trays lined with parchment paper; ensure the grains are not overlapping.
- Leave the quinoa in a warm place for 24 hours until it is completely dry.
- Once dry, puff the quinoa in oil at 190 °C.
- Drain, soak up the excess oil on paper towel and season with salt while still hot.
- Once cool, season with grated orange zest.

For the crunchy spice bread crumbs

50 g honey spice bread

- Cut off the crust.
- Chop the bread in a liquidiser. Use short, sharp bursts to obtain 3 mm crumbs.
- Place the crumbs in the oven at 110 °C until completely dry.
- Store in an airtight container in a cool, dry place.

For the grated walnuts

20 g walnuts, shelled
1 Microplane grater

- Grate the walnuts with the Microplane grater into long strips.
- Store the threads in a container without piling, so as not to alter their texture.

1131

Earth 2005

Finishing and presentation

15 g cocoa powder
2 g ground toasted hazelnut skin

- Place 2 frozen duck foie gras air rocks in the middle of each of 4 x 25 cm frozen soup plates.
- Cover the foie gras rocks with 40 g of frozen foie gras powder.
- Use a 1.5 cm diameter melon baller to make 4 balls of sweetcorn sorbet. Coat them in cocoa powder.
- Place the following over the foie gras powder, distributed in such a way that they are not in contact with each other: a small mound of 3 g spice bread crumbs, 3 g puffed cocoa, 3 g grated walnut, 3 g red peach powder, 3 g fried crushed almond and a pinch of toasted hazelnut skin.
- Place a sweetcorn sorbet ball coated in cocoa powder in the middle of the dish.
- The final effect should be that of a barren landscape.

NB: This dish is a variation on the theme of *Earth/**936*** from 2003.

Cutlery

- Tapas cutlery.

NB: Tapas cutlery consists of a 14 x 3 cm spoon and fork.

How to eat

- Alternate the different components. The sweetcorn sorbet truffle should be eaten in two non-consecutive mouthfuls.

1132

Almond kernels with elderflower, in egg yolk and lemon

Year
2005

Family
Tapas

Temperature
Cold

Season
March, April

Serves 4

For the almond kernels	• Use a paring knife to open the green almond shells and extract the almond kernels from inside, taking care not to break them.
500 g green almonds	• There should be 12 g of almond kernels for each person.
	• Refrigerate.

For the peeled crystal almonds	• Use the tip of a knife to remove the shells and lift the almonds out, taking care not to break them.
12 crystal almonds	• Make a slit in the almond skin and peel the almonds with your fingers, taking care not to break them.
	• Refrigerate.
	NB: We give the name 'crystal almond' to a very young almond that can be peeled and hold its shape. Its name refers to its transparent appearance.

For the cold elderflower jelly	• Bring the water to the boil and add the elderflower.
	• Remove from the heat and leave to infuse for 1 minute.
100 g water	• Strain and dissolve the well-drained gelatine leaf in it.
30 g elderflower	
10 g Hafi elderflower concentrate	
½ x 2 g gelatine leaf (previously rehydrated in cold water)	• Add the elderflower drink concentrate, mix and transfer to a shallow container to a depth of 5 mm.
	• Refrigerate for 2 hours to set.

For the liquidised lemon juice	• Wash the lemons and cut off both ends.
	• Liquidise the whole lemons and reserve the juice in a deep, narrow container so that the pulp (top) will separate from the liquid (bottom).
3 x 250 g thick-skinned lemons	
	• Discard the pulp from the top and reserve the liquid part of the juice.

For the egg yolk and lemon sauce	• Mix both ingredients with a whisk to obtain a smooth cream.
50 g liquidised lemon juice (previously prepared)	• Refrigerate.
50 g egg yolk	

For the prune kernel oil	• Mix the oils and set aside.
15 g prune kernel oil	
5 g olive oil	

Finishing and presentation	• Pour the cream into a deep 25 cm diameter container. Work a stick blender over the surface until it emulsifies and the air forms. Leave the air to stand for 1 minute.
500 g 35% fat single cream	• Imagining the plate as a clock face, place 2 x 4 g mounds of almond kernels in an O! LUNA deep lunar plate in both the 11 and 3 o'clock positions.
8 acacia flowers	
8 g elderflower petals	
	• Place a 1.5 cm piece of cold elderflower jelly at 6 and 12 o'clock, and sprinkle 2 g of elderflower petals over them.
	• Place a crystal almond at 1, 4 and 9 o'clock.
	• Place 3 acacia flowers at 8 o'clock.
	• Place a spoonful of egg yolk and lemon sauce in the middle of the plate.
	• Make a zigzag using 4 g of prune kernel oil over the sauce.
	• Finish by placing 2 teaspoons of cream air on top of the egg yolk and lemon sauce.

Cutlery	• Dessert spoon and fork.

How to eat	• Alternate the almond kernels and the crystal almonds with the other components of the dish.

1133

Pistachio-LYO with black truffle jellied consommé and mandarin air

Year
2005

Family
Tapas

Temperature
Ambient/cold

Season
All year round

Serves 4

For the peeled green pistachio cream

140 g peeled green pistachios
240 g water
Pacojet

- Blend the peeled green pistachios with the water in the liquidiser to obtain a cream.
- Put the cream in a Pacojet beaker and freeze at -20 °C.
- Once frozen solid, put through the Pacojet 3 times and leave to thaw in the refrigerator for 3 hours until it has the texture of light cream.
- Refrigerate.

For the cold peeled green pistachio foam

250 g peeled green pistachio cream (previously prepared)
1 g salt
1 x 0.5 litre ISI siphon
1 N$_2$O cartridge

- Mix the pistachio cream and season with salt.
- Strain and fill the siphon.
- Refrigerate for 3 hours.

For the freeze-dried peeled green pistachio foam

Cold peeled green pistachio foam (previously prepared)
8 x 60 cc plastic cups

- Fill the plastic cups with green pistachio foam and quickly put them into the freeze-dryer.
- Freeze dry for 48 hours.
- Once the foams are freeze dried, cut each one into 3 even pieces per person. Four pieces are required per person.
- Crush the rest of the freeze-dried foam between 2 sheets of parchment paper to obtain a powder.
- Keep the freeze-dried foam and LYO powder in the dehydrator so that they do not become moist.

For the chicken and veal stock

500 g chicken
1.5 kg chicken carcasses
500 g veal knucklebones
50 g veal shank
20 g carrot
20 g leek
20 g onion
2.5 kg water

- Brown the veal knucklebones in the oven.
- Clean the chicken carcasses of any traces of fat and entrails. Brown in the oven.
- Chop up the veal shank.
- Clean the chicken of fat and entrails but keep whole.
- Peel and slice the onions. Brown them in a frying pan.
- Peel the carrot and clean the leek.
- Put all the ingredients in a pot and cover with water.
- Simmer for 8 hours.
- Strain. There should be about 1.5 kg remaining.

For the chicken and veal consommé

750 g chicken and veal stock (previously prepared)
20 g carrot
10 g leek
50 g ripe tomato
75 g minced veal
100 g egg white
15 g crushed ice

- Bring the stock to the boil. When it breaks into a boil, reduce the heat so it stays warm but does not evaporate.
- To prepare the egg white clarifying mixture, grate the tomato and leave it to drain in a colander. Next, chop the carrot and leek into small dice. Mix the chopped vegetables with the tomato and minced meat. Finally, add the egg whites and beat.
- Mix with the crushed ice.
- Stir the stock to create a swirl and gradually incorporate the egg white mixture.
- Gradually turn up the heat until the liquid breaks into a boil.
- Remove from the heat. Stand for 15 minutes, then make a small hole in the egg white mixture with a spoon so that you can take the consommé out with a ladle. As you take the consommé out of the pot, strain it through a Superbag.
- Refrigerate.

1133

Pistachio-LYO with black truffle jellied consommé and mandarin air

For the black truffle juice with consommé

75 g chicken and veal consommé
(previously prepared)
175 g unsalted black truffle juice
0.1 g Xantana
Salt

- Heat the consommé and mix with the truffle juice.
- Season with salt, add the Xantana and dissolve with a stick blender until lump-free.
- Refrigerate.

For the mandarin juice air base

500 g Simone Gatto mandarin juice
1.5 g soya lecithin powder

- Mix the mandarin juice with the soya lecithin in a deep 25 cm diameter container.

Finishing and presentation

- Work a stick blender over the surface of the mandarin air base until it emulsifies and the air forms.
- Arrange 4 pieces of freeze-dried pistachio foam along the edge of an O! LUNA large eclipse plate, on the side opposite the relief.
- Place a spoon of freeze-dried pistachio powder at the bottom edge of the dish
- Place 3 soup spoonfuls of mandarin juice air between the pieces of freeze-dried pistachio foam.
- Put 40 g of truffle juice per person in a separate jug so that the waiter can serve it in front of the diner.

Cutlery

- Tapas cutlery.

  NB: Tapas cutlery consists of a 14 x 3 cm spoon and fork.

How to eat

- Alternate the freeze-dried pistachio foam with the air and the truffle juice with consommé.

1134

Carrot-LYO foam with hazelnut foam-air and Córdoba spices

Year
2005

Family
Tapas

Temperature
Ambient/cold

Season
All year round

Serves 4

For the carrot juice

1.5 kg carrots

- Peel and liquidise the carrots.
- Pass the juice through a fine strainer and refrigerate.

For the cold carrot juice foam

500 g carrot juice
3.5 x 2 g gelatine leaves (previously rehydrated in cold water)
1 x 0.5 litre ISI siphon
1 N₂O cartridge

- Heat a quarter of the carrot juice and dissolve the gelatine in it.
- Add the remaining carrot juice. Mix, pass through the fine strainer and fill the siphon with the liquid.
- Close the siphon and insert the gas cartridge.
- Keep the siphon in an ice bath in the refrigerator for 6 hours.

For the cold carrot juice foam-LYO

Cold carrot juice foam (previously prepared)
10 x 60 g plastic cups

- Fill the plastic cups with carrot juice foam and quickly put them into the freeze-dryer.
- Freeze-dry for 48 hours.
- Once the foams are freeze dried, cut each one into 3 even pieces per person.
- Keep in the dehydrator so that the freeze-dried foam does not become moist.

For the hazelnut cream

120 g skinned toasted hazelnuts
240 g water
Pacojet

- Blend the hazelnuts with the water in the liquidiser until they have a cream-like consistency.
- Put the hazelnut cream in a Pacojet beaker and freeze at -20 °C.
- Once frozen solid, put through the Pacojet 3 times and leave to thaw in the refrigerator for 3 hours until it has the texture of light cream.
- Refrigerate.

For the cold hazelnut foam

40 g hazelnut paste
120 g 35% fat single cream
80 g hazelnut cream (previously prepared)
¾ x 2 g gelatine leaf (previously rehydrated in cold water)
1 g salt
1 x 0.5 litre ISI siphon
1 N₂O cartridge

- Warm a quarter of the hazelnut cream, dissolve the gelatine in it, then add the rest of the cream and the remaining ingredients.
- Mix and strain.
- Fill the siphon with the mixture, close and charge the gas canister.
- Stand in the refrigerator for 3 hours.

For the pink grapefruit segments

1 x 300 g pink grapefruit

- Slice off the top and bottom of the grapefruit to expose the segments.
- Peel the grapefruit in a spiral to expose the flesh so that there are no traces of zest or pith, but without altering the basic shape of the fruit.
- Remove the segments from their membranes with a sharp knife.
- Slice each segment down the middle so that each piece measures 2.5 x 1 cm. 4 pieces are needed.
- Refrigerate.

For the fermented milk _mató_ cheese

500 g fermented full-cream milk

- Pour the milk into a small pan a heat to 58 °C, stirring constantly with a spatula.
- Leave to stand for 5 minutes and pour the milk through a sieve so that the whey is drained out and the _mató_ cheese remains in the sieve.
- Collect the _mató_ cheese and store in the refrigerator.

For the milk air and Córdoba spice base

500 g milk
1.5 g soya lecithin powder
3.5 g Fatéma Hal's Córdoba spices

- Heat the milk.
- Mix in the spices with a stick blender and allow to infuse for 24 hours.
- Strain the infusion through a Superbag over a deep 25 cm diameter container. Add the lecithin and process with a stick blender.

1134

Carrot-LYO foam with hazelnut foam-air and Córdoba spices

For the toasted saffron powder

3 g saffron threads

- Toast the saffron threads in a frying pan.
- Break up the saffron to make a rough powder.

For the fried hazelnuts

4 shelled and skinned hazelnuts
100 g x 0.4° olive oil
Salt

- Put the hazelnuts and oil into a cold pan and fry, stirring constantly.
- Once fried, drain off excess oil on a paper towel and season with salt while hot.
- Split the hazelnuts in half and set aside.

Finishing and presentation

20 g pure hazelnut paste
4 g Fatéma Hal's Córdoba spices
10 g coriander shoots
2 g fresh chopped fennel
2 g virgin fennel seed oil

- Heat the milk air and Córdoba spice mixture to 50 °C and work a stick blender over the surface until it emulsifies and the air forms.
- Put 1 drop of virgin fennel seed oil and a pinch of chopped fresh fennel over each grapefruit segment. Place the grapefruit segment in the middle of a plate.
- Place a teaspoon of mató cheese to the right of the grapefruit, but without touching it.
- Place a spoonful of milk and spice air in the middle of the plate. Then place 4 x 3 g spots of cold hazelnut foam and 3 fried half hazelnuts over it.
- Apply the hazelnut paste over the foam-air in a zigzag pattern.
- Place 3 pieces of freeze-dried carrot foam in the upper section of the plate, just above the air.
- Sprinkle a pinch of saffron powder over the air, lightly place 2 g coriander shoots over one side of the air and finish by sprinkling a little Córdoba spice around the air.

Cutlery

- Tapas cutlery.

  NB: Tapas cutlery consists of a 14 x 3 cm spoon and fork.

How to eat

- Alternate the pieces of freeze-dried carrot foam with the other ingredients.

1135

Jellied *tucupi* consommé with frozen passion fruit crumbs

Year
2005

Family
Tapas

Temperature
Ambient/frozen

Season
All year round

Serves 4

For the chicken breast consommé

2 x 300 g free-range chicken breasts
800 g water

- Remove any excess fat or skin from the chicken breasts and chop them into 2 cm pieces.
- Cover the chicken with water, bring to the boil and simmer, constantly skimming off the scum and fat to obtain 400 g of stock.
- Strain through a Superbag to keep the consommé clear.
- Skim off the fat and refrigerate.

For the *tucupi* broth

400 g chicken breast consommé
(previously prepared)
15 g fresh coriander
1 stalk fresh lemongrass
1 kaffir lime zest
1 lime zest
2 kaffir lime leaves
0.2 g toasted saffron threads
3 g fresh pressed yeast
2 g Szechuan button
Salt

NB: The real *tucupi* is the stock resulting from cooking the juice obtained from fermented cassava It originates from Brazil.

- Chop the fresh coriander, lemongrass and kaffir lime leaves.
- Mix the previous ingredients with the toasted saffron in the chicken breast consommé and bring to the boil gradually.
- When it breaks into a boil, remove from the heat and stand for 5 minutes to infuse.
- Add the kaffir lime and lime zests (it is essential that there should be no pith at all on either so as not to turn the consommé bitter), leave to infuse for 2 minutes and strain through a Superbag.
- Add the yeast and the crumbled Szechuan button, and season with salt.
- Bring to the boil to prevent the consommé from fermenting, then refrigerate.

NB: The Szechuan button causes an electrical effect on the palate. It is the flower of the *Spilanthes oleracea*, native of Sichuan (formerly Szechuan) province in China. It is also found in Madagascar and the Amazon region. It is also known as *jambu* in certain areas of South America.

For the cold *tucupi* consommé jelly

250 g *tucupi* consommé (previously prepared)
1¼ x 2 g gelatine leaves (previously rehydrated in cold water)

- Drain the gelatine well then dilute it in one quarter of the hot consommé.
- Remove from the heat and add the rest of the consommé.
- Mix and pour 50 g of consommé with gelatine into 4 x 21 cm O! LUNA deep lunar plates.
- Leave to set in the refrigerator for 3 hours on a perfectly flat surface.

For the passion fruit juice

20 x 50 g passion fruits

- Cut the passion fruits in half and scoop out the flesh with a teaspoon over a chinois to catch and strain the juice.
- Process the passion fruit seeds with a stick blender on the lowest speed so that they release all their juice without being crushed.
- Strain the juice through a Superbag and refrigerate.

1135

Jellied *tucupi* consommé with frozen passion fruit crumbs

For the frozen passion fruit crumbs

225 g passion fruit juice (previously prepared)
45 g water
2 g soya lecithin powder

- Mix the passion fruit juice with the water in a deep 25 cm diameter container.
- Add the soya lecithin and process with a stick blender.
- Work the stick blender over the surface of the mixture until it emulsifies and the air forms.
- Leave to stabilise for 1 minute, then collect the air with a large spoon and fill an ice cream tub until the air protrudes 3 cm above the tub.
- Fill 2 tubs.
- Cover with a sheet of paper and freeze.

For the chilli oil

50 g sunflower oil
0.5 g dried chilli

- Chop the chillies, add them to the oil and heat to 70 °C.
- Remove from the heat and refrigerate for 24 hours.
- Strain and fill a pipette with the oil.

Finishing and presentation

10 g coriander shoots
1 lime
1 Microplane grater

- Remove the dishes of jelly from the refrigerator and temper at room temperature for 5 minutes.
- Place 1 spot of chilli oil at the top and bottom of the dishes.
- Place 3 g of coriander shoots on the left and 1 g of grated lime zest on the right.
- Keep the frozen passion fruit crumbs separate so that the waiter can serve them in front of the diner.

Cutlery

- Tapas cutlery.

  NB: Tapas cutlery consists of a 14 x 3 cm spoon and fork.

How to eat

- Alternate the *tucupi* consommé jelly with the frozen passion fruit crumbs.

1136

Músico

Year
2005

Family
Tapas

Temperature
Cold

Season
March, April

Serves 4

For the almond milk

250 g crushed almonds
300 g water

- Use a stick blender to process the crushed almonds thoroughly with the water.
- Stand in the refrigerator for 12 hours.
- Blend the water and almond mixture in the liquidiser to obtain a cream.
- Squeeze firmly through a Superbag to release all the liquid and create a thick, tasty almond milk.
- Strain and refrigerate.

For the almond milk sorbet balls

250 g almond milk (previously prepared)
¼ x 2 g gelatine leaf (previously rehydrated in cold water)
Salt

- Season the almond milk with salt.
- Heat a quarter of the almond milk and dissolve the gelatine in it.
- Add the remaining almond milk, mix and leave in the refrigerator for 2 hours.
- Process the mixture in the sorbet maker and store the resulting sorbet at -20 °C.
- When the sorbet has gained in substance, use a 1.5 cm diameter melon baller to make 8 balls.
- Store the almond sorbet balls at -10 °C.

For the almond bombs

200 g water
10 g Sosa powdered vegetable gelling agent
8 almond milk sorbet balls (previously prepared)

- Dissolve the vegetable gelling agent in the water and bring to the boil while whisking constantly.
- Remove from the heat and leave the mixture to cool to 75 °C.
- Use a thin needle to prick the almond sorbet balls, allowing you to dip them in the gelling mixture. Coat the balls with a 1 mm layer of jelly.
- Carefully remove the needle. Refrigerate the coated balls for 2 hours so that the sorbet melts, leaving the balls with a liquid centre.

For the green almond water

140 g green almonds
140 g water
0.2 g ascorbic acid

- Process the 3 ingredients with a stick blender until the green almonds are thoroughly crushed.
- Stand in the refrigerator for 12 hours.
- Grind to a paste in a liquidiser.
- Strain the paste through a Superbag, squeezing firmly to release all the liquid.
- Refrigerate.

For the cold green almond water jelly

110 g green almond water (previously prepared)
½ x 2 g gelatine leaf (previously rehydrated in cold water)
2 g sugar
0.1 g ascorbic acid

- Heat a third of the green almond water with the sugar and dissolve the drained gelatine in it.
- Add in the remaining green almond water and ascorbic acid. Mix.
- Pour into a container and leave to set in the refrigerator for 3 hours.

For the hazelnut savoury praline

50 g skinned toasted hazelnuts
5 g sunflower oil
Salt

- Blend the hazelnuts with the water in a liquidiser to obtain a fine cream.
- Strain and season with salt.
- Fill a squeeze bottle and set aside.

For the prune kernel oil

15 g prune kernel oil
5 g olive oil

- Mix the oils and set aside.

For the peeled crystal almonds

12 crystal almonds

- Use the tip of a knife to remove the shells and lift the almonds out, taking care not to break them.
- Make a slit in the almond skin and peel the almonds with your fingers, taking care not to break them.
- Refrigerate.

NB: We give the name 'crystal almond' to an almond in its skin when it can be peeled and hold its almond shape. Its name refers to its crystal-like appearance.

1136

Músico

Finishing and presentation

2 g ground toasted hazelnut skin
4 peeled walnut halves
10 g virgin pine nut oil
Maldon sea salt

- Carefully arrange 2 almond bombs in the middle of an O! LUNA deep lunar plate with a 5 cm space between them without breaking them.
- Place a soup spoon of cold green almond jelly between the bombs.
- Place 3 crystal almonds and 4 drops of prune kernel oil over the jelly.
- Put 2 x 2 g spots of hazelnut savoury praline to the sides of the jelly without touching the bombs. Sprinkle a pinch of ground toasted hazelnut skin over them.
- Place 1 walnut half at the top of the plate, in contact with the jelly.
- Finish with 2 g of pine nut oil around the jelly and a pinch of Maldon salt over each crystal almond.

Cutlery

- Tapas cutlery.

  NB: Tapas cutlery consists of a 14 x 3 cm spoon and fork.

How to eat

- Alternate the bombs with the jelly and the other components of the dish. The bombs should be eaten in a single mouthful so that they explode in the diner's mouth.

1137

Passion for olives

Year
2005

Family
Tapas

Temperature
Ambient

Season
All year round

Serves 4

For the green olive juice

500 g green Verdial olives

- Drain the olives and pit them.
- Blend the olives in the liquidiser, then strain through a Superbag.
- Set aside the obtained juice.

For the green olive 'fat'

250 g green olive juice (previously prepared)

- Decant the olive juice in a tall, narrow container for 24 hours at room temperature to allow the 'fat' to rise to the top.
- Remove the 'fat', taking care it does not mix with the water at the bottom.
- Set aside both the olive water and 'fat' separately.

For the passion fruit seeds

6 x 100 g passion fruits

- Cut the passion fruits in half with a knife and scoop out the flesh with a spoon.
- Refrigerate.

For the extra virgin olive oil air

200 g extra virgin olive oil
400 g water
2 g soya lecithin powder

- Mix the ingredients in a deep 25 cm diameter container.

Finishing and presentation

- Work a stick blender over the surface of the extra virgin olive oil until it emulsifies and the air forms.
- Spread a thick line of olive 'fat' around a 21 cm diameter soup plate.
- Make 4 small spots with the passion fruit seeds over the olive 'fat'.
- Place a spoon of extra virgin olive oil air in the middle of the dish.

Cutlery

- Tapas cutlery.

  NB: Tapas cutlery consists of a 14 x 3 cm spoon and fork.

How to eat

- Start with a spoonful of olive 'fat' with air and alternate with the passion fruit seeds.

1138

Carrot-LYO desert

Year
2005

Family
Tapas

Temperature
Frozen/cold/ambient

Season
All year round

Serves 4

For the carrot juice

1.5 kg carrots

- Peel and liquidise the carrots.
- Pass the juice through a fine strainer and refrigerate.

For the cold carrot juice foam

250 g carrot juice (previously prepared)
1¾ x 2 g gelatine leaves (previously rehydrated in cold water)
1 x 0.5 litre ISI siphon
1 N₂O cartridge

- Heat a quarter of the carrot juice and dissolve the gelatine in it.
- Add the remaining carrot juice. Mix, pass through the fine strainer and fill the siphon with the liquid.
- Close the siphon and insert the gas cartridge.
- Keep the siphon in an ice bath in the refrigerator for 6 hours.

For the freeze-dried cold carrot juice foam

Cold carrot juice foam (previously prepared)
10 x 60 g plastic shot glasses

- Fill the plastic cups with carrot juice foam and quickly put them into the freeze-dryer.
- Freeze dry for 48 hours.
- Once the foams are freeze-dried, remove them from the moulds and cut out 8 x 1.5 cm cubes. Crush the rest of the freeze-dried foam between 2 sheets of parchment paper to obtain a powder.
- Make 4 x 3 g portions of powder.
- Keep in the dehydrator so that the freeze-dried foam does not become moist.

For the fennel bulb juice

1 x 150 g fennel bulb
2 sprigs fresh fennel flowers

- Discard the outer layer of the bulb and chop the rest into coarse 2 cm chunks.
- Blanch the fennel in boiling water tor 3 minutes, then drain and quickly refresh in iced water.
- Drain, dry over paper towel and liquidise.
- Add the fennel flowers to the juice and process with a stick blender.
- Strain through a Superbag and refrigerate.

For the cold fennel bulb juice jelly

100 g fennel bulb juice (previously prepared)
½ x 2 g gelatine leaf (previously rehydrated in cold water)

- Heat a quarter of the fennel bulb juice and dissolve the well-drained gelatine in it.
- Remove from the heat and add the rest of the fennel bulb juice.
- Pour into a container to a thickness of 1 cm.
- Leave to set in the refrigerator for 3 hours.

For the carrot sorbet

250 g carrot juice (previously prepared)
1 x 2 g gelatine leaf (previously rehydrated in cold water)

- Heat a quarter of the carrot juice to 45 °C and dissolve the well-drained gelatine in it.
- Remove from the heat and add the rest of the carrot juice.
- Process in the sorbet maker and keep at -8 °C.

  NB: This preparation should be made immediately before finishing and presentation.

For the grated macadamia

20 g macadamia nut
1 Microplane grater

- Grate the macadamia with the Microplane grater to make strings as long as possible.
- Store the threads in a container without piling, so as not to alter their texture.

For the coconut air base

200 g water
90 g coconut milk powder

- Heat the water and mix both ingredients in a deep 25 cm diameter container.

For the fresh fennel flower seeds

4 sprigs fresh fennel flowers

- Use a pair of scissors to snip off the fresh fennel flower seeds.
- Refrigerate.

1138

Carrot-LYO desert

Finishing and presentation

30 g double cream
8 x 1.5 cm fresh tarragon shoots
16 g Pral yogurt powder
2 g citric acid granules

- Work a stick blender over the surface of the coconut air base until it emulsifies and the air forms.
- Imagining the plate as a clock face, place 2 g of yogurt powder on an O! LUNA large eclipse plate in the 6 o'clock position. Place a teaspoon of double cream to the left.
- Place a soup spoon of cold fennel bulb jelly at 8 o'clock, taking care not to break it.
- Place a piece of freeze-dried carrot with 2 citric acid granules at 11 and 1 o'clock, arranging a flattened quenelle of carrot sorbet in the space between them.
- Cover the remaining space on the left side of the plate with a spoon of coconut air.
- Cover all the ingredients with a thin layer of freeze-dried carrot powder.
- Sprinkle 4 g of grated macadamia below and on top of the carrot powder to create an elongated form.
- Arrange 2 tarragon shoots on the dish and finish by sprinkling a little yogurt powder and the fresh fennel seeds over the carrot powder.

Cutlery

- Tapas cutlery.

  NB: Tapas cutlery consists of a 14 x 3 cm spoon and fork.

How to eat

- Eat without disordering the dish so that the different components under the freeze-dried powder do not become mixed.

1139

Soy sauce nest with sesame, miso and wasabi sweets

Year
2005

Family
Tapas

Temperature
Ambient/cold

Season
All year round

Serves 4

For the plain liquid caramel

500 g Isomalt

- Melt the Isomalt in a pan over a medium heat until the temperature reaches 120 °C.

For the sesame oil sweets

500 g plain liquid caramel (previously prepared)
50 g raw sesame oil
50 g toasted sesame oil
1 No. 8 plain piping nozzle

- Place 2 g of raw sesame oil in each of 4 hemispherical measuring spoons.
- Dip the tip of the nozzle in the liquid caramel at 120 °C and slowly remove it so that a fine caramel film forms across the base.
- Quickly pour the oil from the spoon through the still-hot film on the nozzle. In this way, the oil will be coated in a thin layer of caramel.
- With scissors, cut the sugar thread that forms on top of the sweet to a length of 4 cm. Make 4 raw sesame oil sweets.
- Repeat the operation with the toasted sesame oil to make 4 sweets.
- Keep the oil sweets in an airtight container in a cool, dry place.

  NB: It is important to keep the plain caramel at 120 °C to give the sweet a fine, even coating.

For the cold soy sauce jelly nests

200 g water
100 g soy sauce
5.4 g Kappa Carrageenan
1½ x 2 g gelatine leaves (previously rehydrated in cold water)

- Mix the water with the soy sauce.
- Add the Kappa Carrageenan and bring to the boil while stirring constantly with a whisk until lump-free.
- Remove from the heat, skim off the froth and add the well-drained gelatine.
- While the mixture is still hot, fill a syringe with a 0.1 mm diameter needle. Place an ice cube over the needle so that jelly sets as it passes through, forming very fine strings that are as long as possible. Place the strings on a tray lined with parchment paper so that they do not stick together, and form nests from the string without rolling them too tightly. Make 32 x 8 cm diameter nests.
- Refrigerate.

For the grated fresh wasabi

20 g fresh wasabi
1 Japanese wasabi grater

- Peel the fresh wasabi.
- Grate.
- Put the grated wasabi in a piping bag to make it easier to handle.
- Refrigerate. This preparation should be made immediately before finishing and presentation.

  NB: If fresh wasabi is not available, substitute with wasabi paste.

For the black sesame savoury praline

50 g black sesame seeds
5 g sunflower oil
Salt

- Toast the black sesame in a frying pan.
- Blend the toasted black sesame seeds with the sunflower oil in a liquidiser until a fine, lump-free cream is obtained.
- Strain, season with salt and put in a squeeze bottle.

For the mandarin juice concentrate

1 x 500 g carton of frozen Simone Gatto mandarin juice

- Thaw the mandarin juice without moving for 48 hours to decant, so that the concentrate (pulp) separates from the liquid.
- Use a syringe to discard the liquid from the top until the pulp is reached so as not to touch the carton, preventing the concentrate from mixing with the water again.
- Remove the concentrate that has settled at the bottom of the carton.
- Refrigerate.

1139

Soy sauce nest with sesame, miso and wasabi sweets

Finishing and presentation

15 g white miso paste

- Place 2 mounds of 4 soy sauce nests each in a small soup plate, one on the upper part the other in the lower part.
- Make 2 x 2 g mounds of miso paste on the left side of the plate, against the edge. Flatten them lightly with a small spatula. Pipe a little grated fresh wasabi over the miso, also flattening with the spatula.
- Place 1 drop of toasted black sesame praline on the right, against the edge of the plate.
- At the base of the plate, place a raw sesame oil sweet on the left side and a toasted sesame oil sweet on the right.
- Serve a medicine spoon filled with mandarin concentrate for each diner.

Cutlery

- Tapas spoon and wooden tweezers.

How to eat

- Alternate the nests with the sweets and other components. Eat the sweets in a single mouthful, and finish with the mandarin concentrate to refresh the palate.

1140

Dulse nest with sea urchins and lime caviar

Year
2005

Family
Tapas

Temperature
Cold

Season
January, February, March, April, May, June

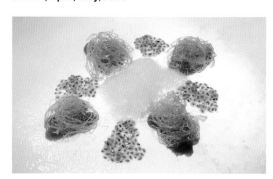

Serves 4

For the dulse water

500 g dulse seaweed
500 g water

- Rinse the seaweed in plenty of water to remove excess salt.
- Blend the dulse with the water in a liquidiser.
- Strain through a Superbag and set aside.

For the cold dulse water jelly nests

200 g dulse water (previously prepared)
3.6 g Kappa Carrageenan
1 x 2 g gelatine leaf (previously rehydrated in cold water)

- Add the Kappa Carrageenan to the dulse water and bring to the boil while stirring constantly with a whisk until lump-free.
- Remove from the heat, skim off the froth and add the well-drained gelatine.
- While the mixture is still hot, fill a syringe with a 0.1 mm diameter needle. Place an ice cube over the needle so that jelly sets as it passes through, forming very fine strings that are as long as possible. Place the strings on a tray lined with parchment paper so that they do not stick together, and form nests from the string without rolling them too tightly. Make 32 x 6 cm diameter nests.
- Refrigerate.

For the dulse water air base

250 g dulse water (previously prepared)
1 g soya lecithin powder

- Mix both ingredients in a deep 25 cm diameter container.

For the sea urchin roe

6 x 70 g sea urchins

- Kill the sea urchins by scalding them in boiling water for 10 seconds.
- Cut along the bottom of the sea urchins with a pair of scissors, making a 2 cm diameter circle.
- Remove the roe from inside the sea urchins and place each one in the sea urchin liquor previously strained through a Superbag.
- Choose the 16 largest pieces of roe.
- Refrigerate.

For the lima caviar

10 g basil seeds
110 g water
20 g lime juice
1 lime
1 Microplane grater

- Soak the basil seeds in the water for 10 minutes.
- Once they are hydrated, add the lime juice and the grated zest of half a lime.
- Mix and refrigerate.

Finishing and presentation

- Work the stick blender over the surface of the dulse water air base until it emulsifies and the air forms.
- Place 1 piece of sea urchin roe over each of the 16 dulse nests and wrap them with the 16 remaining nests in such a way that the strings are loose and voluminous.
- Arrange 4 dulse nests with sea urchin roe as a cross on a 21 cm soup plate.
- Place a teaspoon of lime caviar in the spaces between the nests.
- Finish by covering the middle of the dish with a teaspoon of dulse water air.

NB: Another version of this dish has also been created in which each piece of sea urchin roe is substituted with 4 g of beluga caviar.

Cutlery

- Tapas spoon and wooden tweezers.

How to eat

- Pick up the nests with the tweezers and alternate each group of nests with the lime caviar and the air.

1141

'Folie' salad

Year
2005

Family
Tapas

Temperature
Ambient

Season
All year round

Serves 4

For the artichokes-CRU

4 x 60 g baby globe artichokes
100 g water
25 g extra virgin olive oil
25 g 25-year-old sherry vinegar
Salt

- Remove the leaves from the artichokes, leaving the heart and a small section of the stem.
- Mix the water with the vinegar and oil to make a vinaigrette and season with salt.
- Put the vinaigrette in a vacuum-pack bag and add the artichokes.
- Vacuum seal the bag.
- Refrigerate for 6 hours.

For the garlic-CRU

4 x 6 g cloves garlic
15 g 25-year-old sherry vinegar
45 g extra virgin olive oil
1 sprig dried rosemary
1 bay leaf
Salt
Water

- Peel the garlic cloves and blanch 3 times in water.
- Cool in iced water and dry.
- Make a vinaigrette with the oil and vinegar and season with salt.
- Put the vinaigrette in a vacuum-pack bag and add the garlic and herbs.
- Vacuum seal the bag.
- Refrigerate for 48 hours.

For the sodium alginate base

1 kg water
5 g sodium alginate

- Mix the ingredients in a liquidiser until a lump-free mixture is obtained.
- Strain and set aside.

For the spherical-I goat's milk yogurt nodules

50 g goat's milk yogurt
500 g sodium alginate solution
(previously prepared)

- Pour the sodium alginate solution into a container to a depth of 4 cm.
- Beat the yogurt to produce a smooth, lump-free cream. Do not whip it.
- Take a syringe with a 2 mm opening and fill with the beaten goat's milk yogurt.
- Pipe the goat's milk yogurt into the sodium alginate solution to form nodules with a 1 cm diameter. Make 4 nodules.
- Allow them to 'cook' in the sodium alginate solution for 1 minute.
- Take the nodules out of the mixture and dip them in water to clean them.
- Drain the nodules without breaking them and keep them in a container lined with parchment paper.
- Refrigerate.

For the black olive juice

500 g black Aragón olives

- Pit the olives.
- Process the olives in the liquidiser and strain through muslin. Squeeze well to release all of the juice from the olives.
- Refrigerate the juice.

For the spherical-I black olive base

100 g black olive juice (previously prepared)
0.5 g calcium chloride
0.2 g Xantana

- Dilute calcium chloride in the olive juice.
- Add Xantana to the juice and process with a stick blender until it is lump-free. Stand for 2 hours to release any air bubbles that may have formed during the blending.

For the spherical-I black olives

500 g sodium alginate base
(previously prepared)
100 g spherical-I black olive solution
(previously prepared)
100 g extra virgin olive oil

- Using a 1 cm diameter hemispherical measuring spoon, make 8 spherical black olive balls and place them into the sodium alginate base. Leave them for 1 minute.
- Take the olives out of the sodium alginate base and submerge them in water.
- Remove from the water and place in the extra virgin olive oil.
- Do not refrigerate.

1141

'Folie' salad

For the fermented milk *mató* curd cheese

500 g fermented full-cream milk

- Pour the milk into a small pan and heat to 56 °C, stirring constantly with a spatula. Leave to stand for 5 minutes.
- Gently pour the milk through a sieve to drain away the whey, leaving the *mató* cheese in the sieve.
- Refrigerate.

For the preserved tuna water and oil

1 kg tinned tuna preserved in olive oil
300 g water

- Pour the oil from the tin and set aside.
- Combine the tuna with the water and gently break it up with a stick blender.
- Strain through a Superbag and collect the tuna water that is released.
- Refrigerate.

For the preserved tuna oil air

400 g preserved tuna oil (previously prepared)
400 g preserved tuna water (previously prepared)
2.5 g soya lecithin powder

- Mix the ingredients together in a deep 25 cm diameter container with a stick blender

For the preserved cat's claw shoots

4 preserved cat's claw shoots

- Cut the cat's claw shoots into 2 cm lengths.
- Refrigerate.

  NB: Cat's claw, *Uncaria tomentosa*, is a creeper that grows in the central areas of Peru, Colombia and Bolivia, as well as in the Alicante region of Spain. It grows in tall forests in sunny areas. It is a liana that can grow to 20 m in length. It is known to have medicinal properties. In the Alicante area it is known as *raimet de pastor* (shepherd's grapes).

For the peeled green walnuts

2 whole green walnuts

- Peel the walnuts. Use a small pointed knife and gloves to remove the skin.
- Break the walnuts in half with a nutcracker.
- Remove the nut halves in one piece and peel them with a short pointed knife to obtain 4 half walnuts.
- Refrigerate.

For the flowering mini-cucumbers

4 flowering mini-cucumbers

- Remove the bumps from the cucumber skin by hand.
- Clean the cucumbers with paper towel and refrigerate.

For the 'air-bag' dough

250 g plain flour
70 g strong bread flour
190 g cold milk
5 g salt
10 g fresh yeast

NB: This is the minimum recommended amount to ensure a good result.

- Combine all the ingredients (except the salt) in a mixer with a dough hook.
- Knead for 9 minutes at medium speed.
- Add the salt and knead for 2 more minutes.
- Knead by hand for 1 minute. Keep the dough well covered in a bowl in the refrigerator.
- Leave to rise for 4 hours.

For the 'air-bags'

200 g 'air bag' dough (previously prepared)

- Roll the dough out through a rolling machine at maximum thickness.
- Leave the dough to stand for approximately 1 minute, covered with a damp cloth.
- Roll the dough out twice more to 0.5 cm.
- Cut into 1.5 cm rounds.
- Bake at 240 °C for 1 minute. Turn over and bake for another minute until the dough has risen and is golden brown.
- Take out of the oven, leave to cool and keep in an airtight container in a cool, dry place.

1141

'Folie' salad

For the savoury macadamia nut praline

50 g raw macadamia nuts
10 g sunflower oil
Salt

- Process the pine nuts with the oil in the liquidiser until a lump-free cream is obtained.
- Strain, season with salt and put in a squeeze bottle.

For the tuna roe vinaigrette

20 g dry tuna roe
30 g extra virgin olive oil

- Peel the roe.
- Chop the peeled roe in the liquidiser. Use short, sharp bursts to obtain a granular powder.
- Mix with the extra virgin olive oil and refrigerate.

For the shaved toasted hazelnuts

30 g peeled hazelnuts
1 Microplane grater

- Toast the hazelnuts and shave them with a Microplane grater to produce the longest thread possible.
- Place the threads in an airtight container without piling them up, so as not to alter the texture.
- Store in a cool, dry place.

For the dressed *pa-ha*

1 *pa-ha* stem
Extra virgin olive oil
25-year-old sherry vinegar
Salt

- Peel the *pa-ha* stem with a paring knife.
- Cut the stem into 4 x 2 cm pieces on a slight angle at one of the ends.
- Dress the *pa-ha* pieces with extra virgin olive oil, 25-year-old sherry vinegar and salt.

NB: *Pa-ha* is a long and thick-stemmed vegetable with a very porous interior and an unusual texture.

For the bread with oil

4 x 2.5 cm slices rustic bread, crusts removed
30 g extra virgin olive oil

- Soak the bread in the oil.

NB: The bread must be soaked just before presentation and finishing.

1141

'Folie' salad

Finishing and presentation

8 pickled daisy buds
8 fresh *ficoïde glaciale* shoots
4 purslane shoots
4 fresh bergamot flowers
10 g 25-year-old sherry vinegar
Maldon sea salt

- Work a stick blender over the surface of the preserved tuna oil air mixture until it emulsifies and the air forms.
- Cut the artichokes-CRU in half lengthways and stand them on the right-hand side of the base of an O! LUNA deep lunar plate.
- Place a garlic-CRU clove on the left-hand side of the plate. Place a teaspoonful of home-made *mató* cheese in the upper section of the plate.
- Place an 'air-bag' beside the *mató* cheese. Place a flowering mini-cucumber opposite the garlic.
- Place an oil-soaked piece of bread opposite the 'air-bag', and the cat's claw and a halved green walnut beside it.
- Place a piece of dressed *pa-ha* in the middle of the plate.
- Place 1 spherical-I nodule and 2 pickled daisy buds in the lower part of the plate, to the left of the artichoke.
- Cover the base of the dish with 2 spoons of preserved tuna oil air.
- Arrange 2 spherical olives, 2 *ficoïde glaciale* shoots, 1 purslane shoot and 1 bergamot flower over it.
- Without touching any other ingredients, make a 4 cm long and 1 cm wide line of shaved hazelnut on one side of the dish.
- Without touching any other ingredients, make a 4 cm long and 1 cm wide line of shaved hazelnut on one side of the dish.
- Place a 3 g pile of savoury macadamia nut praline beside the 'air-bag', ensuring that they do not touch.
- Dress the artichokes with a spoon of tuna roe vinaigrette.
- Finish by sprinkling a pinch of salt over the bread, garlic and *pa-ha*, and 3 drops of sherry vinegar over the air.

NB: If any of the ingredients are not available, they can be substituted by other ingredients that resemble them, as long as the flavour and texture are similar.

NB: We served the first salads with home-made caviar from serla roe.

NB: We made some versions with tuna foam and air-foam instead of tuna air.

Cutlery

- Tapas cutlery.

NB: Tapas cutlery consists of a 14 x 3 cm spoon and fork.

How to eat

- Eat each component separately, combined with the air, in order to appreciate the different textures and flavours.

1142

Sprouting quinoa with *tucupi* and *kefir* chicken 'tripe'

Year
2005

Family
Tapas

Temperature
Hot

Season
All year round

Serves 4

For the free-range chicken stock

1 x 2 kg free-range chicken
1.5 kg water
Salt

NB: This is the minimum amount recommended for a good result.

- Discard the head, legs and wingtips before quartering the chicken.
- Clean the chicken under running water to remove the entrails and blood.
- Put the chicken in a pot and cover it with the water and a little salt.
- Boil on a medium heat for 2 hours, constantly skimming off impurities and fat, to obtain a flavoursome clear stock.
- Strain through a Superbag, remove excess fat again and refrigerate.

For the *tucupi*

400 g free-range chicken stock (previously prepared)
15 g fresh coriander
1 stalk fresh lemongrass
1 kaffir lime zest
1 lime zest
2 kaffir lime leaves
0.2 g toasted saffron threads
3 g fresh pressed yeast
2 g Szechuan button
Salt

NB: The real *tucupi* is the stock resulting from cooking the juice obtained from fermented cassava. It originates from Brazil.

- Chop the fresh coriander, lemongrass and kaffir lime leaves.
- Mix the previous ingredients with the toasted saffron in the chicken stock and bring to the boil gradually.
- When it breaks into a boil, remove from the heat and stand for 5 minutes to infuse.
- Add the kaffir lime and lime zests (it is essential that there should be no pith at all on either so as not to make the consommé bitter), leave to infuse for 2 minutes and strain through a Superbag.
- Add the yeast and the crumbled Szechuan button, and season with salt.
- Bring to the boil to prevent the consommé from fermenting, then refrigerate.

NB: The Szechuan button causes an electrical effect on the palate. It is the flower of the *Spilanthes oleracea* and is native to the Chinese region of Sichuan (formerly Szechuan). It is also found in Madagascar and the Amazon region. It is given the name *jambu* in certain parts of South America.

For the chicken 'tripe'

20 free-range chicken wings
Water
Salt

- Cut the wings into 3 pieces at the joints.
- Keep the middle and tip for other dishes. This preparation only makes use of the first wing segment, from where the 'tripe' will be removed.
- Simmer the first wing segments in water with salt for 3 hours.
- Use your fingers to remove the bones and separate out the tendons found at the end of the segment.
- Each segment contains 1 large tendon and 1 small one.
- Set aside 5 of each type of tendon per person.

For the boiled quinoa

30 g quinoa
200 g water
Salt

- Boil the quinoa for 13 minutes in salted water.
- Drain and separate 8 g of boiled quinoa per person.

For the hot *kefir* foam

150 g *kefir*
50 g water
1 g methylcellulose
1 x 0.5 litre ISI siphon
1 N$_2$O cartridge

- Mix the ingredients and process with a stick blender to obtain a lump-free mixture.
- Place it in the freezer to reduce the temperature quickly to 3°C.
- Once at this temperature, blend again and fill the siphon.
- Close it and insert gas cartridge.
- Set aside in a bain-marie at 45°C.

1142

Sprouting quinoa with *tucupi* and *kefir* chicken 'tripe'

For the tamarind seed stock

4 tamarind pods
50 g water

- Shell the tamarind pods and remove the seeds. Save the pulp for the purée.
- Mix the seeds with the water, bring to a boil and leave to infuse.
- Strain and set aside.

For the tamarind purée

Tamarind pulp (previously prepared)
15 g tamarind seed stock (previously prepared)

- Boil the tamarind pulp in the tamarind seed stock for 1 minute.
- Strain through a fine strainer, squeezing so that nothing remains in the strainer.
- Refrigerate.

For the fresh herbs

32 x 5 mm fresh tarragon leaves
32 x 5 mm fresh coriander leaves
32 x 5 mm fresh chervil leaves

- Divide the leaves into 4 equal portions.
- Cover them with a damp paper towel and refrigerate.

Finishing and presentation

40 g germinated quinoa
Salt

- Cook the chicken 'tripe' with 200 g of *tucupi* for 5 minutes on a low heat.
- Mix the boiled quinoa with the quinoa shoots and boil in a little water until the shoots are cooked. Season with salt.
- Place the chicken 'tripe' at the bottom of a warmed bowl with the *tucupi*.
- Divide the boiled quinoa and quinoa shoots among the 4 bowls, arranging them so they form a small pile climbing the sides of the bowls.
- Place 10 g of hot *kefir* foam beside the quinoa, also climbing the wall of the bowl.
- Use a small spatula to place 4 g of tamarind purée on the opposite side of the bowl to the foam.
- Sprinkle with the herbs and serve.

Cutlery

- Tapas cutlery.

  NB: Tapas cutlery consists of a 14 x 3 cm spoon and fork.

How to eat

- Alternate the components without mixing.

1143

Green almond *empanadilla* with Szechuan button and cucumber balls in liquorice and yuzu

Year
2005

Family
Tapas

Temperature
Hot

Season
All year round

Serves 4

For the yogurt water

3 x 125 g tubs yogurt

- Freeze the yogurt.
- Once frozen, remove from the tubs and leave over a fine strainer in the refrigerator to thaw. In this way, clear yogurt water will be obtained. Strain through a Superbag.
- Refrigerate.

For the hot yogurt water jelly with Szechuan button

100 g yogurt water (previously prepared)
0.3 g powdered agar-agar
½ x 2 g gelatine leaf (previously rehydrated in cold water)
3 Szechuan buttons

- Dilute the agar-agar with half of the yogurt water and bring to the boil, stirring constantly with a whisk.
- Remove from the heat, add the rest of the yogurt water and dissolve the drained gelatine in the mixture.
- Quickly add the crumbled Szechuan buttons.
- Pour into a container to a thickness of 5 mm.
- Refrigerate for 3 hours to set.

  NB: The Szechuan button causes an electrical effect on the palate. It is the flower of the *Spilanthes oleracea* and is native to the Chinese region of Sichuan (formerly Szechuan). It is also found in Madagascar and the Amazon region. It is given the name *jambu* in certain parts of South America.

For the methycellulose solution

100 g water
3 g methylcellulose

- Blend the ingredients together at room temperature in a liquidiser until they form a smooth, even mixture.
- Strain and stand in the refrigerator for 24 hours.

For the *empanadillas* of green almond and hot yogurt water jelly with Szechuan button

150 g peeled green almonds
20 g methylcellulose solution (previously prepared)
Hot yogurt water jelly with Szechuan button (previously prepared)

- Slice the almonds into 1 mm slices.
- Place the slices on clingfilm lightly coated with the methylcellulose solution to form 4 x 7 cm circles. The slices should overlap slightly.
- Lightly brush the almond circles with the methylcellulose solution.
- Place a 4 g piece of hot yogurt water jelly with Szechuan button in the middle of each circle.
- Seal the disc as if it were a turnover and refrigerate.

For the cucumber soup with almond oil

2 x 250 g cucumbers
60 g almond oil
Pacojet
Salt

- Peel and de-seed the cucumbers, then purge the flesh with salt for 15 minutes.
- Rinse, dry and chop up the cucumber flesh, then transfer it to a Pacojet beaker.
- Freeze at -20 °C.
- Once it is frozen, process in the Pacojet 4 times and leave in a strainer so that the water will drain off by its own weight.
- Weigh 200 g of the cucumber water and process it with the almond oil using a stick blender.
- Add a little more cucumber flesh, if required, to obtain a creamier juice.
- Season with salt.

For the coated diced lemon

1 x 150 g lemon

- Slice off the top and bottom of the lemon exposing the actual segments.
- Peel them in a spiral to expose the flesh and so that there are no traces of rind or pith, without altering the basic shape of the lemon.
- Remove the segments from their membranes with a sharp knife.
- Cut 4 x 3 mm cubes.
- Remove the zest and chop it into tiny 1 mm dice.
- Coat each lemon cube in the diced lemon zest.
- Refrigerate.

1143

Green almond *empanadilla* with Szechuan button and cucumber balls in liquorice and yuzu

For the cucumber and methylcellulose *albóndigas*

1 x 200 g cucumber
20 g methylcellulose solution
(previously prepared)
Salt

- Peel the cucumber, slice in half and de-seed.
- Purge the cucumber in salt for 15 minutes.
- Rinse in plenty of water and dry.
- Cut into 3 mm cubes.
- Mix 75 g of the cubes with 15 g of the methylcellulose solution.
- Make 8 x 7 g cucumber and methylcellulose *albóndigas*.
- Refrigerate.

Finishing and presentation

5 g liquorice paste
4 g ground dehydrated yuzu zest
20 g almond oil
Maldon sea salt
Water
Salt

- Steam the *empanadillas* to warm so that the methylcellulose sets and allow them to be handled easily.
- Cook the cucumber and methylcellulose *albóndigas* in water at 90 °C for 15 seconds. Drain and season with salt.
- Place 1 *empanadilla* at the base of a warm bowl.
- Place 2 g of liquorice paste on the upper part of the bowl so that it falls towards the base. Sprinkle a little dehydrated yuzu zest over the liquorice paste.
- Place 1 coated lemon cube at the lower end of the liquorice paste.
- Drizzle the *empanadilla* with 5 g of almond oil and a few flakes of Maldon sea salt.
- Place 1 cucumber and methylcellulose *albóndiga* at each end of the *empanadilla*.
- Pour the hot cucumber and almond oil soup in a jug so that the waiter can serve it in front of the diner.

NB: Yuzu is an Asian citrus fruit that tastes like a cross between mandarin and lemon. It is used particularly for its highly aromatic zest.

Cutlery

- Tapas cutlery.

NB: Tapas cutlery consists of a 14 x 3 cm spoon and fork.

How to eat

- Eat the *empanadilla* whole, followed by the soup and other components.

1144

Thai soup with coconut tofu

Year
2005

Family
Tapas

Temperature
Hot

Season
All year round

Serves 4

For the free-range chicken stock

1 x 2 kg free-range chicken
1.5 kg water
Salt

NB: This is the minimum amount recommended
for a good result.

- Discard the head, legs and wingtips before
  quartering the chicken.
- Clean the chicken under running water to remove
  the entrails and blood.
- Put the chicken in a pot and cover it with the water
  and a little salt.
- Simmer for 2 hours, constantly skimming
  off impurities and fat, to obtain a flavoursome
  clear stock.
- Strain through a Superbag, remove excess
  fat again and refrigerate.

For the Thai chicken stock

1 kg free-range chicken stock
(previously prepared)
30 g fresh lemongrass
15 g kaffir lime leaves
10 g fresh coriander leaves
12 g fresh ginger
4 g lime zest
3 g kaffir lime zest
30 g langoustine claws
1 g red curry paste
Salt

- Chop the lemongrass and crush in a mortar.
- Chop the kaffir lime and fresh coriander leaves.
- Chop the fresh ginger in a liquidiser.
- Bring the stock to the boil and add the lemon-
  grass, kaffir lime leaves, fresh coriander,
  fresh ginger and the lime and kaffir lime zests.
  Simmer for 5 minutes.
- Strain the stock and allow to cool down.
- When the temperature reaches 40 °C, add the
  langoustine claws previously crushed in a mortar
  and bring to the boil. Simmer for 5 minutes.
- Strain through a Superbag and season with salt
  and red curry paste.

For the hot coconut jelly cubes

125 g water
60 g coconut milk powder
½ x 2 g gelatine leaf (previously rehydrated
in cold water)
0.6 g powdered agar-agar

- Add the agar-agar to the sea water and bring
  to the boil, stirring constantly with a whisk.
- Remove from the heat, add the drained gelatine
  leaf and dissolve.
- Add the coconut milk powder and mix with
  a stick blender until the mixture is lump-free.
- Pour into a container to a thickness of 2 cm.
- Refrigerate for 2 hours to set.
- Once set, cut out 12 2 x 2 cm cubes.

NB: The aim of this preparation is to reproduce
the texture and appearance of fresh tofu, but with
a different flavour.

For the pink grapefruit segments

2 x 400 g pink grapefruits

- Slice off the top and bottom of the grapefruits
  exposing the actual segments.
- Peel the grapefruit in a spiral to expose the flesh
  so that there are no traces of zest or pith,
  but without altering the basic shape of the fruit.
- Remove the segments from their membranes
  with a sharp knife.
- Slice each segment down the middle so that
  each piece measures 1.5 x 1.5 cm. Prepare
  2 pieces per person.
- Refrigerate.

1144

Thai soup with coconut tofu

For the fresh herbs

20 x 5 mm fresh basil leaves
24 x 5 mm fresh mint leaves
32 x 5 mm fresh coriander leaves

- Divide the leaves into 4 equal portions.
- Cover them with a damp paper towel and refrigerate.

Finishing and presentation

1 lime
1 Microplane grater

- Heat the hot coconut jelly cubes covered in a little Thai chicken soup.
- Heat the remaining Thai chicken soup separately.
- Place 3 hot coconut jelly cubes in a bowl, taking care not to break them.
- Arrange 2 pink grapefruit segments beside the hot jelly.
- Sprinkle the fresh herbs, grated lime zest and a few drops of lime juice over the top.
- Finish by bathing the components with 50 g of hot Thai chicken soup.

Cutlery

- Tapas spoon.

How to eat

- Smell the aroma given off by the soup. Alternate the soup with the coconut jelly.

1145

Spherical-I yogurt nodules with ice plant, capers and black butter

Year
2005

Family
Tapas

Temperature
Hot

Season
All year round

Serves 4

For the sodium alginate solution

1 kg water
5 g sodium alginate

- Mix the ingredients in a liquidiser until a lump-free mixture is obtained.
- Strain and set aside.

For the spherical-I goat's milk yogurt nodules

2 x 200 g tubs yogurt
1 kg sodium alginate solution
(previously prepared)

- Pour the sodium alginate solution into a container to a depth of 4 cm.
- Beat the yogurt to produce a smooth, lump-free cream. Do not whip it.
- Take a syringe with a 3 mm opening and fill with the beaten goat's milk yogurt.
- Pipe the goat's milk yogurt into the sodium alginate solution to form nodules with a 2 cm diameter. Make 3 nodules per person.
- Allow them to 'cook' in the sodium alginate solution for 2 minutes.
- Take the nodules out of the mixture and dip them in water to clean them.
- Drain the nodules without breaking them and keep them in a container lined with parchment paper.
- Refrigerate.

For the de-salted capers

36 x 3 mm diameter salted capers

- Soak the capers in water until they reach the desired level of salinity.
- Drain and refrigerate.

For the *ficoïde glaciale* stalks, shoots and leaves

150 g *ficoïde glaciale*

- Use scissors to cut 4 x 2 cm long leaves, 8 x 1.5 cm long shoots and 8 x 2.5 cm long tender, fibre-free stalks.
- Refrigerate.

  NB: Use scissors to cut the *ficoïde glaciale* so as to delay oxidation at the points where the cut is made.

For the black butter sauce

120 g 25-year-old sherry vinegar
150 g butter

- Reduce the vinegar to 20 g.
- Place the butter in a pan on a medium heat and cook it until its temperature reaches 140 °C. Remove from the heat.
- Mix the butter with the reduced vinegar to obtain a split sauce.
- Set aside.

Finishing and presentation

Maldon sea salt
Freshly ground black pepper

- Arrange 3 nodules to make a triangle in a 21 cm diameter soup plate.
- Season the nodules with Maldon sea salt and freshly ground black pepper.
- Arrange 9 capers between the nodules without touching them.
- Place under the salamander grill until it is hot.
- Place 1 leaf, 2 shoots and 2 stalks of *ficoïde glaciale* on the dish without touching the nodules.
- Heat again under the salamander grill and finish by drizzling a line of black butter sauce over the nodules.

Cutlery

- Tapas cutlery.

  NB: Tapas cutlery consists of a 14 x 3 cm spoon and fork.

How to eat

- Alternate the nodules with the rest of components.

1146

Peas and ham with creamy fresh mint and eucalyptus air ravioli

Year
2005

Family
Tapas

Temperature
Hot

Season
March, April, May

Serves 4

For the peeled peas

250 g fresh shelled peas
Water
Salt

- Blanch the peas in salted water.
- Drain and chill in iced water.
- Peel the peas and refrigerate.

For the hot water jelly sheet

600 g water
3 g gellan gum
10 g powdered agar-agar

- Mix the agar-agar and gellan gum with the water and bring to the boil, stirring constantly with a whisk.
- Skim off the froth and pour the jelly mixture over a preheated 60 x 40 cm stainless steel tray.
- Drain off the excess mixture quickly to make a very fine (0.5 mm) jelly layer.
- Leave to set at room temperature, then refrigerate for 30 minutes.

For the cold fresh mint-infused cream

125 g 35% fat single cream
20 g fresh mint leaves

- Mix the fresh mint with the cream.
- Transfer to an airtight container and refrigerate for 24 hours to infuse.

  NB: It is important that the mint leaves are not broken so as not to oxidise the cream.

For the whipped fresh mint-infused cream

100 g cold fresh mint-infused cream
(previously prepared)

- Strain without applying pressure.
- Whip the cream in the electric mixer.
- Fill a piping bag and refrigerate.

For the creamy ravioli

Hot water jelly sheet (previously prepared)
Whipped fresh mint-infused cream
(previously prepared)
Sunflower oil

- Cut the hot water jelly sheet into 12 x 5 cm squares.
- Pipe 5 g of whipped cream on each jelly square.
- Fold the sides of the hot water jelly squares in towards the middle to obtain 12 neat square ravioli.
- Place in a container greased with sunflower oil so that the jelly does not stick. Set aside at room temperature.

For the *jamón ibérico* stock

50 g *jamón ibérico* offcuts
100 g water

- Cut the ham into 1 cm pieces and cover with the water.
- Boil on medium heat for 15 minutes, skimming continuously.
- Strain, discard the excess fat and set aside.

For the *jamón ibérico* lard

50 g *jamón ibérico* fat

- Remove any lean or rancid bits from the fat.
- Simmer until the solid fat is fully rendered into lard.
- Strain the liquid lard and set aside.

For the *jamón ibérico* cream

50 g *jamón ibérico* stock (previously prepared)
30 g *jamón ibérico* lard (previously prepared)
0.2 g Xantana

- Mix the ingredients and emulsify with a stick blender to obtain a smooth, lump-free cream.
- Refrigerate.

For the *jamón ibérico* fat cubes

50 g *jamón ibérico* fat

- Remove any lean or rancid bits from the fat.
- Cut the fat into 24 x 5 mm cubes.

For the eucalyptus oil

100 g sunflower oil
10 g tender eucalyptus leaves

- Put the oil and chopped eucalyptus leaves in a pan.
- Infuse at 70 °C for 1 hour. Remove from the heat and leave to stand for 3 hours.
- Strain.

  NB: When making eucalyptus oil, you should use the round leaves that are found at the bottom of the trunk. The oil produced from the long leaves is too spicy.

1146

Peas and ham with creamy fresh mint and eucalyptus air ravioli

For the eucalyptus air base

15 g eucalyptus oil (previously prepared)
400 g water
0.8 g soya lecithin powder

- Mix the ingredients in a deep 25 cm diameter container with a whisk.

Finishing and presentation

- Work a stick blender over the surface of the eucalyptus air base until it emulsifies and the air forms.
- Arrange 3 creamy ravioli on a plate with a 2 cm space between them.
- Mix the peeled peas with the ham cream in a frying pan and cook on low heat for 3 minutes. Season with salt if required.
- Heat the *jamón ibérico* fat cubes in a frying pan until they sweat and the fat is warm and soft. Do not allow them to melt.
- Place the plates with the ravioli under the salamander grill until they are heated through.
- Place the peas cooked in the ham cream on the plate, taking care that the ravioli do not become stained and so as to integrate them with the peas. Lightly coat the ravioli with the ham cream.
- Arrange the fat cubes over the peas.
- Finish with 4 spots of eucalyptus air around the edge of the plate without touching the peas.

Cutlery

- Tapas cutlery.

  NB: Tapas cutlery consists of a 14 x 3 cm spoon and fork.

How to eat

- Alternate the components. Eat the ravioli whole.

1147

Warm murex snails with *kikurage*, hot vinaigrette and basil-flavoured kombu

Year
2005

Family
Tapas

Temperature
Hot

Season
All year round

Serves 4

For the boiled murex snails

20 x 40 g murex snails
1 kg sea water
1 bay leaf

- Wash the sea snails in water to remove any dirt from inside.
- Bring the sea water with bay leaf to the boil.
- Add the sea snails and cook for 25 minutes. Leave them to stand in their water for 1 hour.
- Clean the sea snails, separating their bodies from the entrails.
- Keep the bodies in the cooking water.

For the murex snail essence

40 g boiled murex snail entrails (previously prepared)
10 g murex snail cooking water (previously prepared)
10 g water

- Blend all 3 ingredients in a liquidiser and strain.

For the rice stock

20 g round rice
20 g spring onion
1 garlic clove
1 bay leaf
1.2 kg water
Salt

- Peel the onion and garlic.
- Combine the water, onion, garlic and bay leaf and bring to the boil. Then add the rice.
- Boil on a medium heat for 40 minutes.
- Strain and season with salt.
- Set aside.

For the *kikurage* cooked in rice stock

4 dried *kikurage* mushrooms
500 g rice stock (previously prepared)
Water

- Soak the *kikurage* in water for 30 minutes to hydrate.
- Cut each one into 4 x 2 cm pieces.
- Cook the drained *kikurage* in the rice stock for 20 minutes on a medium heat.

  NB: *Kikurage* is the Japanese name for the *Auricularia auricula* (cloud ear) mushroom, appreciated for its gelatinous texture. It is usually dried and can be reconstituted by soaking it in hot water or another liquid.

For the mustard oil vinaigrette

300 g water
150 g mustard oil
150 g virgin olive oil
1.5 g Xantana
Freshly ground black pepper
Salt

- Dilute the Xantana in the water and process with a stick blender until a lump-free cream is obtained.
- Add the 2 oils while emulsifying continuously with the stick blender.
- Season with salt and freshly ground black pepper.
- Set aside.

For the *shiraita* kombu strips in rice vinegar syrup

2 6 x 19 cm strips *shiraita* kombu
80 g rice vinegar
120 g water
4 g sugar
1.5 g salt

- Mix the water with the rice vinegar, salt and sugar.
- Place the *shiraita* kombu slices in a pan and cover with this mixture.
- Bring to the boil and then remove from the heat.
- Refrigerate for 24 hours.

  NB: *Shiraita* kombu is the Japanese name for the slices taken from the middle section of kombu seaweed.

1147

Warm murex snails with *kikurage*, hot vinaigrette and basil-flavoured kombu

For the *shiraita* kombu and fresh basil ravioli

4 sliced *shiraita* kombu in rice vinegar syrup
(previously prepared)
84 x 5 mm fresh basil leaves

- Drain the *shiraita* kombu slices and lay them out over baking trays.
- Cut them into 12 3.5 x 7 cm rectangles.
- Place 7 fresh basil leaves in the middle of each rectangle.
- Fold the seaweed rectangle like a turnover.
- Keep the ravioli covered in paper towel moistened with the water and rice vinegar syrup mixture used to cook the seaweed to keep from drying out.

Finishing and presentation

10 g 25-year-old sherry vinegar

- Heat 4 x 24 cm soup plates.
- Place 4 pieces of hot *kikurage* in the middle of each plate to form a bouquet.
- Arrange 5 hot snails in a circle around the *kikurage*.
- Bathe the snails with the hot mustard oil vinaigrette.
- Pour a little murex snail essence between the snails.
- Place 3 kombu and basil ravioli between the snails, leaning against the *kikurage* to give the final composition volume.
- Finish with 3 drops of sherry vinegar between the snails.

Cutlery

- Tapas cutlery.

  NB: Tapas cutlery consists of a 14 x 3 cm spoon and fork.

How to eat

- Alternate the different components.

1148

**Rock mussels with seaweed
and fresh herbs**

Year
2005

Family
Tapas

Temperature
Cold

Season
April, May, June

Serves 4

For the rock mussels

32 x 15 g rock mussels

- Plunge the rock mussels a few at a time in boiling water for 10 seconds.
- Remove the mussels from the water and leave them to cool at room temperature.
- Use a paring knife to cut the muscle joining each mussel to its shell.
- Lift the rock mussels out, taking care they do not break.
- Cover the mussels with their own liquor, which has been previously strained through a Superbag. Refrigerate.

For the thickened mussel water

100 g rock mussel liquor (previously prepared)
0.4 g Xantana

- Strain the mussel liquor through a Superbag to remove any impurities.
- Mix the mussel liquor and Xantana in a container.
- Process with a stick blender to obtain a smooth, lump-free cream.
- Refrigerate.

**For the sliced *shiraita* kombu
in rice vinegar syrup**

2 *shiraita* kombu slices measuring 6 x 19 cm
80 g rice vinegar
120 g water
4 g sugar
1.5 g salt

- Mix the water with the rice vinegar, salt and sugar.
- Place the sliced *shiraita* kombu in a small pan and cover with the vinegar mixture.
- Bring to the boil and then remove from the heat.
- Keep refrigerated for 24 hours.
- Cut the seaweed into 12 x 2 cm squares.

NB: *Shiraita* kombu is the Japanese name for the slices taken from the middle section of kombu seaweed.

For the seaweed

20 g fresh nori seaweed
20 g fresh samphire
20 g fresh wakame seaweed
20 g dulse seaweed
20 g red tosaka seaweed
20 g green tosaka seaweed
8 stems fresh samphire
4 x 3 cm stems of pasteurised sea grapes

- Clean all the seaweed (apart from the sea grapes) under running water to remove excess salt.
- Refrigerate.
- Select the 8 x 4 cm samphire stems.
- Hydrate the sea grapes under plenty of running water until it is smooth and moist.

NB: The samphire variety used, purple glasswort, *Salicornia ramosissima,* is an annual herb from the chenopodiaceae family that grows in saline soils. The branches have a number of nodes and are fleshy and green, except towards the end of its cycle when the plant turns a reddish colour. It grows in places close to the sea or in marshy areas occasionally flooded with sea water.

NB: Sea grapes, *Umi budo,* take their name from the clusters of liquid-filled globules along the seaweed. They have a crisp texture and originate from Japan, specifically the Okinawa region. It can be bought fresh or pasteurised.

NB: The sea grapes should be hydrated just before finishing and presentation.

1148

Rock mussels with seaweed and fresh herbs

Finishing and presentation

4 fresh basil shoots
4 fresh 1.5 cm chervil leaves
4 fresh mint shoots
4 fresh tarragon shoots

- Arrange the seaweed salad on the right side of an O! LUNA deep lunar plate in the following order: kombu, green tosaka, dulse, kombu, samphire, nori, samphire, wakame, red tosaka and finally kombu.
- Arrange the 8 mussels on the left-hand side following the edge of the dish to complete the circle started by the seaweed.
- Arrange the fresh herbs over the seaweed.
- Cover each mussel with a spoon of thickened mussel water and fill the middle of the dish with another spoon of the same sauce.
- Finally, place a sea grape stem in the space between the rock mussels and the seaweed salad.

Cutlery

- Tapas cutlery.

  NB: Tapas cutlery consists of a 14 x 3 cm spoon and fork.

How to eat

- Alternate the mussels with each type of seaweed. Take a little mussel water with every mussel.

1149

Tender pine nut risotto in pine nut oil

Year
2005

Family
Tapas

Temperature
Hot

Season
April, May

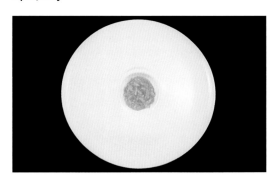

Serves 4

For the shelled tender pine nuts

3 x 300 g green pine cones

- Peel the pine cones and split them open length-ways to extract the pine nuts.
- Open the shells and carefully take out the tender pine nut kernels without breaking them.
- Prepare 12.5 g per person and refrigerate.

For the unshelled tender pine nuts

1 x 200 g green pine cone

- Peel the pine cone and split it lengthways to extract the pine nuts in their tender shell.
- Prepare 16 unshelled tender pine nuts.
- Refrigerate.

For the tempura batter

50 g glutinous rice flour
80 g water

- Mix both ingredients with a whisk and refrigerate.

For the virgin pine nut oil cream

100 g water
3 g tapioca flour
50 g virgin pine nut oil
Salt

NB: The tapioca flour can be substituted with 0.4 g of Xantana.

- Mix the water and tapioca flour and bring to the boil, stirring constantly with a whisk.
- When the mixture thickens, remove from the heat, add the virgin pine nut oil and mix in such a way that the oil emulsifies with the thickened water.
- Season with salt.

NB: This preparation should be made immediately before finishing and presentation.

For the green pine cone oil

1 x 200 g green pine cone
100 g sunflower oil

- Chop the green pine cone into 2 cm chunks.
- Cover in sunflower oil and cook at 65 °C for 2 hours to make a confit.
- Refrigerate for 24 hours to infuse.
- Strain before use.

Finishing and presentation

500 g olive oil
Salt

- Heat the olive oil to 170 °C.
- Coat the unshelled tender pine nuts in the tempura batter and fry in the oil until the batter is crisp. Take them out with a slotted spoon and drain the excess oil on a paper towel. Season with salt.
- Place 12.5 g of shelled tender pine nuts at the base of a hot O! LUNA small eclipse plate.
- Add 2 soup spoons of hot virgin pine nut oil cream soup to the tender pine nuts and mix so that the pine nuts and soup become a risotto.
- Serve 4 tempura pine nuts separately on a slate with a medicine spoon half full of green pine cone oil per person.

Cutlery

- Tapas cutlery.

NB: Tapas cutlery consists of a 14 x 3 cm spoon and fork.

How to eat

- Alternate the risotto with the tempura pine nuts and the green pine cone oil.

1150

White asparagus with virgin olive oil capsules and lemon marshmallow

Year
2005

Family
Tapas

Temperature
Hot

Season
March, April, May

Serves 4

For the boiled white asparagus tips and stalks

12 x 1.2 cm diameter white asparagus
Water
Salt

- Peel the asparagus leaving the tips intact.
- Cut off the asparagus tips with a slightly diagonal slice, leaving a length of 4.5 cm.
- Cut off and discard the woody end of the stalks.
- Boil the asparagus tips for 1 minute in lightly salted water. Drain and chill in salted iced water.
- Cool the cooking water down and keep the boiled asparagus tips in it.
- Boil the trimmed asparagus stalks in salted water for 7 minutes.
- Drain and chill in salted iced water.
- Cool the cooking water down and keep the boiled asparagus stalks in it.

For the boiled white asparagus juice

Boiled white asparagus stalks
(previously prepared)

- Liquidise the boiled asparagus stalks.
- Strain and refrigerate.

For the white asparagus cream

100 g boiled white asparagus juice
(previously prepared)
2 g potato starch
Salt

- Dissolve the potato starch in the white asparagus juice and bring to the boil while stirring constantly with a whisk.
- Remove from the heat and season with salt.

For the spherical olive oil capsule base

270 g water
240 g extra virgin olive oil
3 g sodium alginate
3 g sucrose ester
2.4 g monoglyceride
1 x 0.5 litre ISI siphon
1 N_2O cartridge

- Mix the water and sucrose ester with a stick blender.
- Once the sucrose ester is thoroughly dissolved, add the sodium alginate and mix again with the stick blender until lump-free.
- Heat the oil to 70 °C and add the monoglyceride.
- Process with a stick blender.
- Combine both mixtures, mix with a whisk and strain.
- Stand in the refrigerator for 24 hours.
- Fill the siphon, close it and insert the gas cartridge.

For the calcium chloride solution

1 kg water
10 g calcium chloride

- Mix both ingredients together with a whisk.

For the lemon marshmallows

250 g full cream milk
4.5 x 2 g gelatine leaves (previously rehydrated in cold water)
13 g lemon juice
½ lemon
1 Microplane grater

- Heat 50 g of milk and dissolve the well-drained gelatine leaves. Leave at room temperature until it cools to 20 °C.
- Lower the temperature of the remaining 200 g of milk to 3 °C by leaving it in the freezer.
- When the gelatine and milk mixture is at 20 °C, place it in the electric mixer on medium speed.
- Gradually add the milk at 3 °C to the mixture in the mixer.
- Whip until the texture is similar to that of a meringue.
- Once it is whipped, add the lemon juice and the zest of half a lemon grated using a Microplane grater.
- Mix everything together and fill a piping bag. Use a 1 cm plain nozzle.
- Pipe 12 4 x 1 cm strips of marshmallow over a transparent sheet.
- Refrigerate for 1 hour.

1150

White asparagus with virgin olive oil capsules and lemon marshmallow

Finishing and presentation

10 g dehydrated yuzu zest
Maldon sea salt
Freshly ground black pepper

- Pipe the spherical olive oil capsule base in the calcium chloride solution as 1 cm diameter strips. Quickly cut them into 3.5 cm lengths with scissors.
- 'Cook' them in the calcium chloride on all sides for 1½ minutes.
- Remove the spherical capsules from the calcium chloride solution and immerse them in water at 80 °C for 1 minute to heat.
- Heat the asparagus tips in their cooking water. Once they are hot, drop them in the hot white asparagus cream.
- Use tweezers to remove the asparagus tips from the cream and arrange 3 of them on a rectangular tray with a 5 cm separation between them.
- Use a slotted spoon to drain the capsules and place 1 capsule next to each asparagus tip.
- Season the capsules with freshly ground black pepper and Maldon sea salt.
- Coat the tops of the marshmallows with the yuzu zest and place 1 over each asparagus and olive oil capsule set.

NB: Yuzu is an Asian citrus fruit that tastes like a cross between mandarin and lemon. It is used particularly for its highly aromatic zest.

Cutlery

- Spoon and dessert fork.

How to eat

- Eat each asparagus, olive oil capsule and marshmallow set in a single mouthful without breaking.

1151

Green almond and tamarillo crunch, in eucalyptus, with mangosteen

Year
2005

Family
Tapas

Temperature
Hot

Season
June, July, August

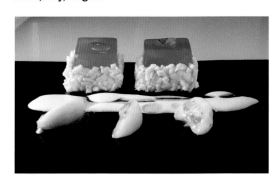

Serves 4

For the methylcellulose solution

100 g water
3 g methylcellulose

- Mix the ingredients at room temperature in a liquidiser until they form a smooth, even mixture.
- Strain and leave in the refrigerator for 24 hours.

For the green almond cubes

110 g green almonds

- Peel and dice the green almonds into 1.5 mm cubes.
- Refrigerate.

For the tamarillo water

500 g Jugolandia tamarillo pulp

- Thaw the tamarillo pulp and place it in a fine strainer lined with paper towel in the refrigerator to separate the liquid from the solids.
- Reserve the pulp left in the strainer for other dishes.
- Strain the liquid through a Superbag to obtain crystal clear tamarillo water.
- Refrigerate.

NB: The tamarillo is a Peruvian fruit also known as the tree tomato. It tastes like a cross between a tomato and a strawberry. We use frozen tamarillo pulp because its ripeness and flavour are more reliable.

For the hot tamarillo water jelly

150 g tamarillo water (previously prepared)
0.6 g powdered agar-agar
1 x 2 g gelatine leaf (previously rehydrated in cold water)

- Mix the agar-agar with 50 g of tamarillo water and bring to the boil, stirring constantly with a whisk.
- Remove from the heat, add the drained gelatine leaf, mix and add the rest of the tamarillo water.
- Mix and pour into a container to a thickness of 2 cm.
- Leave to set in the refrigerator for 2 hours.
- Once it has set, slice into 8 x 2 cm cubes.

For the green almond and hot tamarillo water jelly crunch

100 g green almond cubes (previously prepared)
60 g methylcellulose solution (previously prepared)
8 hot tamarillo water jelly cubes (previously prepared)

- Mix the green almond cubes with the methylcellulose base to obtain an even mixture.
- Spread the almond and methylcellulose mixture over parchment paper to a thickness of 1.5 mm.
- Place 1 tamarillo jelly cube on the almond. Use a small spatula to coat first the base of the cube and then the sides to a height of 1.5 cm only, making sure the almond sticks to the jelly.
- Repeat this operation for all the jelly cubes. Place them on parchment paper for easy handling later.
- Refrigerate.

For the almond milk

500 g crushed almonds
450 g water

- Use a stick blender to process the crushed almonds thoroughly with the water.
- Stand in the refrigerator for 12 hours.
- Blend the water and almond mixture in the liquidiser to obtain a cream.
- Squeeze firmly through a Superbag to release all the liquid and create a thick and tasty almond milk.
- Strain and refrigerate.

For the almond milk cream

250 g almond milk (previously prepared)
¼ x 2 g gelatine leaf (previously rehydrated in cold water)
Salt
Pacojet

- Season the almond milk with salt.
- Dissolve the gelatine in one quarter of the almond milk.
- Add the remaining almond milk, mix and pour into a Pacojet beaker.
- Freeze at -20 °C.
- Process the frozen almond milk in the Pacojet 3 times, then leave to thaw in the refrigerator without stirring so as not to alter the texture.

1151

Green almond and tamarillo crunch, in eucalyptus, with mangosteen

For the mangosteen wedges

4 x 75 g mangosteens

- Peel the mangosteens.
- Separate the segments, setting aside the wedges with a pit inside.
- Choose the largest 12 mangosteen wedges without a pit.
- Refrigerate.

NB: The mangosteen is a fruit originating in Malaysia. It is round, red and thick-skinned. It has 5–6 segments of very delicate and perfumed white flesh.

For the tender eucalyptus leaf oil

100 g sunflower oil
50 g tender eucalyptus leaves

- Chop the tender eucalyptus leaves and cover them with the sunflower oil.
- Heat to 70 °C and refrigerate in an airtight container for 24 hours.
- Strain as required.

Finishing and presentation

4 x 1 cm fresh basil leaves
10 g toasted almond oil
20 g prune kernel oil

- Place the almond and jelly crunches together with the parchment paper in a non-stick frying pan and heat until the methylcellulose softens and the crunches are easily unstuck from the paper.
- Place the crunch under the salamander grill until the jelly is very hot.
- Cook the mangosteen wedges in a frying pan on both sides until golden.
- Heat 4 O! LUNA deep lunar plates. Place 2 hot crunches on the right with a 4 cm space between them.
- Make a fan with 3 mangosteen wedges on the opposite side of the plate.
- Place a soup spoon of almond milk cream at the centre of the plate without touching the crunches or mangosteen wedges.
- Place 1 drop of toasted almond oil on the leftmost crunch together with a fresh basil leaf.
- Place 1 drop of tender eucalyptus oil on the other crunch.
- Finish by drizzling a little prune kernel oil over the almond milk cream.

NB: We have made another version of this dish substituting the hot tamarillo water jelly with hot truffle juice jelly.

Cutlery

- Tapas cutlery.

NB: Tapas cutlery consists of a 14 x 3 cm spoon and fork.

How to eat

- Eat the crunch with almond oil first, followed by the almond cream, alternating with the mangosteen. Finish by eating the crunch with eucalyptus oil. Eat the crunches in a single mouthful.

1152

**Baby broad bean *albóndigas*
in their juice with broad bean flowers**

Year
2005

Family
Tapas

Temperature
Hot

Season
March, April, May

Serves 4

For the blanched and peeled baby broad beans

300 g fresh shelled baby broad beans
Water
Salt

- Blanch the baby broad beans in the salted water for 5 seconds.
- Peel the beans and refrigerate.
- Set aside their skins.

**For the baby broad bean *albóndigas*
and the raw baby broad bean juice**

300 g peeled raw baby broad beans
1 Green Star juice extractor

- Introduce the baby broad beans into the juice extractor.
- Set aside the juice obtained for finishing and presentation.
- Make 8 x 6.5 g *albóndigas* with the shredded pulp.
- Refrigerate.

For the blanched baby broad bean skin juice

Blanched baby broad bean skins
(previously prepared)
Green Star juice extractor

- Introduce the baby broad bean skins into the juice extractor and set aside the juice obtained for finishing and presentation.

For the methylcellulose solution

100 g water
3 g methylcellulose

- Mix the ingredients at room temperature in a liquidiser until they form a smooth, even mixture.
- Strain and leave in the refrigerator for 24 hours.

**For the baby broad bean *albóndigas*
with methylcellulose**

65 g peeled baby broad beans (previously prepared)
20 g methylcellulose solution
(previously prepared)

- Mix the cooked peeled baby broad beans with the methylcellulose solution.
- Make 8 x 8.5 g *albóndigas*.
- Refrigerate.

For the *jamón ibérico* stock

400 g *jamón ibérico* bones
1.2 kg water

- Remove any rancid bits from the ham bones.
- Blanch the bones in water and drain.
- Place the blanched ham bones in the water and simmer until 400 g of ham stock is obtained.
- Strain, discard excess fat and season with salt if necessary.

For the *jamón ibérico* lard

200 g *jamón ibérico* bones
20 g water

- Remove any lean or rancid bits from the fat.
- Simmer until the water evaporates and the solid fat is fully rendered into lard.
- Strain the liquid lard and set aside.

For the *jamón ibérico* cream

60 g *jamón ibérico* stock (previously prepared)
60 g *jamón ibérico* lard (previously prepared)
60 g 35% fat single cream
Instant cornflour
Salt

- Heat the ham stock and add the 60 g of cream.
- Thicken the mixture with a little instant cornflour. Remove from the heat and add the lard.
- Season with salt and fill a squeeze bottle.

For the *jamón ibérico* stock air base

250 g *jamón ibérico* stock (previously prepared)
0.8 g soya lecithin powder

- Mix the *jamón ibérico* stock with the soya lecithin in a deep 25 cm diameter container.

For the soft *jamón ibérico* fat cubes

50 g *jamón ibérico* fat

- Remove any lean or rancid bits from the fat.
- Dice the ham fat into 0.5 cm cubes.
- Heat the ham fat cubes in a frying pan until they sweat and the fat is warm and soft.
- Drain and lay on paper towel to soak up the excess fat.

1152

**Baby broad bean *albóndigas*
in their juice with broad bean flowers**

For the fresh mint oil

40 g fresh mint leaves
40 g sunflower oil
Water

- Blanch the mint leaves for 2 seconds in
  boiling water.
- Drain and refresh immediately in iced water.
- Drain the blanched mint leaves well, then blend
  with the sunflower oil in a liquidiser.
- Strain and fill a squeeze bottle.
- Refrigerate.

Finishing and presentation

20 fresh broad bean flowers
Salt
Water

- Work the stick blender over the surface of the
  jamón ibérico stock air base until it emulsifies and
  the air forms.
- Carefully transfer the baby broad bean *albóndigas*
  to a pan without breaking and place next to
  the heat to warm.
- When they are warm, place a spoon of ham
  stock air over them, covering them completely
  in an air layer.
- Heat the salted water to 90 °C and immerse
  the peeled baby broad bean *albóndigas*
  with methylcellulose. Leave to cook for 1 minute.
- Drain and season with salt.
- Place two spoons of hot baby broad bean juice
  in the base of a preheated 24 cm soup plate.
- Place a spoon of hot baby broad bean skin juice
  over it.
- Make 4 spots of hot ham cream and 3 of mint
  oil over the 2 juices.
- Arrange 8 soft ham cubes over the plate.
- Place 2 *albóndigas* covered in ham stock air
  on the right and left of the plate, over the juice.
  Place the baby broad bean *albóndigas* with
  methylcellulose at the top and bottom of the dish.
- Arrange 5 broad bean flowers in the middle
  of the dish.

Cutlery

- Tapas cutlery.

  NB: Tapas cutlery consists of a 14 x 3 cm
  spoon and fork.

How to eat

- Eat all the components separately, alternating
  with the sauce.

1153

Walnuts in their cream, hot yogurt jelly, apple velvet and mint aroma

Year
2005

Family
Tapas

Temperature
Hot/ambient

Season
**January, February, March,
April, May, October,
November, December**

Serves 4

For the stewed walnuts

16 x 8 g Franquette walnut halves, shelled
150 g water
Salt

- Soak the walnuts in water for 72 hours.
- Then cook the walnuts in a pressure cooker for 14 minutes in salted water.
- Set the walnuts aside in their cooking water until finishing and presentation.

NB: The Franquette variety of walnuts should be used to ensure a good result.

For the walnut milk

200 g walnuts, shelled
200 g water

- Mix the walnuts with the water in a container and lightly crush them with a stick blender.
- Stand in the refrigerator for 24 hours.
- Blend in the liquidiser to a smooth paste.
- Strain through a Superbag. Press well to release all the liquid.

For the walnut cream

150 g walnut milk (previously prepared)
100 g walnut oil
0.6 g Xantana
Salt

- Blend the walnut milk with the Xantana until lump-free. Add the walnut oil and emulsify the mixture to obtain a cream.
- Season with salt and set aside.

For the plain yogurt water

6 x 125 g tubs plain yogurt

- Freeze the yogurt.
- Once frozen, remove from the tubs and leave over a fine strainer in the refrigerator to thaw. In this way, clear yogurt water will be obtained. Strain through a Superbag.
- Refrigerate.

For the plates set with hot yogurt water jelly

100 g yogurt water (previously prepared)
0.3 g powdered agar-agar

- Dissolve the agar-agar with a third of the yogurt water and bring to the boil, stirring constantly with a whisk.
- Remove from the heat and add the rest of the yogurt water.
- Position 4 O! LUNA deep lunar plates at a 20% tilt and pour 25 g of the jelly base into each.
- Leave to set at room temperature without moving the plates.

For the fresh tarragon water

40 g fresh tarragon leaves
Water

- Blanch the leaves in water for 15 seconds.
- Drain and chill in iced water.
- Blend the blanched tarragon leaves in a liquidiser with 120 g of the water used to chill them.
- Strain and refrigerate in an airtight container.

For the fresh tarragon concentrate

140 g fresh tarragon water (previously prepared)

- Pour 70 g of the tarragon water into each of 2 centrifuge tubes and 70 g of water in the other 2 tubes.
- Spin in the centrifuge for 5 minutes at 100 rpm.
- When the process is complete, separate the water from on top of the concentrated pulp that has settled at the bottom of each tube.
- Discard the water.
- Transfer the concentrate to a piping bag, vacuum seal and refrigerate.

For the apple velvet

4 x 250 g Granny Smith apples

- Clean and core the apples. Cut into 8 wedges.
- Liquidise the apples and transfer the juice to a deep, narrow container.
- The pulp that remains at the top is the apple velvet and will be used in the finishing and presentation.

NB: This preparation should be done at the time of finishing and presentation to prevent the apple velvet from oxidising.

1153

**Walnuts in their cream,
hot yogurt jelly, apple velvet
and mint aroma**

For the mint aroma spoons

4 aroma spoons
4 x 8 cm shoots fresh mint with budding leaves

- Insert the fresh mint shoots in the aroma spoons leaving the budding leaves exposed.

Finishing and presentation

10 g Pral yogurt powder
2 g citric acid granules
Maldon sea salt

- Heat the stewed walnuts in their cooking water.
- Heat the 4 plates set with hot yogurt water jelly under the salamander grill until the jelly is very hot.
- Arrange 4 hot walnut halves on the side of the plate where there is no jelly with a 2 cm space between them.
- Place 2 spots of tarragon concentrate over the hot yogurt water jelly with a 4 cm space between them.
- Make 2 spots with pinches of yogurt powder between the 2 tarragon concentrate spots and place 4 granules of citric acid over them.
- Coat the stewed walnuts with the hot walnut cream and place 2 Maldon sea salt flakes on top of each.
- Place a spoon of apple velvet in the middle of the plate, in the space created between the yogurt water jelly and the walnuts.
- Serve the aroma spoons so that diners can smell the mint aroma while eating the dish.

Cutlery

- Tapas fork and aroma spoon.

How to eat

- Alternate the different components without mixing.

1154

Green walnuts[3], smoked tea and wasabi

Year
2005

Family
Tapas

Temperature
Hot/ambient

Season
August, September

Serves 4

For the peeled green walnuts

12 x 30 g green walnuts
20 g walnut oil

- Use a paring knife to peel the shells, then break the shells with a nutcracker.
- Use a knife to remove the two walnut halves from each shell without breaking them.
- Peel the walnuts to make 24 peeled green walnut halves.
- Set them aside in the refrigerator covered with walnut oil.

For the stewed green walnuts

12 peeled green walnut halves (previously prepared)
150 g water
Salt

- Salt the water.
- Place the walnuts and the salted water in a pressure cooker.
- Cook for 14 minutes and leave the walnuts in their cooking water until finishing and presentation.

For the walnut milk

200 g walnuts, shelled
200 g water

- Mix the walnuts with water in a container and break them up with a stick blender.
- Stand in the refrigerator for 24 hours.
- Blend in the liquidiser to a fine paste.
- Strain through a Superbag, squeezing well to obtain as much liquid as possible.

For the walnut cream

150 g walnut milk (previously prepared)
100 g walnut oil
0.6 g Xantana
Salt

- Blend the walnut milk with the Xantana until lump-free. Add the walnut oil and emulsify the mixture to obtain a cream.
- Season with salt and set aside.

For the smoked tea infusion

12 g Grand Lapsang Souchong smoked tea
250 g water

- Bring the water to the boil, add the tea and leave to infuse for 5 minutes.
- Strain through a Superbag.
- Set aside.

For the smoked tea air base

200 g smoked tea infusion (previously prepared)
0.8 g soya lecithin powder

- Dissolve the soya lecithin in the tea in a deep 25 cm container.

For the grated Cantonese-style candied walnuts

10 x 2 cm walnut halves, shelled
450 g water
345 g sugar
675 g rosemary honey
500 g sunflower oil
1 Microplane grater

- Place 150 g of the water, 115 g sugar and 225 g of rosemary honey in each of 3 pans.
- Put the walnuts into one of the pans and slowly bring to the boil. Skim off the froth, remove the nuts and put them in next pan.
- Repeat the same operation, leaving the walnuts in the last pan.
- Slowly bring to the boil and skim off the froth. Keep the walnuts covered in the syrup in a container and refrigerate for 24 hours.
- Drain the walnuts, then fry them in sunflower oil at 165 °C until caramelised.
- Remove them from the oil and allow them to cool on a tray lined with parchment paper so that the sugar crystallises and their crunchy coating is enhanced.
- When they are cold, grate with the Microplane grater to make long strings.
- Store the walnut strings in a container without piling, so as not to alter their texture.

For the walnut oil cream

100 g water
3 g tapioca flour
50 g walnut oil
Salt

- Mix the water and tapioca flour and bring to the boil, stirring constantly with a whisk.
- When the mixture thickens, remove from the heat, add the oil and mix in such a way that the oil emulsifies with the thickened water.
- Season with salt.

NB: The tapioca flour can be substituted with 0.4 g of Xantana.

NB: This preparation should be made immediately before finishing and presentation.

1154

Green walnuts³, smoked tea and wasabi

For the grated fresh wasabi

20 g fresh wasabi
1 Japanese wasabi grater

- Peel the fresh wasabi.
- Grate.
- Put the grated wasabi in a piping bag to make it easier to handle.
- Refrigerate. This preparation should be made immediately before finishing and presentation.

NB: If fresh wasabi is not available, substitute with wasabi paste.

Finishing and presentation

Maldon sea salt

- Work a stick blender over the surface of the smoked tea air base until it emulsifies and the air forms.
- Heat 4 O! LUNA deep lunar plates under the salamander grill. Arrange 3 peeled raw green walnut halves in a triangle at the base of the plate.
- Place 1 spot of grated fresh wasabi on each followed by 2 flakes of Maldon sea salt.
- Place 3 teaspoons of hot walnut cream between the raw walnuts to form a circle.
- Place 1 hot stewed walnut half on top of each spot of cream.
- Fill the base of the plate with a spoon of hot walnut oil cream.
- Without touching any of the other components, place 2 spoons of smoked tea air on the right and left sides of the plate.
- Finish by spreading a 1 x 4 cm strip of grated walnut along the top edge of the plate.

Cutlery

- Tapas cutlery.

NB: Tapas cutlery consists of a 14 x 3 cm spoon and fork.

How to eat

- Alternate the different components without mixing.

1155

**Stewed walnuts with
daisy buds, beurre noisette
air-foam and mint aroma**

Year
2005

Family
Tapas

Temperature
Hot/ambient

Season
**January, February, March,
April, May, October,
November, December**

Serves 4

For the stewed walnuts	• Soak the walnuts in water for 72 hours.
	• Then cook the walnuts in a pressure cooker
16 x 8 g Franquette walnut halves, shelled	for 14 minutes in salted water.
150 g water	• Set the walnuts aside in their cooking water
Salt	until finishing and presentation.
	NB: The Franquette variety of walnuts should
	be used to ensure a good result.

For the beure noisette	• Cook the butter in a pan until the temperature
	reaches 140 °C.
300 g butter	• Leave to cool away from the heat and set aside.

For the hot beurre noisette foam	• Emulsify the melted butter at room temperature
	with the egg white and yolk as if making
275 g beurre noisette (previously prepared)	a mayonnaise.
100 g pasteurised egg yolk	• Strain, season with salt and fill the siphon.
80 g pasteurised liquid egg white	• Close it and insert gas cartridge.
Salt	• Leave the siphon in a bain-marie at 55 °C.
1 x 0.5 litre ISI siphon	• Shake the siphon every 10 minutes to prevent
1 N₂O cartridge	the foam from separating.

For the beurre noisette air base	• Melt the 2 types of butter and mix all the ingredients
	in a deep 25 cm diameter container.
375 g beurre noisette (previously prepared)	
125 g butter	
375 g water	
4 g soya lecithin powder	

For the daisy buds	• Drain the daisy buds and refrigerate.
40 pickled daisy buds	

For the mint aroma spoons	• Insert the fresh mint shoots in the aroma
	spoons leaving the budding leaves exposed.
4 aroma spoons	
4 x 8 cm shoots fresh mint with budding leaves	

1155

**Stewed walnuts with
daisy buds, beurre noisette
air-foam and mint aroma**

Finishing and presentation

30 g walnut oil
Maldon sea salt

- Work the stick blender over the surface
  of the beurre noisette air base until it emulsifies
  and the air forms.
- Heat 4 O! LUNA deep lunar plates.
- Arrange 10 daisy buds climbing in a line from
  the bottom edge of the base up the gentler
  sloping side.
- Arrange 4 stewed walnuts around the base
  of the plate with a 3 cm space between them.
- Squirt 15 g of hot beurre noisette foam in
  the middle. Spread a spoon of hot beurre noisette
  around the foam.
- Season each walnut half with 2 drops of walnut
  oil and a pinch of Maldon sea salt.
- Finish by placing a spoon of beurre noisette
  air over the hot beurre noisette foam.
- Serve the aroma spoons separately so that diners
  can smell the mint aroma while eating the dish.

Cutlery

- Dessert fork and aroma spoon.

How to eat

- Eat the walnuts with the foam and the beurre
  noisette, alternating with the daisy buds.
  Smell the aroma spoon while eating the dish.

1156

Warm spherical dashi cloud with fairy ring mushrooms flavoured with purple shiso, sesame and yuzu

Year
2005

Family
Tapas

Temperature
Hot

Season
April, May, September, October

Serves 4

For the dashi stock

500 g water
30 g shaved *katsuobushi*
20 g dried kombu seaweed

- Cut the kombu seaweed into 1 cm pieces, mix with the water and bring to the boil.
- Remove from the heat. Leave to stand for 5 minutes, then take out the kombu.
- Bring the resulting stock back to the boil. Add the shaved *katsuobushi* and when it comes back from the boil, remove from heat.
- Leave to stand for 5 minutes and strain through a Superbag.
- Set aside.

NB: *Katsuobushi* is the Japanese name for dried bonito (tuna) that has been smoked and cured with the *Aspergillus glaucus* fungus.

For the sodium alginate solution

100 g water
2 g sodium alginate

- Blend both ingredients in a liquidiser until lump-free.
- Set aside.

For the calcium chloride solution

1 kg water
10 g calcium chloride

- Dissolve the calcium chloride in the water with a whisk.
- Set aside.

For the warm spherical dashi cloud

300 g dashi (previously prepared)
3 x 2 g gelatine leaves (previously rehydrated in cold water)
75 g sodium alginate solution (previously prepared)
1 kg calcium chloride solution (previously prepared)

- Place 225 g of dashi in the freezer to lower its temperature to 1 °C.
- Preheat the remaining 75 g of dashi and dissolve the gelatine into it.
- Transfer the dashi from the freezer to the electric mixer and whip on medium speed. Gradually add the dashi and gelatine mixture that has been allowed to cool to 25 °C.
- Whip until the texture is similar to that of a meringue.
- Add the sodium alginate solution and whip for 10 more seconds.
- Pour 20 g of cloud in each of 4 x 20 cm diameter hemispherical Flexipan moulds and refrigerate for 30 minutes to set.
- Remove the clouds from their moulds without breaking and place in the calcium chloride solution.
- 'Cook' the mixture on all sides for 5 minutes.
- Drain the cooked clouds and rinse them.

NB: The clouds should be 'cooked' in the calcium chloride solution 10 minutes before finishing and presentation.

For the toasted white sesame cream

50 g white sesame seeds
60 g water

- Lightly toast the sesame seeds in a frying pan.
- Mix the sesame with the water in a liquidiser and blend to obtain a fine cream.
- Strain through a Superbag. Press well to release all the liquid.
- Set aside.

NB: We use white Japanese sesame seeds for their very delicate flavour.

For the purple shiso infusion

20 g purple shiso
100 g water

- Chop the purple shiso.
- Bring the water to the boil and add the shiso. Remove from the heat and leave to infuse for 5 minutes.
- Strain and refrigerate.

NB: Shiso is a kind of Asian herb similar to basil and mint. There are 2 varieties, purple and green.

1156

Warm spherical dashi cloud with fairy ring mushrooms flavoured with purple shiso, sesame and yuzu

For the hot purple shiso infusion jelly

100 g purple shiso infusion (previously prepared)
0.3 g powdered agar-agar
½ x 2 g gelatine leaf (previously rehydrated in cold water)

- Mix the agar-agar with half of the infusion and bring to the boil, stirring constantly with a whisk.
- Remove from the heat, dissolve the gelatine leaf and add the remaining infusion.
- Pour into a container to a thickness of 5 mm.
- Leave to set in the refrigerator for 3 hours.
- Once set, cut out 4 x 1 cm cubes.

For the hot yuzu juice jelly

50 g yuzu juice
25 g water
0.3 g powdered agar-agar
½ x 2 g gelatine leaf (previously rehydrated in cold water)

- Mix the water and yuzu juice.
- Dissolve the agar-agar in a third of the liquid and bring to the boil, stirring constantly with a whisk.
- Remove from the heat and dissolve the gelatine into it. Mix in the rest of the juice.
- Pour into a container to a thickness of 3 mm.
- Leave to set in the refrigerator for 3 hours.
- Once set, cut out 8 x 3 mm cubes.

NB: Yuzu is an Asian citrus fruit that tastes like a cross between mandarin and lemon. It is used particularly for its highly aromatic zest.

For the clean fairy ring mushrooms

100 g 8 mm diameter fairy ring mushrooms

- Remove the stalks from the mushrooms.
- Rinse the mushrooms to clean and lay them out on paper towel to dry well.
- Make 4 x 20 g portions.
- Refrigerate.

For the fairy ring mushroom cream

75 g broken up fairy ring mushrooms
Olive oil
25 g water
Salt

- Rinse the mushrooms and lay them out on paper towel to dry well.
- Cook the mushrooms in a pan over low heat with a little oil and moisten with the water.
- Cook for 5 minutes, then blend in a liquidiser.
- Press firmly through a fine strainer and season with salt.
- Refrigerate.

Finishing and presentation

20 g toasted Japanese white sesame seeds
4 g chopped purple shiso
Olive oil
Salt

- Cook the mushrooms in a little oil. Remove from the heat when they start to release water. Add 4 spoons of fairy ring mushroom cream and season with salt. The cooked mushrooms should be in a consistent and flavoursome sauce.
- Place a warm spherical dashi cloud in the middle of an O! LUNA deep lunar plate and heat under the salamander grill for 10 seconds.
- Fill a syringe with the warm white sesame cream and carefully inject 8 g into the cloud without breaking it.
- Heat the hot shiso and yuzu jellies separately.
- Place 2 spoons of cooked mushrooms and sauce around the cloud.
- Place 1 cube of hot shiso jelly and 2 cubes of hot yuzu jelly over the mushrooms each separated by the same distance.
- Sprinkle a pinch of chopped purple shiso over the hot shiso jelly.
- Finish by sprinkling toasted Japanese white sesame seeds over the cloud.

Cutlery

- Tapas cutlery.

NB: Tapas cutlery consists of a 14 x 3 cm spoon and fork.

How to eat

- Break the spherical cloud and eat, alternating with the components.

1157

Sea tomatoes

Year
2005

Family
Tapas

Temperature
Hot

Season
June, July

Serves 4

For the cherry tomato confit

12 x 3 cm diameter ripe cherry tomatoes
500 g extra virgin olive oil
Salt

- Make a small cross on the top of each tomato and blanch them in boiling water for 5 seconds.
- Drain and chill in iced water.
- Peel the tomatoes.
- Cut off the top and use a 5 mm melon baller to hollow out the tomatoes, removing all the seeds.
- Season with salt. Place the tomatoes in a pan covered with the oil.
- Cook at 70 °C for 15 minutes to make a confit.
- Drain the tomatoes and leave them upside down for 1 minute over a sieve to drain the oil from the inside.

For the rock mussels

10 x 15 g rock mussels

- Plunge the rock mussels a few at a time in boiling water for 10 seconds.
- Remove them from the water and leave them to cool at room temperature.
- Use a paring knife to cut the muscle joining each mussel to its shell.
- Lift the rock mussels out, taking care they do not break.
- Cover the mussels with their own liquor, which has been previously strained through a Superbag. Refrigerate.

For the sea urchin roe

2 x 70 g sea urchins

- Kill the sea urchins by scalding them in boiling water for 10 seconds.
- Cut along the bottom of the sea urchins with a pair of scissors, making a 2 cm diameter circle.
- Remove the roe from inside the sea urchins and place each one in the sea urchin liquor previously strained through a Superbag.
- Refrigerate.

For the hot sea water, rock mussel and sea urchin infusion jelly

125 g sea water
10 rock mussels (previously prepared)
15 sea urchin roe (previously prepared)
0.3 g powdered agar-agar
¼ x 2 g gelatine leaf (previously rehydrated in cold water)

- Add the agar-agar to the sea water and bring to the boil, stirring constantly with a whisk.
- Remove from the heat, add the mussels and sea urchin roe and break them up with a short sharp burst with the stick blender.
- Leave the infuse for 30 seconds, then filter quickly through a fine strainer. Press firmly so the mussels and roe release all their liquid. This jelly will be used immediately to fill the tomatoes.

1157

Sea tomatoes

For the cherry tomatoes filled with hot sea water, rock mussel and sea urchin infusion jelly

12 cherry tomato confit (previously prepared)
Hot sea water, rock mussel and sea urchin infusion jelly (previously prepared)

- Fill a syringe with the hot jelly and fill the tomatoes to capacity one at a time.
- Leave to set at room temperature.
- Once the jelly has set, return the tomatoes to the confit oil at room temperature to keep them moist.

For the nori water

500 g salted nori seaweed
500 g water

- Rinse the seaweed in plenty of water to remove excess salt.
- Blend the seaweed with the water in a liquidiser.
- Strain through a Superbag and set aside.

For the nori water air base

250 g nori water (previously prepared)
1 g soya lecithin powder

- Mix both ingredients in a deep 25 cm diameter container.

For the lemon zest purée

60 g lemon zest
10 g sugar
10 g water
65 g lemon juice
14 g butter, softened

- Blanch the lemon zest 3 times, starting with cold water each time.
- Drain, change the water and boil for 30 minutes.
- Drain the water from the zest and blend it in the Thermomix at 50 °C together with the lemon juice, water and sugar to obtain a smooth paste.
- Emulsify with the butter to give the purée a creamy texture.
- Strain and refrigerate.

For the green tomato juice

2 x 250 g green tomatoes
Salt

- Peel the tomatoes and remove the stalk.
- Chop the tomatoes and blend their flesh in the liquidiser to obtain a lump-free juice.
- Season with salt.

NB: This preparation should be made immediately before finishing and presentation to prevent it from oxidising.

For the grated green almond

10 green almonds
1 Microplane grater

- Peel the green almonds and grate them with a Microplane grater to make long threads.
- Store the threads in an airtight container without piling, so as not to alter their texture.

1157

Sea tomatoes

Finishing and presentation

Freshly ground black pepper
4 flowering sprigs chocolate mint
Extra virgin olive oil

- Work the stick blender over the surface of the nori water air base until it emulsifies and the air forms.
- Heat the tomatoes in the oil at 70 °C. Do not let the jelly melt.
- Heat the green tomato juice on a low heat.
- Place 2 tablespoons of hot green tomato juice in the middle of an O! LUNA deep lunar plate.
- Drain the oil from 3 hot tomatoes and arrange them in an equilateral triangle with their openings face down on the plate.
- Season the tomatoes with freshly ground black pepper.
- Carefully make a small mound of grated green almond on top of the middle tomato without damaging its airy texture.
- Place a teaspoon of hot lemon zest purée on one side of the plate, lightly touching the green tomato juice. Use a small spatula to flatten the purée slightly, giving it the shape of a teardrop.
- Drizzle a little extra virgin olive oil over the green tomato juice.
- Place a spoon of nori water air on top of the tomatoes without the grated almond.
- Finish by placing a sprig of flowering chocolate mint on the tomato juice.

NB: There is another version of this dish where the tomatoes are filled with hot seaweed jelly.

Cutlery

- Tapas cutlery.

NB: Tapas cutlery consists of a 14 x 3 cm spoon and fork.

How to eat

- Alternate the components. Eat the tomatoes in a single mouthful.

1158

Warty venus clam with watermelon and yuzu in a saffron and kombu broth

Year
2005

Family
Tapas

Temperature
Hot

Season
June, July, August

Serves 4

For the warty venus clams

12 x 30 g warty venus clams

- Plunge the clams a few at a time in boiling water for 15 seconds.
- Use an oyster opener to open the clams. Keep all their liquor.
- Smell them one by one.
- Cut through the muscle holding the oyster to the shell and remove the oyster.
- Choose the 8 most attractive clams for finishing and presentation and use the rest for the sauce.
- Strain the clams through a Superbag and keep them in their own liquor.
- Refrigerate.

For the warty venus clam sauce

4 warty venus clams (previously prepared)
50 g warty venus clam liquor (previously prepared)

- Process the clams in their liquor with a stick blender to obtain a fine cream.
- Strain and refrigerate.

For the yuzu sauce

50 g yuzu juice
0.3 g Xantana

- Mix the ingredients and process with a stick blender to obtain a thick, lump-free cream.
- Fill pipettes and refrigerate.

  NB: Yuzu is an Asian citrus fruit that tastes like a cross between mandarin and lemon. It is used particularly for its highly aromatic zest.

For the saffron infusion

50 g water
0.6 g saffron threads

- Bring the water to the boil, toast the saffron threads and add them to the boiling water.
- Remove from the heat and leave to infuse in the refrigerator for 24 hours.
- Strain through a fine strainer. Press the threads firmly to obtain as much infusion as possible.
- Refrigerate.

For the saffron sauce

50 g saffron infusion (previously prepared)
0.3 g Xantana

- Mix the ingredients with a stick blender to obtain a thick, lump-free cream.
- Fill pipettes and refrigerate.

For the kombu broth

500 g water
100 g dried kombu seaweed

- Chop the kombu, add to the water and bring to the boil.
- Remove from the heat and leave to infuse for 30 minutes.
- Strain through a Superbag and refrigerate.

For the methylcellulose solution

100 g water
3 g methylcellulose

- Mix the ingredients at room temperature in a liquidiser until they form a smooth, even mixture.
- Strain and leave in the refrigerator for 24 hours

For the watermelon in methylcellulose

1 x 200 g piece of seedless watermelon
20 g methylcellulose solution (previously prepared)

- Peel the watermelon and cut the flesh into 2 mm dice.
- Weigh out 100 g of watermelon dice and mix them with the methylcellulose solution.

  NB: The watermelon should be cut just before finishing and presentation so it does not release water.

1158

Warty venus clam with watermelon and yuzu in a saffron and kombu broth

Finishing and presentation

Olive oil
Maldon sea salt

- Cover the upper side of the clams with a layer of watermelon dice in methylcellulose.
- Heat 4 O! LUNA deep lunar plates. Make 9 spots of clam sauce, 5 of yuzu sauce and 5 of saffron sauce to form a circle around the edge of the base of the plate. Do not let them touch each other.
- Cook the clams watermelon side down in a non-stick frying pan in a little oil until the watermelon turns golden.
- Remove the clams from the pan and place 2 of them in the middle of each plate. Do not let them touch the sauces.
- Place 2 Maldon sea salt flakes on top of each clam.
- Place the kombu broth in a separate dish so that the waiter can serve it in front of the diner.

Cutlery

- Tapas cutlery.

  NB: Tapas cutlery consists of a 14 x 3 cm spoon and fork.

How to eat

- Alternate the components. Eat the clams in a single mouthful to appreciate the texture of the watermelon.

1159

Earthy

Year
2005

Family
Tapas

Temperature
Hot/ambient

Season
June, July, August

Serves 4

For the methylcellulose solution

100 g water
3 g methylcellulose

- Mix the ingredients at room temperature in a liquidiser until they form a smooth, even mixture.
- Strain and stand in the refrigerator for 24 hours.

For the summer truffle purée

50 g peeled summer truffle
15 g 35% fat single cream
15 g white truffle oil
Salt

- Heat the cream and blend it with the truffle and the white truffle oil in the liquidiser until it forms a smooth purée.
- Strain and season with salt to taste.
- Refrigerate.

For the summer truffle *empanadillas*

1 x 35 g peeled summer truffle
20 g summer truffle purée (previously prepared)
20 g methylcellulose solution (previously prepared)
Salt

- Slice the truffles into 1 mm slices.
- Place the slices on clingfilm lightly coated with the methylcellulose solution to form 4 x 4 cm circles. The slices should overlap slightly.
- Lightly coat the circle with the methylcellulose solution and a little salt.
- Put 5 g of summer truffle purée in the middle of the summer truffle circle.
- Seal the disc as if it were a turnover and refrigerate.

For the Venus rice stock

50 g Venus rice
250 g water

- Cook the rice in the recommended amount of water for 30 minutes.
- Strain and reserve the cooking liquid.

For the Venus rice stock jelly

100 g Venus rice stock (previously prepared)
0.4 g powdered agar-agar
1/3 x 2 g gelatine leaf (previously rehydrated in cold water)
Salt

- Season the Venus rice stock with salt.
- Add the agar-agar to the stock and bring to the boil, stirring constantly with a whisk.
- Remove from the heat, add the drained gelatine and pour into a container to a depth of 2 cm.
- Refrigerate for 3 hours.
- Once it has set, cut the jelly into 2 cm cubes. This will give 1 cube per person.

For the fresh liquorice infusion

50 g fresh liquorice stick
300 g water
1 g ascorbic acid

- To prevent oxidisation, peel the liquorice and place in the water into which the ascorbic acid has been dissolved.
- Break up the liquorice and the water in the liquidiser and infuse for 24 hours in the refrigerator.
- Strain through a Superbag.

NB: Ascorbic acid (vitamin C) is used as an antioxidant.

For the fresh liquorice infusion jelly lasagne

200 g fresh liquorice infusion (previously prepared)
2.3 g powdered agar-agar
1 x 2 g gelatine leaves (previously rehydrated in cold water)
5 g liquorice paste

- Mix the agar-agar with half of the liquorice infusion and bring to the boil, stirring constantly with a whisk.
- Remove from the heat, add the remaining infusion and dissolve the gelatine into it.
- Pour the jelly onto a 20 x 20 cm flat wooden tray to a depth of 1 mm.
- Wait 5 minutes and pour the jelly onto the tray again to create another 1 mm thick layer.
- Repeat this operation twice more to create 4 x 1 mm gelatine layers.
- Refrigerate for 1 hour and cut into 3 cm squares.
- Place 1 drop of liquorice paste between the third and fourth layers. There should be 1 lasagne per person. Refrigerate.

1159

Earthy

For the cep *albóndigas*

50 g ceps
8 g methylcellulose solution (previously prepared)

- Clean the ceps and cut the stems into 3 mm cubes.
- Mix 25 g of the cubes with 8 g of the methylcellulose solution.
- Make 4 *albóndigas* weighing 8 g each.
- Refrigerate.

For the peanut oil marshmallow

250 g milk
5 x 2 g gelatine leaves (previously rehydrated in cold water)
40 g virgin peanut oil

- Put 200 g of milk in the freezer to cool to 3 °C.
- Meanwhile, mix the gelatine with the remaining 50 g milk in a pan.
- Dissolve the gelatine leaves at 40 °C and pour into the electric mixer bowl.
- Start to whip. After 30 seconds, add all the cooled milk in one go.
- Continue to whip for 3 minutes and add the virgin peanut oil.
- Keep whipping for another 30 seconds and spread out over a transparent tray to a thickness of 2 cm.
- Refrigerate for 2 hours.
- Cut into cubes with 2 cm sides.
- Store refrigerated in an airtight container.

For the grated peanuts

40 g peeled toasted peanuts
1 Microplane grater

- Grate the peanuts with a Microplane grater.
- Keep in an airtight container.

For the toasted black sesame savoury praline

50 g black sesame seeds
5 g sunflower oil
Salt

- Toast the black sesame in a frying pan.
- Process the toasted black sesame seeds with the sunflower oil in a liquidiser until a fine, lump-free cream is obtained.
- Strain, season with salt and put in a squeeze bottle.

For the beetroot shoot juice

300 g beetroot shoots
1 Green Star juice extractor

- Put the beetroot shoots through the Green Star.
- Set aside the juice obtained.

For the beetroot shoot juice air base

100 g beetroot shoot juice (previously prepared)

- Pour the beetroot shoot juice into a deep 15 cm diameter container.

For the freeze-dried cold white miso foam

125 g water
35 g white miso paste
1 x 2 g gelatine leaf (previously rehydrated in cold water)
1 x 0.5 litre ISI siphon
1 N_2O cartridge
5 x 60 cc plastic cups

- Dilute the white miso paste in the water with a whisk and strain.
- Heat a third of the liquid obtained and dissolve the gelatine into it.
- Add the remaining liquid, strain and put in the siphon.
- Close it and insert gas cartridge.
- Refrigerate for 3 hours.
- Fill 5 x 60 g cups with chilled miso foam and freeze dry for 48 hours.
- Remove the freeze-dried foam from the cup moulds and cut each one in half vertically.
- Keep vacuum sealed until just before serving.

For the potato stock

400 g potatoes
500 g water
Salt

- Clean and cut the potatoes, skin on, into 5 mm slices.
- Cover with water and boil over a medium heat for 1 hour. Remove the froth continuously.
- Strain carefully to prevent the stock from becoming cloudy.
- Season with salt and set aside.

1159

Earthy

Finishing and presentation

20 g red cabbage shoots
Olive oil
Salt

- Work a stick blender over the top of the beetroot shoot juice air base so it emulsifies and the air forms.
- Steam the Venus rice jelly.
- Cook the cep *albóndigas* for 30 seconds in lightly salted water at 80 °C. Drain and season with salt.
- Sauté the red cabbage shoots in a little olive oil and season with salt.
- Coat the peanut marshmallow with grated peanut.
- Place a summer truffle *empanadilla* in the 11 o'clock position on an O! LUNA large eclipse plate. Place 1 cube of hot Venus rice jelly at 12 o'clock and a liquorice lasagne at 2 o'clock.
- Put a cep albóndiga at 3 o'clock and a sesame praline at 4 o'clock.
- Place a coated peanut marshmallow at 5 o'clock. Put a teaspoon of beetroot shoot air at 7 o'clock.
- Place a piece of freeze-dried miso foam at 8 o'clock.
- Arrange a small pile of sautéed red cabbage shoots in the middle of the plate.
- Present the hot potato broth separately so that the waiter can serve it in front of the diners.

Cutlery

- Tapas cutlery.

  NB: Tapas cutlery consists of a 14 x 3 cm spoon and fork.

How to eat

- Eat the *empanadilla* whole and alternate with the other components, without mixing them.

1160

Monkfish liver fondue with ponzu and white sesame-flavoured kumquat

Year
2005

Family
Tapas

Temperature
Hot/ambient/cold

Season
All year round

Serves 4

For the ponzu sauce

150 g water
15 g sliced *katsuobushi*
6 g dried kombu seaweed
60 g lime juice
75 g soy sauce

- Combine the water with the kombu and bring to the boil.
- Remove from the heat and leave to infuse for 2 minutes.
- Take the kombu out and bring the kombu-infused water to the boil. Then add the shaved *katsuobushi*. Take off the heat and infuse for 5 minutes.
- Squeeze through a Superbag and cool at room temperature.
- Add the lime juice and soy sauce when cold.
- Refrigerate.

NB: *Katsuobushi* is the Japanese name for dried bonito (tuna) that has been smoked and cured with the *Aspergillus glaucus* fungus.

For the ponzu sauce air base

200 g ponzu sauce (previously prepared)
0.4 g soya lecithin powder

- Combine both ingredients in a deep 25 cm diameter container.

For the soy sauce vinaigrette, toasted sesame oil and yuzu

150 g soy sauce
100 g toasted sesame oil
15 g rice vinegar
10 g yuzu juice

- Mix all of the ingredients together with a whisk.

NB: Yuzu is an Asian citrus fruit that tastes like a cross between mandarin and lemon. It is used particularly for its highly aromatic zest.

For the monkfish liver slices

1 x 500 g piece of monkfish liver
Water
Ice

- Cut off the ends of the liver and remove the outer veins.
- Cover the liver with water and plenty of ice and leave in the refrigerator for 48 hours for the blood to drain away. Change the water and ice every 8 hours.
- Drain and dry the liver well. Cut into 2 mm slices.
- Divide into 4 servings of 6 slices each. Slightly overlap each slice over the next.
- Refrigerate.

For the dashi stock

1 kg water
50 g shaved *katsuobushi*
40 g dried kombu seaweed

- Cut the kombu into 1 cm pieces and bring to the boil in the water.
- Remove from the heat. Leave to stand for 5 minutes, then take out the kombu.
- Bring the resulting stock back to the boil. Add the shaved *katsuobushi* and when it comes back to the boil, remove from heat.
- Leave to stand for 5 minutes and strain through a Superbag.
- Set aside.

For the candied kumquats

4 x 30 g kumquats
150 g water
45 g sugar

- Mix the sugar and water and bring to the boil, simmering until the sugar dissolves completely.
- Clean the kumquats and remove any stems.
- When the syrup boils, add the kumquats and remove from heat.
- Cool the kumquats in the syrup in the refrigerator.

For the kumquat juice

6 x 30 g kumquats

- Clean the kumquats, cut into quarters and remove any seeds from inside.
- Liquidise the kumquat pulp and refrigerate.

1160

Monkfish liver fondue with ponzu and white sesame-flavoured kumquat

For the candied kumquats filled with kumquat juice and sesame

4 candied kumquats (previously prepared)
40 g kumquat juice (previously prepared)
10 g toasted sesame oil
15 g toasted Japanese white sesame seeds

- Make a cut in the top of each kumquat with a knife.
- Use tweezers to remove the flesh from the fruit.
- Using a syringe, fill the kumquats with previously prepared kumquat juice.
- Put 2 drops of sesame oil inside each kumquat.
- Finish by covering the cut with the toasted Japanese white sesame seeds

Finishing and presentation

- Work a stick blender over the surface of the ponzu sauce air mixture until it emulsifies and the air forms.
- Put 2 spoons of soy and sesame vinaigrette into 4 bowls.
- Cover the vinaigrette with 2 spoons of ponzu sauce air.
- Place the 4 filled kumquats on 4 individual serving trays.
- Place the monkfish liver on 4 slates accompanied by tweezers.
- Heat the dashi stock well and place in a jug.
- The waiter will bring a spirit burner and a hot pan separately.

Cutlery

- Silver tweezers.

How to eat

- Take a slice of monkfish liver and dip into the boiling dashi for 2 seconds. Remove from the dashi and dip into the bowl with vinaigrette and the ponzu sauce air. Eat the whole filled kumquat last.

1161

Almonds/beans with small squid, daisy buds, mustard, bitter almond and fennel

Year
2005

Family
Tapas

Temperature
Hot

Season
June, July, August

Serves 4

For the small squid

12 x 8 cm squid

- Separate the bodies from the tentacles.
- Peel and clean the bodies.
- Clean the tentacles, discarding the 'beak'.
- Set aside the cleaned bodies and tentacles in the refrigerator.

For the hot bean water jelly

200 g bean cooking water
0.6 g powdered agar-agar
¾ x 2 g gelatine leaf (previously rehydrated in cold water)
Salt

- Season the bean cooking water with salt.
- Add the agar-agar and bring to the boil, stirring constantly with a whisk.
- Remove from the heat, skim off the froth and add the drained gelatine.
- Pour into a container to a thickness of 7 mm.
- Leave to set in the refrigerator for 3 hours.
- Once set, cut out 8 x 2 cm cubes.

For the boiled green almonds

28 green almonds
300 g water

- Peel and halve the green almonds.
- Use a pressure cooker to boil them in the water for 40 minutes.
- Set aside in their cooking water.

For the almond milk

250 g crushed almonds
225 g water
Salt

- Use a stick blender to process the crushed almonds with the water thoroughly.
- Stand in the refrigerator for 12 hours.
- Blend the water and almond mixture in the liquidiser to obtain a cream.
- Squeeze firmly through a Superbag to release all the liquid and make a thick, tasty almond milk.
- Season with salt and refrigerate.

For the almond milk cream

250 g almond milk (previously prepared)
¼ x 2 g gelatine leaf (previously rehydrated in cold water)
Pacojet

- Dissolve the gelatine in one quarter of the almond milk.
- Add the remaining almond milk, mix and pour into a Pacojet beaker.
- Freeze at -20 °C.
- Process the frozen almond milk in the Pacojet 3 times, then leave to thaw in the refrigerator without stirring so as not to alter the texture.

For the fresh fennel flower seeds

2 sprigs fresh fennel flowers

- Use scissors to snip off the fresh fennel flower seeds.
- Refrigerate.

1161

Almonds/beans with small squid, daisy buds, mustard, bitter almond and fennel

Finishing and presentation

10 g wholegrain Dijon mustard
10 g prune kernel oil
20 pickled daisy buds
Olive oil
150 g bean cooking water
Salt

- Season the squid bodies and tentacles with salt and cook them in a little oil in a non-stick frying pan. The tentacles should be slightly crunchy and the bodies golden and juicy.
- Heat the hot bean cooking water jelly cubes and the boiled green almonds.
- Place 2 hot bean cooking water jelly cubes at the base of an O! LUNA small eclipse plate together with 14 boiled green almond halves and a spoon of bean cooking water.
- Place the squid tentacles inside their corresponding bodies and position them on the edge of the plate with a 2 cm space between them.
- Place 1 spot of wholegrain mustard, 2 drops of prune kernel oil, a pinch of fresh fennel seeds and a teaspoon of almond cream over the almond and been jelly stew.
- Finish by arranging 5 daisy buds at the well opening.

Cutlery

- Tapas cutlery.

  NB: Tapas cutlery consists of a 14 x 3 cm spoon and fork.

How to eat

- Alternate the squid with the almond and bean stew without mixing the components.

1162

Sweetcorn snow egg with Mexican broth and *coquina* clams

Year
2005

Family
Tapas

Temperature
Hot

Season
All year round

Serves 4

For the sweetcorn water

5 x 300 g tins of sweetcorn

- Open the tins and drain the water.
- Set the sweetcorn and its water aside separately.

For the corn juice

500 g drained boiled sweetcorn
(previously prepared)

- Liquidise the sweetcorn.
- Strain the juice and refrigerate.

For the cold sweetcorn juice foam

110 g sweetcorn juice (previously prepared)
40 g 35% fat single cream
0.4 g Xantana
½ x 2 g gelatine leaf (previously rehydrated
in cold water)
1 x 0.5 litre ISI siphon
1 N$_2$O cartridge

- Blend the Xantana with the sweetcorn juice
until lump-free.
- Dissolve the gelatine in half of the hot sweetcorn
juice and add the rest, stirring well.
- Add the cream, mix and strain.
- Fill the siphon, close it and insert the gas cartridge.
- Stand in the refrigerator for 3 hours.

For the sweetcorn water methylcellulose cloud

250 g sweetcorn water (previously prepared)
3 g methylcellulose
3 x 2 g gelatine leaves (previously rehydrated
in cold water)

- Process 200 g of sweetcorn water with
the methylcellulose with a stick blender
until lump-free.
- Place the mixture in the freezer to reduce
the temperature quickly to 3 °C.
- Dissolve the drained gelatine leaves in 50 g
of sweetcorn water previously heated to 45 °C.
- Once the sweetcorn water and methylcellulose
solution has reached 3 °C, remove from
the freezer and leave in a warm place until
the temperature increases to 14 °C.
- Put the solution into the mixer and begin beating
at medium speed.
- When it starts to foam, add the sweetcorn
water mixture, which has been heated to 39 °C.
- Whip for about 7 minutes until the mixture forms
peaks like beaten egg whites.

For the sweetcorn snow egg

Sweetcorn water methylcellulose cloud
(previously prepared)
Cold sweetcorn juice foam (previously prepared)
10 g sunflower oil

- Fill a piping bag with the sweetcorn water
methylcellulose cloud. Use a No. 8 plain nozzle.
- Cover with clingfilm the base of 4 large soup
spoons previously greased with sunflower oil.
- Fill the base of the spoons with a 7 mm layer of
the methylcellulose cloud, making a 6 x 4 cm oval.
- Place a 10 g mound of cold sweetcorn juice foam
in the middle.
- Completely cover the foam with a 5 mm layer
of sweetcorn water methylcellulose cloud.
- You should have a shape similar to that of
a snow egg.
- Refrigerate for 5 minutes.

For the free-range chicken stock

1 x 2 kg free-range chicken
1.5 kg water
Salt

NB: This is the minimum recommended
amount to ensure a good result.

- Discard the head, legs and wingtips before
quartering the chicken.
- Clean the chicken under running water
to remove the entrails and blood.
- Put the chicken in a pot and cover it
with the water and a little salt.
- Simmer for 2 hours, constantly skimming
off impurities and fat, to obtain a flavoursome,
clear stock.
- Strain through a Superbag, remove excess
fat again and refrigerate.

1162

Sweetcorn snow egg with Mexican broth and *coquina* clams

For the Mexican broth

200 g free-range chicken stock (previously prepared)
75 g sweetcorn water (previously prepared)
15 g fresh coriander
0.3 g dried chilli
Salt

- Combine the chicken stock with the sweetcorn water, bring to the boil and add the chopped chilli and coarsely chopped coriander.
- Infuse for 10 minutes and strain.
- Season with salt and set aside.

For the cleaned *coquina* clams

32 x 8 g *coquina* clams

- Plunge the clams a few at a time in boiling water for 6 seconds.
- Remove them from the water and leave them to cool at room temperature.
- Use a paring knife to slice off the muscle joining the clam to the shell.
- Carefully remove the clams from their shells without breaking them.
- Strain the clam liquor through a Superbag, cover the clams with it and refrigerate.

NB: Before opening all the clams, make sure they do not contain sand. If so, cover them with sea water and leave them to release all the sand.

Finishing and presentation

Maldon sea salt

- Place the snow egg at the base of an O! LUNA deep lunar plate.
- Heat under the salamander grill until it is hot and the inside is liquid.
- Steam the clams to warm and arrange 8 in a row on one side of the egg.
- Keep both the hot Mexican broth and the Maldon sea salt separate so that the waiter can serve the broth in front of the diner and season the snow egg with the salt.

NB: A different version of this dish has been created without either coriander or chilli in the Mexican broth. Instead, they are incorporated into the dish as chilli oil and fresh coriander leaves on top of the clams.

Cutlery

- Tapas cutlery.

NB: Tapas cutlery consists of a 14 x 3 cm spoon and fork.

How to eat

- Alternate the snow egg with the clams and broth.

1163

Creamy cannellone with Spanish bacon, anchovy caviar and black olive

Year
2005

Family
Tapas

Temperature
Hot

Season
All year round

Serves 4

For the smoked streaky Spanish bacon slices

1 x 350 g piece smoked streaky Spanish bacon

- Remove the rind and any rancid bits from the bacon.
- Square off the sides of the bacon to form a 2 x 3.5 cm rectangular block. Reserve the trimmings for the stock.
- Wrap the block in clingfilm and freeze.
- Once frozen, cut 24 x 1 mm thin slices with a meat slicer.
- Lay them over parchment paper to form 4 strips, each of which consisting of 6 slightly overlapping slices and with an overall length of 11 cm.
- Refrigerate.

For the smoked streaky Spanish bacon stock

150 g smoked streaky Spanish bacon trimmings (previously prepared)
250 g water

- Cut the trimmings into 1 cm chunks and simmer for 1 hour, constantly skimming off the scum and fat.
- Strain, remove the excess fat and set the stock aside.

For the hot smoked streaky Spanish bacon jelly cubes

125 g smoked streaky Spanish bacon stock
0.4 g powdered agar-agar
¼ x 2 g gelatine leaf (previously rehydrated in cold water)

- Dissolve the agar-agar in the smoked streaky Spanish bacon stock and bring to the boil, stirring constantly with a whisk.
- Remove from the heat, add the drained gelatine leaf, mix and skim off the froth.
- Pour into a container to a thickness of 1 cm.
- Leave to set in the refrigerator for 2 hours.
- Once it has set, cut the jelly into 8 x 1.5 cm cubes.

For the hot water jelly sheet

600 g water
3 g gellan gum
10 g agar-agar

- Mix the agar-agar and gellan gum with the water and bring to the boil, stirring constantly with a whisk.
- Skim off the froth and pour the jelly mixture over a preheated 60 x 40 cm stainless steel tray.
- Drain off the excess mixture quickly to make a very fine (0.5 mm) jelly layer.
- Leave to set at room temperature, then refrigerate for 30 minutes.

For the whipped cream

100 g 35% fat single cream

- Whip the cream in the electric mixer and fill a piping bag. Refrigerate.

For the creamy cannelloni

100 g whipped cream (previously prepared)
Hot water jelly sheet (previously prepared)
8 hot smoked streaky Spanish bacon jelly cubes (previously prepared)

- Cut the hot water jelly sheet into 4 11 x 6 cm rectangles.
- Place 1 bacon stock jelly cube at both ends of the rectangles and fill the resulting space with a 1.5 cm thick line of whipped cream.
- Roll the jelly sheets to form cannelloni, ensuring there is no air trapped inside and that the ends are well sealed with the jelly.

For the anchovy sauce caviar

10 g basil seeds
80 g water
20 anchovy sauce

- Put the basil seeds in the water and leave to hydrate for 30 minutes.
- Add the anchovy sauce, stir and refrigerate.

NB: Anchovy sauce (colatura di alici) is a product sold in Italy consisting of the brine leftover from curing anchovies.

1163

Creamy cannellone with Spanish bacon, anchovy caviar and black olive

For the black olive juice

250 g black Aragón olives

- Pit the olives.
- Process the olives in the liquidiser and strain through muslin. Squeeze well to release all of the juice from the olives.

For the black olive 'fat'

70 g black olive juice (previously prepared)

- Decant the escabeche jus into a tall, narrow container to allow the 'fat' (the oil) to separate.

Finishing and presentation

56 x 5 mm fresh basil leaves

- Carefully lay a cannellone on a rectangular tray without breaking it.
- Heat under the salamander grill until it is hot and the cream begins to melt.
- Place a smoked streaky bacon strip over the cannellone, covering it completely.
- Place 3 x 3 g spots of anchovy sauce caviar around the tray without touching the cannellone.
- Sprinkle 14 fresh basil leaves around the cannellone.
- Spread a spoon of black olive 'fat' on both sides of the cannellone.

Cutlery

- Tapas cutlery.

  NB: Tapas cutlery consists of a 14 x 3 cm spoon and fork.

How to eat

- Alternate the cannellone with the black olive 'fat', the anchovy caviar and the basil.

1164

Macaroni with egg yolk, miso, sesame and green shiso

Year
2005

Family
Tapas

Temperature
Hot

Season
All year round

Serves 4

For the hot soy sauce jelly macaroni

800 g water
200 g soy sauce
30 g powdered agar-agar
1 metal rod for making macaroni

- Mix the ingredients and bring to the boil, stirring constantly with a whisk.
- Remove from the heat, skim off the froth and leave the mixture to cool to 40 °C.
- Then immerse the metal rod into the mixture for 5 seconds.
- Remove the rod and drain so that there are no bumps.
- Once the jelly has set, remove the rod carefully without breaking the jelly tube.
- Place the jelly tubes on a flat tray.
- Refrigerate for 30 minutes.
- Cut the jelly tubes with a slightly diagonal slice into 18 cm lengths.
- Prepare 4 macaroni per person.

For the miso sauce

50 g white miso paste
75 g water

- Mix both ingredients and heat while stirring constantly with a whisk to make a fine, lump-free cream.
- Set aside.

For the miso air base

500 g water
125 g white miso paste
1.5 g soya lecithin powder

- Heat the water and dissolve the miso paste in it.
- Transfer to a deep 25 cm diameter container and mix with the lecithin until lump-free.

For the grated horseradish

1 x 10 g piece horseradish root
1 Japanese wasabi grater

- Peel the horseradish and grate with a Japanese wasabi grater.

For the green shiso shoots

2 punnets green shiso shoots
10 g rice vinegar

- Trim the shiso shoots with scissors to make 5 cm lengths.
- Make 4 bunches of 10 green shiso shoots.
- Dress the leaves with a few drops of rice vinegar just before use.

NB: Shiso is a kind of Asian herb similar to basil and mint. There are 2 varieties, purple and green.

1164

Macaroni with egg yolk, miso, sesame and green shiso

Finishing and presentation

200 g extra virgin olive oil
4 x 80 g eggs
20 g raw white sesame oil
Maldon sea salt
20 g rice vinegar

- Work a stick blender over the surface of the miso air base until it emulsifies and the air forms.
- Separate the eggs and place the yolks in a container covered with oil. Warm them to 50 °C without allowing the yolk to cook.
- Place 4 soy sauce macaroni in the middle of a rectangular tray and heat under the salamander grill.
- Make 3 spots of grated horseradish on top of the macaroni and cover the macaroni with a spoon of hot miso sauce and 5 g of raw white sesame oil.
- Cover the macaroni with a spoon of miso air.
- Use a slotted spoon to remove the yolks from the oil carefully without breaking and place 1 yolk over the middle of the group of 4 macaroni.
- Season the yolks with a few Maldon sea salt flakes.
- Finish by placing the green shiso shoot salad dressed with rice vinegar at one end of the tray.

Cutlery

- Tapas cutlery.

  NB: Tapas cutlery consists of a 14 x 3 cm spoon and fork.

How to eat

- Break the egg yolk and mix the macaroni with it. Finally, refresh the palate with the green shiso.

1165

Mock tartufo of Iberian pork and green olive

Year
2005

Family
Tapas

Temperature
Hot/ambient

Season
June, July, August

Serves 4

For the mock tartufo slices

1 x 5 cm diameter summer truffle
20 g white truffle oil
Salt

- Brush the truffle under a little water to remove any soil.
- Peel with a paring knife.
- In the slicer cut the truffle into 12 x 1.5 mm slices.
- Use a 3 cm pastry cutter to make 12 circular sheets.
- Season the slices of summer truffle with white truffle oil and salt just before use.

For the summer truffle dice

2 x 60 g summer truffles

- Brush the truffles under a little water to remove any soil.
- Peel with a paring knife.
- Cut them into 1.5 mm dice.

For the methylcellulose solution

100 g water
3 g methylcellulose

- Mix both ingredients at room temperature in a liquidiser until they form a smooth, lump-free mixture.
- Strain and leave in the refrigerator for 24 hours.

For the summer truffle mock slices

50 g summer truffle dice (previously prepared)
15 g methylcellulose solution (previously prepared)

- Mix the summer truffle dice with the methylcellulose solution.
- Make 12 x 7.5 g mounds over parchment paper.
- Use a small spatula to flatten the mounds to the extent that no summer truffle dice overlap, obtaining discs 1.5 mm in thickness.
- Use a 3 cm pastry cutter to trim the discs and make them even.
- Lay the mock slices out on parchment paper and refrigerate.

For the green olive juice

1 kg green Verdial olives

- Drain and pit the olives.
- Blend the olives in the liquidiser, then strain through a Superbag.
- Decant the olive juice in a tall, narrow container for 24 hours at room temperature to allow the 'fat' to rise to the top.
- Remove the 'fat', taking care it does not mix with the water at the bottom.
- Set aside both the olive water and 'fat' separately.

For the green olive air

100 g green olive 'fat' (previously prepared)
400 g green olive water (previously prepared)
4 g soya lecithin powder

- Mix the ingredients in a deep 25 cm diameter container.

For the Iberian pork rib sauce

1 kg Iberian pork ribs
100 g olive oil
500 g water
Salt
Freshly ground black pepper

- Chop the pork into roughly 1.5 cm pieces and season them lightly with salt.
- Heat the oil in a pan and brown the ribs until well caramelised.
- Remove the excess fat and add the water.
- Cook on a medium heat until the sauce is reduced and well flavoured.
- Strain and season with salt if required.

1165

**Mock tartufo of Iberian pork
and green olive**

Finishing and presentation

White truffle oil
Salt

- Work a stick blender over the surface
  of the green olive air base until it emulsifies
  and the air forms.
- Arrange 3 mock truffle slices in an equilateral
  triangle on a round flat plate.
- Season the mock slices with white truffle oil
  and salt, and place under the salamander grill
  for the methylcellulose to react and turn to jelly.
- Take out the mock slices and carefully arrange
  them without breaking in the spaces between
  the mock truffle slices to form a circle. Do not let
  them touch.
- Spread a spoon of Iberian pork rib sauce over
  the mock truffle.
- Place a teaspoon of olive 'fat' in the middle
  of the plate and finish with 2 soup spoons
  of green olive air as series of random lines over
  the dish.

Cutlery

- Tapas cutlery.

  NB: Tapas cutlery consists of a 14 x 3 cm
  spoon and fork.

How to eat

- Alternate the sheets and mock slices with the olive
  'fat' and air. Eat the slices in a single mouthful.

1166

Parmesan-LYO mini French toasts with onion-flavoured ham fat, egg yolk and coffee

Year
2005

Family
Tapas

Temperature
Hot/ambient

Season
All year round

Serves 4

For the Parmesan water

500 g grated Parmesan cheese
800 g water

- Bring the water to the boil in a pot and add the grated Parmesan cheese.
- Stir until it forms an elastic paste.
- Remove from the heat and leave to infuse for 1 hour.
- Strain through a Superbag and refrigerate.
- After 10 hours, skim off the fat (reserve for use in another dish) from the surface of the cheese water.

For the cold Parmesan water jelly

300 g Parmesan water
(previously prepared)
1.4 g powdered agar-agar
36 x 30 ml plastic shot glasses

- Mix the cheese water with the agar-agar in a pan and bring to the boil, stirring constantly.
- Introduce 5 ml of the cold Parmesan water jelly mixture into each shot glass.
- Allow to set, then refrigerate.

For the freeze-dried Parmesan water jelly mini French toasts

36 shot glasses of cold Parmesan water jelly (previously prepared)

- Place in the freeze-dryer for 48 hours.
- Once the freeze-drying process is complete, store in an airtight container in a cool, dry place.

For the onion sauce

2 x 300 g onions
Olive oil
Water
Salt

- Peel the onion and slice into fine julienne.
- Cook the onion in a pan over low heat with a little oil until it is browned.
- Moisten the onion with a little water to caramelise.
- Gradually moisten the caramelised onion with a few drops of water at a time to make a tasty concentrated sauce.
- Strain and season with salt if required.

For the egg yolk sauce

2 x 70 g eggs

- Separate the yolks from the whites.
- Pass the egg yolks through a fine strainer and fill a squeeze bottle.
- Refrigerate.

For the *jamón ibérico* lard

40 g fat

- Remove any lean or rancid bits from the fat.
- Simmer the ingredients on a low heat until the fat becomes clear.
- Remove from the heat and cut the fat confit into 2 mm dice.
- Set aside near a heat source until finishing and presentation.

For the *jamón ibérico* fat confit dice

30 g fat
20 g *jamón ibérico* lard (previously prepared)

- Remove any lean or rancid bits from the fat.
- Simmer the ingredients on a low heat until the fat becomes clear.
- Remove from the heat and cut the fat confit into 2 mm dice.
- Set aside near a heat source until finishing and presentation.

For the coated lemon cubes

1 x 150 g lemon

- Cut off the ends of the lemon to expose the segments.
- Peel them in a spiral to expose the flesh and so that there are no traces of rind or pith, without altering the basic shape of the lemon.
- Remove the segments from their membranes with a sharp knife.
- Cut 4 x 5 mm cubes.
- Remove the zest and chop it into tiny 1 mm cubes.
- Coat each lemon cube in the diced lemon zest.
- Refrigerate.

1166

Parmesan-LYO mini French toasts with onion-flavoured ham fat, egg yolk and coffee

Finishing and presentation

Freshly ground black pepper
2 espresso coffees

- Cover the Parmesan mini French toasts with Parmesan water and warm on the stove until they soak up the water and acquire the texture of real French toast.
- Make 3 vertical lines containing 3 mini French toasts each in a 21 cm diameter soup plate.
- Season with freshly ground black pepper.
- Spread a line of hot onion sauce around the French toasts.
- Place a 3 g quenelle of *jamón ibérico* lard confit over the first line of French toast.
- Place 6 spots of egg yolk sauce around the French toasts.
- Place 1 spot of espresso coffee cream on the right of the French toast and 1 coated lemon cube on the left.

Cutlery

- Tapas cutlery.

NB: Tapas cutlery consists of a 14 x 3 cm spoon and fork.

How to eat

- Eat the first French toast with the lard, then alternate the remaining French toasts with the onion sauce and egg yolk. Halfway through the dish, eat the coated lemon cube and finish with the coffee cream.

1167

**Pavé of St George's mushrooms
with samphire and *kefir***

Year
2005

Family
Tapas

Temperature
Hot/ambient

Season
April, May

Serves 4

For the methylcellulose solution

100 g water
3 g methylcellulose

- Blend the ingredients together at room temperature in a liquidiser until they form a smooth, even mixture.
- Strain and stand in the refrigerator for 24 hours.

For the St George's mushroom dice

24 x 5 g St George's mushrooms

- Remove the stalks and clean the mushrooms with a cloth.
- Cut the clean mushrooms into 2 mm dice.
- Refrigerate.

For the pavés of St George's mushroom

100 g St George's mushroom dice
(previously prepared)
25 g methylcellulose solution (previously prepared)

- Mix the mushroom dice with the methylcellulose solution.
- Make 8 x 12 g groups with the mixture.
- Use a small spatula to make 8 2.7 x 3.5 x 1.5 cm compact portions.
- Refrigerate.

For the St George's mushroom slices

12 x 1 cm diameter St George's mushrooms

- Remove the stalks and clean the mushrooms with a cloth.
- Use a mandolin to slice the mushrooms into 1 mm thicknesses.

NB: Slice the mushrooms just before use to prevent their oxidation.

For the whole St George's mushrooms

60 g 6 mm diameter St George's mushrooms

- Remove the stalks and clean the mushrooms with a cloth.
- Divide 12 g portions per person.
- Refrigerate.

**For the St George's mushrooms
with the elBullisetas brand**

4 x 2 cm diameter St George's mushrooms
elBullisetas stamp

- Remove the stalks and clean the mushrooms with a cloth.
- Heat the stamp over a fire and brand each mushroom.
- Set aside.

For the samphire

40 g fresh samphire

- Trim the tips, then choose 7 x 3 cm samphire shoots per person.
- Refrigerate.

NB: The samphire variety used, purple glasswort *Salicornia ramosissima*, is an annual herb from the Chenopodiaceae family that grows in saline soils. The branches have a number of nodes and are fleshy and green, except towards the end of its cycle when the plant turns a reddish colour. It grows in places close to the sea or in marshy areas occasionally flooded with sea water.

For the hot *kefir* foam

200 g *kefir*
60 g egg white
1 x 0.5 litre ISI siphon
1 N$_2$O cartridge

- Mix the *kefir* and egg white with a whisk.
- Strain and fill the siphon.
- Close it and insert gas cartridge.
- Set aside in a bain-marie at 60 °C.

1167

Pavé of St George's mushrooms with samphire and *kefir*

Finishing and presentation

Olive oil
Salt
Water
Freshly ground black pepper
20 g virgin pine nut oil

- Cook the pavés of St George's mushroom in salted water at 90 °C for 30 seconds. Drain them without breaking them.
- Sauté the whole mushrooms and the mushrooms with the brand, seasoning with salt.
- Sauté the samphire in a little olive oil.
- Take an O! LUNA large eclipse plate and arrange the following inside the well under the ridge: 1 bunch of salted samphire on the left, 1 small mound of St George's mushroom slices seasoned with salt in the middle, and the whole sautéed mushrooms on the right.
- Arrange 2 pavés of St George's mushroom with a 5 cm space between them on the opposite side of the well. Place a sautéed mushroom with the elBullisetas brand between them.
- Squirt 15 g of hot *kefir* foam in the middle of the plate. Sprinkle 5 g of virgin pine nut oil and a pinch of freshly ground black pepper over it.

Cutlery

- Tapas cutlery.

  NB: Tapas cutlery consists of a 14 x 3 cm spoon and fork.

How to eat

- Eat the pavés in a single mouthful, alternating with the other components.

1168

Cep blocks with hot cep jelly, cat's claw and hazelnut cream

Year
2005

Family
Tapas

Temperature
Hot/ambient

Season
May, June

Serves 4

For the cep stock

100 g cep mushrooms
150 g water
Olive oil
Salt

- Clean the mushrooms and cut into 2 mm slices.
- Cook the ceps in a pan with a little oil.
  When golden, remove the excess fat and moisten
  with the water.
- Cook on a medium heat for 20 minutes,
  then strain.
- Season with salt and set aside.

For the hot cep stock jelly cubes

125 g cep stock (previously prepared)
0.4 g powdered agar-agar
⅔ x 2 g gelatine leaf (previously rehydrated
in cold water)

- Dissolve the agar-agar in the cep stock
  and bring to the boil, stirring constantly with a whisk.
- Remove from the heat and add the drained
  gelatine.
- Pour into a container to a thickness of 7 mm.
- Leave to set in the refrigerator for 2 hours.
- Once it has set, cut into 8 x 1.7 cm cubes.

For the methylcellulose solution

100 g water
3 g methylcellulose

- Mix the ingredients at room temperature in a
  liquidiser until they form a smooth, even mixture.
- Strain and stand in the refrigerator for 24 hours.

For the cep dice

60 g cep mushrooms

- Remove the stalks and wipe each mushroom
  with a damp cloth.
- Cut the mushrooms into 2 mm dice.
- Refrigerate.

For the cep block with hot cep stock jelly

8 hot cep stock jelly cubes (previously prepared)
50 g cep dice (previously prepared)
15 g methylcellulose solution (previously prepared)

- Mix the mushroom dice with the methylcellulose
  solution.
- Coat the hot cep stock jelly cubes with the
  cep dice and methylcellulose mixture, obtaining
  8 blocks, 1.2 cm tall x 2 cm long.
- Lay out on parchment paper and refrigerate.

For the hazelnut oil cream

100 g water
50 g hazelnut oil
3 g tapioca flour
Salt

NB: The tapioca flour can be substituted
with 0.4 g of Xantana.

- Mix the water and tapioca flour and bring
  to the boil, stirring constantly with a whisk.
- When the mixture thickens, remove from the heat.
  Add the hazelnut oil and mix in such a way
  that the oil emulsifies with the thickened water.
- Season with salt.

NB: This preparation should be made immediately
before finishing and presentation.

For the cat's claw with hazelnut oil

30 g preserved cat's claw
30 g hazelnut oil

- Pluck the cat's claw leaves. Discard the stalks.
- Immerse the cat's claw leaves in the hazelnut oil
  and set aside.

NB: Cat's claw, *Uncaria tomentosa*, is a creeper
that grows in the central areas of Peru, Colombia
and Bolivia, As well as in the Alicante region
of Spain. It grows in tall forests in sunny areas.
It is a liana that can grow to 20 m in length.
It is known to have medicinal properties.
In the Alicante area it is known as *raimet
de pastor* (shepherd's grapes).

1168

**Cep blocks with hot cep jelly,
cat's claw and hazelnut cream**

Finishing and presentation

Salt
Freshly ground black pepper
Olive oil

- Season the cep blocks with salt and cook
  on both sides in a non-stick frying pan
  with a little oil.
- Remove from the pan and season with freshly
  ground pepper.
- Heat 4 O! LUNA small eclipse plates under
  the salamander grill. Place 2 soup spoons
  of hot hazelnut cream at the base.
- Arrange 2 hot cep blocks on the edge
  of the well with a 5 cm space between them.
- Drain the cat's claw and make a small bouquet
  between the 2 cep blocks.

Cutlery

- Tapas cutlery.

  NB: Tapas cutlery consists of a 14 x 3 cm
  spoon and fork.

How to eat

- Alternate the components. Eat the blocks
  in a single mouthful.

1169

Papillote of tomatoes in mastic, almond and tarragon oil and kumquat sorbet

Year
2005

Family
Tapas

Temperature
Hot/frozen

Season
August, September

Serves 4

For the peeled Mataró tomatoes

24 x 6 g Mataró tomatoes
Water
Ice

- Blanch the tomatoes in boiling water for 3 seconds.
- Drain and refresh immediately in iced water.
- Peel the tomatoes and remove the stalk.
- Set aside.

For the fresh tarragon water

40 g fresh tarragon leaves
Water

- Blanch the leaves in boiling water for 15 seconds.
- Drain and chill in iced water.
- Blend the blanched tarragon leaves in a liquidiser with 120 g of the water used to chill them.
- Strain and refrigerate in an airtight container.

For the fresh tarragon concentrate

140 g fresh tarragon water (previously prepared)

- Pour 70 g of the tarragon water into each of 2 centrifuge tubes and 70 g of water in the other 2 tubes.
- Spin in the centrifuge for 5 minutes at 4,100 rpm.
- When the process is complete, separate the water from on top of the concentrated pulp that has settled at the bottom of each tube.
- Discard the water.
- Transfer the concentrate to a piping bag, vacuum seal and refrigerate.

For the kumquat purée

20 x 10 g kumquats

- Clean the kumquats and remove the stalk.
- Quarter and de-seed them.
- Liquidise the kumquat flesh.

NB: This preparation should be done immediately before finishing and presentation to prevent the kumquat juice from oxidising.

For the kumquat purée nitro-sorbet

100 g kumquat purée (previously prepared)
500 g liquid nitrogen

- Pour the kumquat purée into a bowl for liquid nitrogen.
- Gradually add the liquid nitrogen while stirring constantly with a whisk until the texture of sorbet is obtained.

NB: This preparation should be made immediately before finishing and presentation so that the sorbet will have the ideal texture.

For the tomato papillote

4 clear papillote sheets, 40 x 40 cm
24 peeled Mataró tomatoes (previously prepared)
8 x 4 cm fresh tarragon sprigs with shoots
8 g fresh tarragon concentrate (previously prepared)
20 g almond oil
50 g water
Salt
Freshly ground black pepper
12 drops mastic essence

- Place the clear papillote sheets in a bowl to make filling easy.
- Each sheet should contain 6 tomatoes seasoned with salt and freshly ground pepper, 2 sprigs of fresh tarragon, 5 g almond oil, 12 g water, 2 x 1 g spots of fresh tarragon concentrate and 3 drops of mastic essence.
- Tie the sheets closed with a thin string to ensure they are completely closed.

NB: Mastic is a gum obtained from mastic resin.

1169

Papillote of tomatoes in mastic, almond and tarragon oil and kumquat sorbet

Finishing and presentation

Maldon sea salt

- Place the papillotes in a fondue pot and heat them slowly.
- When they have been boiling for 1 minute, serve them in the same pot and leave them to cook for 3 minutes in front of the diners.
- Then place the papillote in a bowl and open with scissors in front of the diner so that the aromas given off by the papillote can be enjoyed.
- Allow the open papillote to stand for 2 minutes, then serve the kumquat nitro-sorbet as a quenelle made with a dessert spoon inside the papillote.
- Serve the Maldon sea salt in a separate bowl so that diners can season the tomatoes to taste.

NB: The fondue pot must not exceed 180 °C as the papillote could break at this temperature.

Cutlery

- Tapas cutlery.

NB: Tapas cutlery consists of a 14 x 3 cm spoon and fork.

How to eat

- When the papillote is opened, smell the aroma it gives off. Then eat the tomatoes in a single mouthful with the papillote juices, alternating with the sorbet.

1170

**Baby snails in court-bouillon
with crab escabeche
and amaranth with fennel**

Year
2005

Family
Tapas

Temperature
Hot

Season
June, July, August

Serves 4

For the crab legs and claws

8 x 100 g velvet crabs
Water
Salt

- Boil the crabs for 55 seconds in salted water.
- Remove them from the water and leave to cool at room temperature.
- Remove the legs and claws from the bodies.
- Remove the meat from the claws in one piece, leaving behind the cartilage.
- Set aside the meat from 4 claws per person and refrigerate.

For the crab escabeche

Crab bodies and legs (previously prepared)
20 g dried garlic
60 g onion
50 g ripe tomatoes
200 g olive oil
30 g 25-year-old sherry vinegar
200 g water
3 g dried thyme
3 g dried rosemary
1 bay leaf

- Chop the crab bodies into 8 pieces each.
- Peel and crush the garlic cloves.
- Peel and julienne the onion into very thin slices.
- Roughly grate the tomatoes.
- Brown the garlic in a pot with 75 g oil. Add the onion and stir until soft. Add the tomato and fry gently until well sautéed.
- Add the crab and fry lightly.
- Add the remaining oil and the water, and cook until the sauce is well flavoured.
- Add the vinegar. Leave to evaporate for a few minutes and then strain through a chinois, pressing through well.
- Strain through fine-meshed cloth and refrigerate.

For the escabeche air base

200 g crab escabeche (previously prepared)
0.4 g soya lecithin powder

- Combine the ingredients in a deep 25 cm diameter container.

For the snails and their court-bouillon

250 g baby snails
1 sprig fresh thyme
1 sprig fresh rosemary
1 bay leaf
1 sprig fresh fennel fronds
Water
Salt

- Wash the baby snails in water 3 times and drain.
- To get rid of the slime, add salt and wash once again in water. Repeat until they are no longer slimy.
- Put the snails in a pot and cover with lukewarm water. Gradually bring to a simmer.
- Season the water with salt and add the herbs.
- Cook over a medium heat for 5 minutes, skimming continuously to remove the scum. Leave to cool in the same water.
- Rinse the snails and cover with the strained court-bouillon.

For the boiled amaranth

20 g amaranth grains
300 g water
Salt

- Bring the water to the boil. Add the amaranth, season and cook for 30 minutes.
- Strain to remove as much liquid as possible, and refrigerate.

For the fresh fennel seeds

4 small bunches of fresh fennel flowers

- Snip the seeds from the fennel flowers with scissors.
- Refrigerate.

For the fresh herbs

8 sprigs of fresh basil
12 x ½ cm fresh mint leaves
12 x 1 cm fresh tarragon leaves
8 fresh fennel flowers
12 x 1 cm fresh chervil leaves
16 fresh thyme flowers

- Divide the fresh herbs and flowers into 4 portions.

1170

**Baby snails in court-bouillon
with crab escabeche
and amaranth with fennel**

Finishing and presentation

Freshly ground black pepper
Olive oil
Salt

- Work a stick blender over the surface
  of the escabeche base until it emulsifies
  and the air forms.
- Heat the snails in their court-bouillon.
- Heat the crab claw meat in a little of the escabeche.
  Do not let the meat overcook.
- Sauté the cooked amaranth in a little oil with
  the fresh fennel seeds and season with salt.
- Stand 4 warm crab claws in a row on one side
  of a bowl.
- Arrange the snails at the base of the bowl
  in one layer.
- Season the snails with freshly ground
  black pepper.
- Arrange the fresh flowers and herbs over
  the snails.
- Place a long quenelle of 6 g amaranth and fennel
  seeds beside the crab claws, without touching
  the snails.
- Pour a spoon of court-bouillon over the snails.
- In a separate bowl serve 3 spoons of escabeche
  air per person.

Cutlery

- Tapas cutlery.

  NB: Tapas cutlery consists of a 14 x 3 cm
  spoon and fork.

How to eat

- Alternate the baby snails with the amaranth
  and the crab. Dip the crab into the escabeche air.

1171

Belly of mackerel in chicken escabeche with onions and vinegar caviar

Year
2005

Family
Tapas

Temperature
Ambient

Season
May, June, July, August

Serves 4

For the mackerel belly confit

8 x 200 g mackerel
500 g extra virgin olive oil
Salt

- Use a very sharp knife to remove the bellies from the mackerel. Be careful not to pierce internal organs, as this will give the fish a bitter taste.
- Use paper towels to remove any nerves or tissue that may have stuck to the belly. Ensure that there are no bones left.
- Lightly salt the bellies.
- Place the bellies on a non-stick tray, skin side down.
- Cover with extra virgin olive oil and heat the confit at 70 °C for 2 minutes.
- Store the bellies in the oil until finishing and presentation.

For the chicken escabeche jus and fat

2 kg cleaned chicken cut into 3 cm pieces
100 g onion, julienned
50 g garlic cloves crushed in their skin
2 sprigs dried thyme
2 sprigs dried rosemary
1 bay leaf
500 g olive oil
Salt
50 g 25-year-old sherry vinegar
750 g water
15 g black peppercorns

- Salt the chicken.
- Brown the chicken in a pan with oil.
- Once the chicken is well browned, add the onion and garlic and cook until they are browned.
- Add the dried herbs and peppercorns and cook for 1 more minute.
- Add the vinegar, reduce for 1 minute and add the water.
- Cook for 20 minutes.
- Refrigerate for 24 hours.
- Heat the escabeche and strain. Press well to release all the jus.
- Set aside 50 g for finishing and presentation.
- Decant the escabeche jus into a tall, narrow container to allow the fat to separate.
- Store the escabeche jus and fat separately.

For the chicken escabeche air base

200 g chicken escabeche jus (previously prepared)
50 g chicken escabeche fat (previously prepared)
1 g soya lecithin powder

- Combine all 3 ingredients in a 25 cm deep container.

For the roast onion

1 x 100 g Figueres onion

- Wrap the onion in foil and bake at 180 °C for 25 minutes.
- Peel and cut into 8 x 1.5 cm pieces.
- Store at room temperature.

For the sherry vinegar caviar

10 g basil seeds
120 g water
10 g 25-year-old sherry vinegar

- Put the basil seeds in the water and leave to hydrate for 20 minutes.
- Take 50 g hydrated basil seeds and add the sherry vinegar.
- Mix well and refrigerate.

1171

Belly of mackerel in chicken escabeche with onions and vinegar caviar

Finishing and presentation

10 g chopped chives
8 x 1 cm fresh chervil leaves
8 fresh tarragon shoots
Freshly ground black pepper

- Heat the chicken escabeche air base at 40 °C. Work a stick blender over the top of the liquid until it emulsifies and the air forms.
- Place a soup spoon of chicken escabeche air on each side of a rectangular dish.
- Sprinkle freshly ground black pepper on the meat side of the mackerel bellies and arrange them over the air with the skin side down.
- Sprinkle chopped chives over the roast onion and top each piece with one chervil leaf and one tarragon leaf.
- Place a teaspoon of chicken escabeche air between 2 mackerel belly pieces and arrange 2 pieces of roast onion with herbs over it.
- Put 2 teaspoons of sherry vinegar caviar on top of the onion pieces.
- Finish by lightly sprinkling a few drops of chicken escabeche jus over the mackerel bellies and the onion pieces.

NB: Another version of this dish has also been created in which the roast onion is substituted with *pa-ha* dressed with sherry vinegar, extra virgin olive oil and salt.

Cutlery

- Tapas cutlery.

NB: Tapas cutlery consists of a 14 x 3 cm spoon and fork.

How to eat

- Eat the mackerel belly and the air together, and after each mouthful eat a piece of roast onion with fresh herbs and sherry vinegar caviar.

1172

Grilled oysters with pine jelly, oyster cream and borage shoots

Year
2005

Family
Tapas

Temperature
Hot/cold

Season
May, June, July

Serves 4

For the cleaned oysters

12 x 300 g Napoleon oysters

- Open the oysters with an oyster knife. Retain the liquor.
- Cut through the muscle holding the oyster to the shell and remove the oyster.
- De-beard the oysters with scissors.
- Strain the liquor through a Superbag and add the oysters. Refrigerate.

For the smoked streaky Spanish bacon fat

50 g smoked streaky Spanish bacon

- Slice the bacon into 2 cm pieces and put them in a small saucepan over a low heat to sweat and release the fat. Do not let them fry.
- Strain off the fat and set it aside.

For the oyster cream

25 g cleaned oysters (previously prepared)
30 g oyster liquor (previously prepared)
8 g melted smoked streaky Spanish bacon fat (previously prepared)

- Blend the oysters with the oyster liquor.
- Emulsify the resulting liquid with the melted bacon fat at room temperature.
- Strain and refrigerate.

For the green pine cone infusion

480 g green pine cones
600 g water
75 g sugar
0.6 g ascorbic acid

- Soak the green pine cones in hot water for 1 minute to clean them.
- Coarsely chop the pine cones into 2 cm chunks.
- Bring the water to the boil with the sugar and add the chopped green pine cones.
- Add the ascorbic acid and keep refrigerated for 24 hours.
- Strain through a Superbag and refrigerate.

  NB: Ascorbic acid (vitamin C) is used as an antioxidant.

For the hot green pine come infusion jelly

100 g green pine cone infusion (previously prepared)
0.2 g powdered agar-agar
¼ x 2 g gelatine leaf (previously rehydrated in cold water)

- Mix the agar-agar with a third of the infusion and bring to the boil while stirring constantly.
- Remove from the heat, dissolve the drained gelatine in it and add the rest of the infusion.
- Mix and pour into a container to a thickness of 5 mm.
- Leave to set in the refrigerator for 2 hours.
- Once it has set, cut into 4 rectangles, 2 x 2.5 cm.

For the green pine cone oil

1 x 200 g green pine cone
100 g sunflower oil

- Chop the green pine cone into 2 cm chunks.
- Cover in sunflower oil and cook at 65 °C for 2 hours to make a confit.
- Refrigerate for 24 hours to infuse.
- Strain before use.

For the borage shoots

2 punnets borage shoots

- Use scissors to remove the base of the borage shoots. The stem should be left as long as possible.
- Make 4 bunches of 7 borage shoots.
- Refrigerate.

For the kaffir lime oil

10 kaffir lime leaves
50 g sunflower oil

- Chop the kaffir lime leaves and cover them with the sunflower oil.
- Heat to 70 °C and refrigerate in an airtight container for 24 hours.
- Strain before use.

1172

Grilled oysters with pine jelly, oyster cream and borage shoots

Finishing and presentation

8 Maldon sea salt flakes
Sunflower oil
1 kaffir lime

- Fill 4 medicine spoons with the oyster cream.
- Dress the borage shoots with a few drops of kaffir lime oil and 2 drops of kaffir lime juice.
- Place a piece of green pine cone infusion jelly on a rectangular tray and heat under the salamander grill until the jelly is hot.
- Cook the oysters on one side only for 8 seconds on the Hotstone grill.
- Remove them from the grill and coat lightly with sunflower oil.
- Place an oyster to the left side of the hot green pine cone infusion jelly. Place the spoon filled with oyster cream to the right of the jelly, followed by the remaining oyster. Finish with a bunch of borage shoots dressed with the kaffir lime oil.
- Finally, place a Maldon sea salt flake on top of each oyster and 1 drop of green pine cone oil on the jelly.

NB: A different version of this dish has been created in which the hot green pine cone infusion jelly is substituted with a hot fresh lychee juice jelly.

Cutlery

- Spoon and dessert fork.

How to eat

- Eat the dish from left to right, taking each component separately. Start with an oyster and finish with the borage shoots.

1173

Langoustine with quinoa[3]

Year
2005

Family
Tapas

Temperature
Hot/ambient

Season
All year round

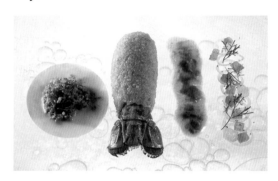

Serves 4

For the langoustine tails

4 x 140 g langoustines

- Remove the heads from the langoustines, and set aside for preparing the essence.
- Peel the tails up to the last ring of the shell.
- Remove the intestinal tract and store the tails in the refrigerator.

For the langoustine essence

Langoustine heads (previously prepared)
Olive oil

- Sauté the langoustine heads in a little olive oil in a frying pan.
- Crush the heads one by one to obtain their jus.
- Add a few drops of olive oil to the essence obtained, without emulsifying it.

NB: This preparation should be made immediately before finishing and presentation.

For the puffed quinoa

50 g quinoa
Water
250 g olive oil
Salt

- Boil the quinoa for 25 minutes in plenty of water.
- Drain, rinse in cold water to stop the cooking process, then drain well.
- Spray the cooked quinoa out over trays lined with parchment paper; ensure the grains are not overlapping.
- Leave the quinoa in a warm place for 24 hours until it is completely dry.
- Once dry, cook the quinoa in oil at 180 °C until it puffs up.
- Drain, soak up the excess oil on paper towel and season with salt while still hot.

For the cooked quinoa

50 g quinoa
200 g water
Salt

- Boil the quinoa in lightly salted water for 14 minutes.
- Drain and lay out on a tray to cool quickly and halt the cooking process.
- Refrigerate.

For the methylcellulose solution

100 g water
3 g methylcellulose

- Blend the ingredients together at room temperature in a liquidiser until they form a smooth, even mixture.
- Strain and leave in the refrigerator for 24 hours.

For the quinoa-coated langoustine

4 langoustine tails (previously prepared)
100 g cooked quinoa (previously prepared)
20 g methylcellulose solution
(previously prepared)

- Mix the cooked quinoa with the methylcellulose solution.
- Coat the langoustine tails with this mixture so that each langoustine is completely covered with a fine layer of it, with only the tail shell remaining uncovered.
- Lay out on parchment paper and put in the refrigerator.

For the spring onion rings

2 x 50 g spring onions
Water
Ice

- Peel and cut the spring onions into 2 mm rings.
- Choose 28 rings with 1.5 cm diameter and soak them in water filled with ice cubes for 2 hours.
- Remove from the water and drain on a paper towel.
- Refrigerate.

For the diced tomato

1 x 100 g ripe tomato
Water

- Blanch the tomato in boiling water, plunge it into iced water and then remove the skin.
- Cut the tomato into quarters and remove the seeds.
- Dice the tomato flesh into 5 mm cubes. Refrigerate.

1173

Langoustine with quinoa[3]

For the lime cubes and chopped zest

2 x 150 g limes

- Slice off the top and bottom of the limes to reveal the segments.
- Peel them in a spiral to expose the flesh and so that there are no traces of rind or pith, without altering the basic shape of the limes.
- Remove the segments from their membranes with a sharp knife.
- Cut the segments into 12 x 5 mm cubes.
- Remove the zest and chop it into tiny 1 mm cubes.
- Refrigerate each ingredient separately.

For the chilli oil

50 g sunflower oil
1 g dried chilli

- Chop the chilli and leave to infuse in the oil for 2 hours at 70 °C.
- Strain and put into a squeeze bottle.

For the quinoa shoots

60 g quinoa shoots
20 g water
Salt

- Boil the quinoa shoots for 5 minutes in the measured water.
- Season with salt and keep hot.

Finishing and presentation

160 g *kefir*
16 fresh, small coriander leaves
Extra virgin olive oil
Olive oil
Salt

- Lightly salt the quinoa-coated langoustine and fry both sides in olive oil.
- On the right-hand side of 4 O! LUNA solar plates, arrange a vertical salad made up of 7 spring onion rings, 7 tomato cubes, 3 lime cubes, 4 small coriander leaves and a little chopped lime zest. Finish with 4 drops of chilli oil, salt and a few drops of extra virgin olive oil.
- Mix 60 g of cooked quinoa shoots with 30 g of puffed quinoa and heat under the salamander grill.
- Divide the mixture among the 4 dishes. Place as a bouquet in the base of the dishes.
- Cut the upper part of the tail off the quinoa-coated langoustine so that the top part of the tail is bare.
- Place a langoustine tail vertically on the left-hand side of the salad, leaving a space of 4 cm in which to arrange vertically a spoon of langoustine essence and oil.
- The *kefir* comes in a separate jug so that the waiter can serve it in front of the diner.

Cutlery

- Spoon, fork and fish knife.

How to eat

- Each ingredient alternately.

1174

Lobster curry with granadilla air-foam and cardamom

Year
2005

Family
Tapas

Temperature
Hot

Season
August, September

Serves 4

For the sweet granadilla juice

8 x 100 g sweet granadillas

- Cut the granadillas in half and scoop out the flesh with a teaspoon over a chinois to catch and strain the juice.
- Process the flesh and seeds with a stick blender on the lowest speed so that they release all their juice without being crushed.
- Strain the juice through a Superbag and refrigerate.

NB: The sweet granadilla, *Passiflora ligularis*, is related to the passion fruit and is native to tropical areas of South and Central America. It is a round, orange fruit with black spots and juicy seeds.

For the hot sweet granadilla juice foam

250 g sweet granadilla juice (previously prepared)
1 g methylcellulose
1 x 0.5 litre ISI siphon
1 N_2O cartridge

- Mix the granadilla juice with the methylcellulose and process with a stick blender until lump-free.
- Cool the mixture to 3 °C and process again with the stick blender.
- Strain and fill the siphon.
- Close it, insert the gas cartridge and set aside in a bain-marie at 45 °C.

For the cardamom-infused milk

250 g milk
2.5 g cardamom seeds

- Lightly crush the cardamom seeds.
- Bring the milk to the boil, add the broken seeds and infuse for 10 minutes.
- Pass the infusion through a fine strainer.
- Set aside.

For the cardamom-infused milk air base

250 g cardamom-infused milk (previously prepared)
3 g sucrose ester

- Combine the infusion and sucrose ester in a deep 25 cm diameter container.

For the lobster

2 x 500 g female lobsters with roe
4 kg sea water

- Bring the sea water to the boil and cook the lobsters in it for 1 minute.
- Remove the lobsters and return them to the water upside down so that only the head and claws are submerged. Cook for 1 more minute.
- Remove the head from the tail and claws.
- Boil the claws for 1 more minute to finish cooking them.
- Clean the claws and reserve the joints for other dishes.
- Remove the feather bone from inside the claws.
- Shell the tails and slice them into 4 x 1.5 cm medallions.
- Make portions of 1 claw, 2 tail medallions per person.
- Refrigerate.

NB: Cooking time will vary according to the lobster weight.

For the lobster essence and roe

Lobster heads (previously prepared)

- Open the lobster heads and carefully extract the partly formed roe sacs without breaking.
- Use a knife to cut the sac containing the roe and empty them out without damaging their texture.
- Remove the remaining coral from the head and pass through a fine strainer.
- Cook the coral in a bain-marie while stirring constantly with a spatula until the temperature reaches 60 °C.
- Cook the water released by the heads in a Thermomix at 60 °C until it turns bright red and thickens. Mix with the roe.

1174

Lobster curry with granadilla air-foam and cardamom

Finishing and presentation

Madras curry powder
Salt
Olive oil
1 lime
1 Microplane grater

- Heat the cardamom-infused milk to 80 °C. Work the stick blender over the surface of the mixture until it emulsifies and the air forms.
- Season the lobster meat with salt and curry powder.
- Cook in a non-stick frying pan with a little oil.
- Place a 10 g mound of hot sweet granadilla foam at the base of a soup plate.
- Place a spoon of cardamom-infused milk air over it, mixing both together.
- Arrange 1 cooked lobster claw and 2 medallions around the air-foam.
- Sprinkle a little grated lime zest over the dish.
- Finish by adding the lobster essence and roe as a sauce between the lobster pieces without touching the air-foam.

Cutlery

- Spoon and dessert fork.

How to eat

- Alternate the components.

1175

Baby monkfish with lemon-scented egg yolk, daisy buds, pine nut oil and beurre noisette

Year
2005

Family
Tapas

Temperature
Hot

Season
All year round

Serves 4

For the baby monkfish fillets 12 x 15 cm baby monkfish	• Remove the head and the skin from the tails. • Use a knife to extract the 2 fillets and peel them. • Refrigerate.
For the liquidised lemon juice 1 x 150 g thick-skinned lemons	• Clean the lemon and remove the stalk. • Quarter the lemon, then liquidise. • Decant the juice into a tall, narrow container. • Remove the pulp from the top and discard.
For the egg yolk and lemon sauce 60 g liquidised lemon juice (previously prepared) 60 g egg yolk	• Pass the egg yolk through a fine strainer and add the liquidised lemon juice. • Mix with a whisk. NB: This preparation should be made immediately before finishing and preparation because the acidity of the lemon 'cooks' the yolk and modifies the texture of the sauce.
For the daisy buds 1 x 200 g jar pickled daisy buds	• Strain the daisy buds and make portions of 8 per person. • Reserve the vinegar from the jar for the vinaigrette.
For the beurre noisette 200 g butter	• Cook the butter in a pan until the temperature reaches 140 °C. • Leave to cool at room temperature and refrigerate in an airtight container.
For the beurre noisette vinaigrette 50 g beurre noisette (previously prepared) 40 g vinegar from the daisy buds (previously prepared)	• Melt the butter, mix with the vinegar and set aside in a warm place.
For the beurre noisette air base 140 g water 140 g beurre noisette (previously prepared) 45 g butter 1.5 g soya lecithin powder	• Melt both butters without cooking. • Combine the butters, water and soya lecithin in a deep 20 cm container.

1175

Baby monkfish with lemon-scented egg yolk, daisy buds, pine nut oil and beurre noisette

Finishing and presentation

Olive oil
75 g pine nut oil
Salt

- Work the stick blender over the surface of the beurre noisette air base until it emulsifies and the air forms.
- Season the baby monkfish fillets with salt and cook in a non-stick frying pan in a little olive oil.
- Heat 4 O! LUNA deep lunar plates.
- Place 2 spoons of the egg yolk and lemon sauce on the right side of the base.
- Arrange the 8 daisy buds on top without letting them touch each other.
- Drizzle the pine nut oil over the egg yolk and lemon sauce.
- Place 6 baby monkfish fillets on the right sloping part of the plate without letting them touch each other.
- Bathe the fillets with a spoon of beurre noisette vinaigrette.
- Finish by spreading a spoon of beurre noisette air in a line across the base of the baby monkfish fillets.

Cutlery

- Spoon and dessert fork.

How to eat

- Alternate the baby monkfish fillets with the air, egg yolk and lemon sauce and daisy buds.

1176

Sole with puffed amaranth, Córdoba air, coriander-flavoured amaranth/popcorn, Chinese garlic flowers and lemon

Year
2005

Family
Tapas

Temperature
Hot

Season
All year round

Serves 4

For the cleaned sole 8 x 12 cm soles	• Remove the skin from the soles and trim off the side fins with scissors • Refrigerate.
For the amaranth/popcorn 100 g amaranth grains	• Place small amounts of amaranth at a time in a pan without piling and cook on a high heat until it puffs. • Transfer immediately to a cold fine strainer to prevent them from burning and remove any grains that may not have puffed. • Store the amaranth/popcorn in an airtight container in a cool, dry place.
For the puffed amaranth 50 g amaranth grains 500 g water 500 g olive oil Salt	• Boil the amaranth for 25 minutes in plenty of water. • Drain, rinse in cold water to stop the cooking process, then drain well. • Spray the cooked amaranth out over trays lined with parchment paper; ensure the grains are not overlapping. • Leave the amaranth in a warm place for 24 hours until it is completely dry. • Once dry, puff the amaranth in oil at 180 °C. • Drain, soak up the excess oil on paper towel and season with salt while still hot.
For the milk air and Córdoba spice base 500 g milk 1.5 g soya lecithin powder 3.5 g Fatéma Hal's Córdoba spices	• Heat the milk to 50 °C. • Mix in the spices with a stick blender and allow to infuse for 24 hours. • Strain the infusion through a Superbag over a deep 25 cm diameter container. Add the soya lecithin and process with a stick blender.
For the garlic oil 30 g dried garlic 100 g extra virgin olive oil	• Peel the garlic cloves and blanch twice in water. • Drain the garlic and slice finely. • Fry the sliced garlic in 50 g of oil. • Remove from the heat and add the remaining oil. • Leave to stand at room temperature for 12 hours, then strain.
For the garlic and lemon split sauce 3 x 300 g thick-skinned lemons 100 g garlic oil (previously prepared)	• Rinse the lemons and remove the stalk. • Quarter and de-seed. • Liquidise and decant the obtained juice in a tall, narrow container. • Separate the top part containing the pulp from the less thick juice in the bottom. • Weigh out 80 g of the juice with pulp and add the garlic oil to make a split sauce. • Keep hot.
For the Chinese garlic shoots 40 Chinese garlic shoots	• Trim the Chinese garlic shoots leaving 2 cm lengths. • Prepare 8 shoots per person.

1176

Sole with puffed amaranth, Córdoba air, coriander-flavoured amaranth/popcorn, Chinese garlic flowers and lemon

Finishing and presentation

24 fresh coriander flowers
Olive oil
Salt
16 g coriander shoots

- Heat the milk air and Córdoba spice mixture to 50 °C and work a stick blender over the surface until it emulsifies and the air forms.
- Season the sole with salt and cook them on both sides in a non-stick frying pan.
- Fillet them carefully without breaking.
- Make a stack with 4 fillets and coat with the puffed amaranth.
- Sauté the Chinese garlic shoots in a little oil and season with salt.
- Use a large spoon to make 4 spoonfuls of milk air and carefully coat them with the amaranth/popcorn.
- Place the milk air coated with amaranth/popcorn on the right side of a slightly tilted rectangular tray.
- Place 2 stacks of the sole fillets coated with puffed amaranth on the left side, with a 2 cm space between them.
- Scatter the Chinese garlic shoots, the coriander shoots and the coriander flowers over and around the sole.
- Finish by spreading garlic and lemon sauce over the sole and around the dish.

  NB: If coriander flower is not available, substitute with tender coriander leaves.

Cutlery

- Spoon and dessert fork.

How to eat

- Dip the individual fillets in the sauce and eat. In the meantime, eat the coated air in two mouthfuls.

1177

Turtle dove with tuna medulla, enokis and samphire

Year
2005

Family
Tapas

Temperature
Hot

Season
August

Serves 4

For the turtle dove breasts

2 x 125 g turtle doves
2 x slices salted Spanish bacon, 0.5 x 7 cm

- Leave the bone in the turtle dove breasts and separate them from the rest of the carcase, which will be used for the sauce together with the wings and feet.
- Discard the entrails.
- Wrap each turtle dove breast in a slice of Spanish bacon and tie with string.
- Set aside.

For the turtle dove sauce

75 g turtle dove bones, wings and feet (previously prepared)
250 g ice cubes
Olive oil
Salt
0.5 g Xantana

- Brown the bones in a pan with a little oil.
- Add the ice cubes.
- Cook on a medium heat for 1 hour.
- Strain as much jus as possible through fine-meshed cloth and remove the excess fat.
- Season with salt.
- Add the Xantana to half of the sauce obtained and process with a stick blender until lump-free.
- Add the other half of the sauce and mix without aerating.
- Set aside.

For the tuna medulla

2 kg tuna spinal cord (from the central part)
Sea water

- Remove as much of the meat from the spine as possible and reserve for another dish.
- Make an incision in the spherical joint between the vertebrae with a short, sharp knife.
- Cut around the joint until it is 80% open, then use a spoon to extract the spinal jelly (medulla). Rinse in the sea water to remove any traces of blood.
- Prepare 12 x 1.5 cm diameter medullas.
- Refrigerate.

For the enokis and samphire

40 g enoki mushrooms
40 g samphire

- Trim the enokis, leaving a 3 cm tip.
- Trim the samphire, leaving 3 cm shoots.
- Prepare 4 g of samphire shoots and 5 g of enokis per person.
- Refrigerate.

NB: The enoki, also known as the velvet stem, is a thin, long and white mushroom with very small caps. Wild and cultivated enokis grow in small bunches on the trunks of trees. The cultivated mushrooms are paler than the wild ones. They have a subtle, delicate flavour and are used widely in Asian cuisine.

NB: The samphire variety used, purple glasswort (*Salicornia ramosissima*), is an annual herb from the Chenopodiaceae family that grows in saline soils. The branches have a number of nodes and are fleshy and green, except towards the end of its cycle when the plant turns a reddish colour. It grows in places close to the sea or in marshy areas occasionally flooded with sea water.

For the nori water

500 g salted nori seaweed
500 g water

- Rinse the seaweed in plenty of water to remove excess salt.
- Blend the seaweed with the water in a liquidiser.
- Strain through a Superbag and set aside.

For the nori water air base

250 g nori water (previously prepared)
1 g soya lecithin powder

- Mix both ingredients in a deep 25 cm diameter container.

1177

Turtle dove with tuna medulla, enokis and samphire

Finishing and presentation

Olive oil
Salt

- Work the stick blender over the surface of the nori water air base until it emulsifies and the air forms.
- Place the turtle dove breast down in a frying pan on a medium heat so it cooks gradually for 2 minutes. Turn it over every 30 seconds. Cover and leave to stand next to the heat for 3 minutes.
- Once it is done (it should be pink), remove the string and the bacon. Cut out both breasts and slice them slightly on the diagonal into 3 pieces.
- Sauté the enokis and samphire seasoned with salt in a frying pan with a little oil.
- Place a tuna medulla on top of each piece of turtle dove breast and heat under the salamander grill.
- Make a small mound with sautéed samphire and enokis in the base of an O! LUNA deep lunar plate.
- On the right of the mound arrange 3 pieces of turtle dove breast with the hot medulla on top.
- Pour a spoon of hot turtle dove sauce over the breast pieces with medulla.
- Finish by placing 1 spot of nori water air over each medulla.

Cutlery

- Tapas cutlery.

  NB: Tapas cutlery consists of a 14 x 3 cm spoon and fork.

How to eat

- Eat the turtle dove together with the medulla and the nori air. Alternate with the enoki and the sautéed samphire.

1178

Tandoori chicken wings with borage shoots, oyster cream and frothy *mató* cheese

Year
2005

Family
Tapas

Temperature
Hot

Season
May, June, July, August

Serves 4

For the chicken wing confit

6 x 100 g free-range chicken wings
20 g olive oil

- Cut off the wing tips at the joint and use the middle section.
- Remove any remaining feathers with tweezers.
- Place the cleaned chicken wings into a vacuum-pack bag with the oil and vacuum seal.
- Slow cook the chicken wings at 63 °C in a Roner for 24 hours.
- Take the wings out of the Roner and trim one end slightly to expose the bone.
- Remove the bones carefully by hand, keeping them whole and without breaking the meat.

For the tandoori chicken sauce

500 g cleaned chicken, cut into 3 cm pieces
30 g onion, julienned
2 g tandoori paste
1 g tandoori powder
200 g water
Olive oil
Salt

- Heat the oil in a pan.
- Add the seasoned chicken pieces and brown well.
- Add the julienned onion and stir until it caramelises.
- Add the tandoori paste and powder. Cook everything together for one minute and add the water.
- Cook on a medium heat until the sauce is reduced and well flavoured.
- Use a fine mesh sieve to strain and season with salt if necessary.

For the fermented milk *mató* cheese

500 g fermented full-cream milk

- Pour the milk into a small pan and heat to 56 °C, stirring continuously with a spatula.
- Leave to stand for 5 minutes.
- Pour the milk through a sieve to drain off the whey. The *mató* cheese curds will remain in the sieve.
- Refrigerate.

For the milk air with Córdoba spice base

500 g milk
2.5 g sucrose ester
3.5 g Fatéma Hal's Córdoba spices

- Mix the ingredients with a stick blender and strain through a Superbag.
- Pour the mixture into a deep 25 cm diameter container.

For the cleaned oysters

3 x 200 g Napoleon oysters

- Open the oysters with an oyster knife. Retain the liquor.
- Cut through the muscle holding the oyster to the shell and remove the oyster.
- De-beard the oysters with a pair of scissors.
- Strain the liquor through a Superbag and add the oysters. Refrigerate.

For the smoked streaky Spanish bacon fat

50 g smoked streaky Spanish bacon

- Slice the bacon into 2 cm chunks and put in a small pan over a low heat to sweat and release the fat. Do not let it fry.
- Strain off the fat and set aside.

For the oyster cream

25 g cleaned oysters (previously prepared)
30 g oyster liquor (previously prepared)
8 g melted smoked streaky Spanish bacon fat (previously prepared)

- Blend the oysters with the oyster liquor.
- Emulsify the resulting liquid with the melted bacon fat at room temperature.
- Strain and refrigerate.

For the green almonds in almond oil

12 green almonds
10 g toasted almond oil

- Peel and split the almonds in half.
- Pour the toasted almond oil over them. Cover and refrigerate.

For the borage shoots

2 punnets borage shoots

- Use scissors to remove the base of the borage shoots. The stem should be left as long as possible.
- Make 8 bunches of 5 borage shoots.
- Refrigerate.

1178

Tandoori chicken wings with borage shoots, oyster cream and frothy *mató* cheese

Finishing and presentation

Freshly ground black pepper
Salt
Olive oil

- Work a stick blender over the surface of the milk and Córdoba spice mixture until it emulsifies and the air forms.
- Season the cooked chicken wings with salt and freshly ground black pepper and fry over a medium heat in a non-stick frying pan with a little oil, keeping the skin in contact with the base of the pan.
- Once the skin is well browned and crisp, turn the wings over and fry for 30 seconds.
- Take the wings out of the pan and trim them on each side. Cut each wing into 2 x 2 cm pieces. Divide into 4 portions with 3 pieces of wing in each one.
- On a rectangular dish make 2 small piles of 3 half almonds in almond oil at each end of the plate.
- Put a small bunch of borage shoots beside each pile of almonds.
- Pour a small amount of oyster cream over the borage shoots.
- Put a teaspoon of mató cheese in the upper central part of the dish.
- Place one portion of chicken wings diagonally across the middle of the dish, leaving a space of 1 cm between each piece of wing.
- Pour hot tandoori chicken sauce over the wings.
- Finish by putting a spoon of milk and Córdoba spice air over the home-made *mató* cheese. Make a hole in the air so that the *mató* can be seen.

NB: If borage shoots are not available, they can be substituted with shoots of wild purslane.

Cutlery

- Tapas cutlery.

NB: Tapas cutlery consists of a 14 x 3 cm spoon and fork.

How to eat

- Alternate the chicken wings with the other components.

1179

Lamb's brains with sea urchin and sea grape

Year
2005

Family
Tapas

Temperature
Hot

Season
January, February, March, April, May

Serves 4

For the vegetable court-bouillon

1 kg water
40 g leek
20 g onion
60 g carrot
10 g black peppercorns
1 bay leaf
Salt

- Peel the onion and chop into 1 cm pieces.
- Peel the leek and cut into 5 mm slices.
- Combine all the ingredients and cook over a medium heat for 30 minutes.
- Strain and season with salt.

For the cleaned lamb's brains

4 x 130 g lamb's brains
Water
Ice

- Carefully devein the brains and separate them into their 2 lobes without breaking.
- Refrigerate for 36 hours in iced water to remove any blood.

For the lamb's brain sauce

150 g cleaned lamb's brains (previously prepared)
50 g water
Salt

- Chop the brains into 1 cm pieces.
- Bring the water to the boil, add the brains, wait until the water boils again and remove from the heat.
- Leave to stand for 5 minutes then blend in a liquidiser to obtain a fine, lump-free sauce.
- Strain and season with salt.

For the sea urchin roe

20 x 70 g sea urchins

- Kill the sea urchins by scalding them in boiling water for 10 seconds.
- Cut along the bottom of the sea urchins with a pair of scissors, making a 2 cm diameter circle.
- Remove the roe from inside the sea urchins and place each one in the sea urchin liquor previously strained through a Superbag.
- Choose the 32 largest pieces of roe.
- Refrigerate.

For the sea grapes

20 x 4 cm stems pasteurised sea grapes

- Hydrate the sea grapes under plenty of running water until it is smooth and moist.

NB: Sea grapes, *Umi budo*, take their name from the clusters of liquid-filled globules along the seaweed. They have a crisp texture and originate from Japan, specifically the Okinawa region. It can be bought fresh or pasteurised.

NB: The sea grapes should be hydrated just before finishing and presentation.

1179

Lamb's brains with sea urchin and sea grape

Finishing and presentation

Vegetable court-bouillon (previously prepared)
Freshly ground black pepper
Salt

- Heat the vegetable court-bouillon to 70 °C and add the lamb's brains seasoned with salt.
- Cook the brains for 15-20 minutes.
- Trim off the ends of the brains and cut the middle part into 2 x 1.5 cm thick slices.
- Arrange 8 pieces of sea urchin roe in a semicircle on the right side of a soup plate.
- Place 5 stems of sea grapes in a semicircle on the left side.
- Place 2 pieces of cooked lamb's brain in the middle of the circle with a 2 cm space between them.
- Finish by pouring 2 spoons of hot lamb's brain sauce over the brain pieces.
- Season the brains with freshly ground black pepper.

NB: If sea grapes are not available, they can be substituted with fresh samphire.

Cutlery

- Tapas cutlery.

NB: Tapas cutlery consists of a 14 x 3 cm spoon and fork.

How to eat

- Alternate the components.

1180

Rack of Iberian pork with Thai aroma

Year
2005

Family
Tapas

Temperature
Hot

Season
All year round

Serves 4

For rack of Iberian pork confit with Thai aroma

1 x 500 g rack of Iberian pork ribs 5 cm thick
1 stalk lemongrass
2 kaffir lime leaves
10 g fresh coriander
20 g fresh ginger
2 g red curry paste
Olive oil

- Square off the rack at the widest point to obtain a 10 x 5 cm rectangle.
- Brush the rack with a little oil and red curry paste.
- Chop the remaining ingredients to release their aroma.
- Place the rack and the other chopped ingredients in a vacuum bag and vacuum seal.
- Cook at 65 °C in a Roner for 24 hours.
- Remove from the Roner and bone the rack without breaking the meat.
- Cut the boned rib meat into 12 2 x 4 x 1 cm blocks.

NB: Bone and cut up the rack just before finishing and presentation to keep it moist.

For the peanut oil with red curry

25 g toasted peanut oil
2.5 g red curry paste

- Mix both ingredients and set aside.

For the boiled *kuzu* spaghetti

40 g *kuzu* spaghetti
Water
Salt

- Boil the spaghetti for 3 minutes in plenty of salted water.
- Drain and refresh in iced water to stop the cooking process.
- Make 4 equal portions of spaghetti.

NB: *Kuzu* is the name given to Japanese starch made from a root of a certain plant similar to arrowroot.

NB: We have created another version with spaghetti made from water jelly with gellan gum and agar-agar instead of *kuzu*.

For the coconut milk

2 x 700 g fresh coconuts

- Split open the coconuts.
- Use an oyster knife to remove the coconut purée from the shell. Discard the shell.
- Peel the coconut purée with a paring knife. Discard the peelings.
- Wash the coconut purée in a little warm water.
- Drain the coconut and liquidise.
- Strain and refrigerate.

For the coconut milk cream

100 g coconut milk
0.6 g Xantana

- Mix both ingredients and process with a stick blender to obtain a fine cream.

For the peanut air base

300 g water
75 g peanut paste
3 g soya lecithin powder

- Combine the peanut paste with the water in a deep 25 cm diameter container.
- Heat so as to dissolve the peanut paste.
- Add the soya lecithin and mix.

For the coriander shoots

20 g coriander shoots

- Remove the seeds from the coriander shoots.
- Cover the shoots with damp paper towel and refrigerate.

For the fres herbs

20 x 1 cm fresh basil leaves
20 x 5 mm fresh mint leaves
20 x 1 cm fresh coriander leaves

- Divide the herbs into 4 equal portions.
- Cover them with a damp paper towel and refrigerate.

1180

**Rack of Iberian pork
with Thai aroma**

Finishing and presentation

4 g coconut milk powder
4 g tamarind paste
4 g Madras curry powder
20 x 2 mm fresh ginger cubes
Salt
1 lime
4 g Japanese white sesame seeds
1 Microplane grater

- Work a stick blender over the surface of the peanut air base until it emulsifies and the air forms.
- Season the pork with salt and steam until hot.
- Warm the coconut milk cream and heat the spaghetti in it.
- Place a mound of *kuzu* spaghetti with coconut milk cream under the ridge of 4 O! LUNA large eclipse plates.
- Sprinkle a pinch of coconut milk powder, the fresh herbs and Japanese white sesame over the spaghetti.
- Arrange 3 pieces of hot Iberian pork rib on the right side of the plate.
- Season the pork with Madras curry powder and grated lime zest.
- Pour a spoon of hot peanut oil with red curry over the pork. Scatter the coriander shoots and finish with 2 spoons of peanut air.

Cutlery

- Tapas cutlery.

  NB: Tapas cutlery consists of a 14 x 3 cm spoon and fork.

How to eat

- Alternate the pieces of pork with the spaghetti.

1181

Red cabbage
with *jamón ibérico* lentils

Year
2005

Family
Tapas

Temperature
Hot

Season
All year round

Serves 4

For the red cabbage juice

1 x 500 g piece red cabbage

- Liquidise the red cabbage.
- Strain the juice and set aside.

For the red cabbage julienne

1 x 200 g piece red cabbage

- Choose the most tender cabbage leaves.
- Cut in a 0.5 mm julienne.
- Make 8 g portions of red cabbage julienne per person.

For the cooked red cabbage

100 g red cabbage juice (previously prepared)
32 g red cabbage julienne (previously prepared)
15 g butter
8 g 25-year-old sherry vinegar
Salt

- Lightly cook the cabbage julienne in the butter.
- Moisten with the vinegar and allow it to evaporate.
- Gradually add the red cabbage juice and stew on a medium heat for 20 minutes.
- The cabbage should be tender and juicy.
- Season with salt.

NB: This preparation should be made immediately before finishing and presentation.

For the *jamón ibérico* stock

250 g *jamón ibérico* offcuts
500 g water

- Remove the excess fat from the ham and cut it into uneven pieces of roughly 1 cm in size.
- Cover the ham with the water and simmer, skimming continuously to remove the fat and scum for 15 minutes.
- Strain through a Superbag. Do not allow the stock to become cloudy or remove any more fat.
- Refrigerate.

For the *jamón ibérico* stock jelly lentils

200 g *jamón ibérico* stock (previously prepared)
4.5 g Kappa Carrageenan

- Mix the water and Kappa Carrageenan and bring to the boil, stirring constantly with a whisk.
- Remove from the heat and skim off the froth. While still hot, fill a syringe and use it to make 5 mm diameter circular drops on a flat sheet of parchment paper.
- Refrigerate for 30 minutes to allow the drops to set.
- Use a flat spatula to unstick the drops from the paper and make 4 x 12 g portions.
- Refrigerate.

For the *jamón ibérico* lard

100 g fat

- Remove any lean or rancid bits from the fat.
- Cut the clean fat into 1 cm chunks.
- Place the fat in a pan on a low heat and render the fat to make lard.
- Strain the liquid lard and set aside.

For the fresh tarragon water

40 g fresh tarragon leaves
Water

- Blanch the leaves in water for 15 seconds.
- Drain and chill in iced water.
- Blend the blanched tarragon leaves in a liquidiser with 120 g of the water used to chill them.
- Strain and refrigerate in an airtight container.

For the fresh tarragon concentrate

140 g fresh tarragon water (previously prepared)

- Pour 70 g of the tarragon water into each of 2 centrifuge tubes and 70 g of water in the other 2 tubes.
- Spin in the centrifuge for 5 minutes at 100 rpm.
- When the process is complete, separate the water from on top of the concentrated pulp that has settled at the bottom of each tube.
- Discard the water.
- Transfer the concentrate to a piping bag, vacuum seal and refrigerate.

1181

**Red cabbage
with *jamón ibérico* lentils**

Finishing and presentation

15 g Dijon mustard
4 g freshly ground cinnamon stick
2 g lightly crushed cardamom seeds
2 g chopped juniper berries

- Place the ham lentils in a pan with 2 spoons of *jamón ibérico* lard and heat, taking care not to melt the lentils.
- Preheat 4 O! LUNA small eclipse plates and place the cooked red cabbage in each base.
- Arrange the different components over the cabbage following the contours of the plate and with even spacing between them.
- Finish by placing the *jamón ibérico* lentils in the well opening resting on the cabbage as an elongated mound.

NB: A different version of this dish has been created by substituting the cooked red cabbage with a hot stewed oxtail sauce jelly.

Cutlery

- Tapas cutlery.

NB: Tapas cutlery consists of a 14 x 3 cm spoon and fork.

How to eat

- Alternate the red cabbage with the different components without mixing them, and with the *jamón ibérico* lentils.

Pre desserts
1182–1186

1182

Tennessee infusion

Year
2005

Family
Pre desserts

Temperature
Hot

Season
All year round

Serves 4

For the Tennessee infusion

80 g Tennessee whiskey barrel wood
300 g water

- Place 3 cm pieces of Tennessee whiskey barrel wood in an infusion jar.
- Boil the water and pour it into the jar. Leave to infuse for 15 minutes.

  NB: Tennessee barrel wood was originally sold for barbecues.

Finishing and presentation

- Serve 30 g of hot infusion in a whisky tumbler.

Cutlery

- None.

How to eat

- Smell and drink a little at a time.

1183

Peach liquid

Year
2005

Family
Pre desserts

Temperature
Frozen/cold

Season
All year round

Serves 4

For the peach liquid

100 g Kuhri peach liqueur
100 g 35% fat single cream
1 kg liquid nitrogen

- Freeze a 5 ml hemispherical measuring spoon, then fill it with peach liqueur and dip it inside the liquid nitrogen tank without letting the nitrogen touch the liqueur, so that only the spoon freezes.
- When the inside edge of the spoon is frozen (some 8 seconds), dip the spoon in completely so that the top layer of liqueur also freezes.
- Freeze for 8 more seconds. Remove from the nitrogen and tap the spoon so that the peach liqueur is released as a hemispherical ice cube.
- Quickly dip the ice cube in the cream, ensuring that no part is uncovered, then put back into the liquid nitrogen for 3 seconds.
- Remove from the nitrogen and store in the freezer at -20 °C.
- Make one liquid per person.

For the vineyard peach juice

100 g Garnier red vineyard peach juice

- Thaw the juice. Strain it and put it in a squeeze bottle.

Finishing and presentation

- Fifteen minutes before serving, remove the peach liquids from the deep freezer at -20 °C and put in the freezer at -8 °C so that the liqueur inside melts.
- Fill a medicine spoon with wild peach juice and place it over one of the slots on a frozen rectangular slate with 2 holes.
- Place the peach liquid over the other slot and serve quickly.

Cutlery

- None.

How to eat

- Eat the liquid whole. Break it gently inside the mouth. Finish with the spoon containing wild peach juice.

1184

Spherical-I mozzarella/burrata with fir honey, fruit-CRU

Year
2005

Family
Pre desserts

Temperature
Cold

Season
All year round

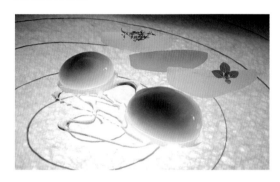

Serves 4

For the mozzarella water

2 balls fresh buffalo mozzarella in 500 g tubs

- Open the tubs. Remove the mozzarella balls and reserve the water from the tubs and the mozzarella balls separately.

For the mozzarella cream

100 g mozzarella water (previously prepared)
60 g buffalo mozzarella balls (previously prepared)

- Heat the mozzarella water to 60 °C and blend it with the mozzarella balls in the liquidiser until a slightly grainy cream forms.

For the mozzarella/burrata base

160 g mozzarella cream (previously prepared)
200 g buffalo mozzarella balls (previously prepared)
15 g double cream

- Crumble the 200 g of mozzarella with your fingers.
- Mix the mozzarella cream with the crumbled mozzarella and the double cream.
- Refrigerate.

For the sodium alginate solution

5 g sodium alginate
1 kg water

- Blend the sodium alginate with the water in the liquidiser until it is lump-free.
- Pour into a container to a thickness of 6 cm.

For the spherical-I mozzarella/burrata

200 g mozzarella/burrata base (previously prepared)
1 kg sodium alginate solution (previously prepared)
1 x 18 g hemispherical measuring spoon
1 x 15 g hemispherical measuring spoon

- Fill the spoons with the mozzarella/burrata base and drop their contents into the sodium alginate solution to form spheres.
- Leave the mozzarella spheres to 'cook' in the sodium alginate solution for 12 minutes.
- Remove the mozzarella spheres with a slotted spoon. Rinse them, then keep them submerged in the mozzarella water.
- Make 4 burrata spheres with each spoon.
- Refrigerate.

For the fruit-CRU

1 Conference pear
1 Granny Smith apple
500 g water
150 g sugar
1.5 g ascorbic acid

- Mix the sugar and water and bring to the boil, simmering until the sugar dissolves completely.
- Remove from the heat and add the ascorbic acid. Leave to cool.
- Peel the peach and cut it into 4 wedges 3 cm long and 1 cm tall.
- Peel the apple and cut it into 4 wedges 3 cm long and 1 cm tall.
- Peel the pear and cut it into 4 wedges 3 cm long and 1 cm tall.
- Cover the 3 different fruits separately with the water, sugar and ascorbic acid mixture and vacuum seal them separately.
- Refrigerate for 6 hours.

Finishing and presentation

100 g fir honey
2 g citric acid granules
2 g fresh chopped fennel
4 fresh basil shoots

- Make a burrata sphere with the 18 g spoon and place on the top left hand side of a soup plate. Make another burrata sphere with the 15 g spoon and place on the bottom left hand side with a 3 cm separation between them.
- Place 1 apple wedge, 1 peach wedge and 1 pear wedge horizontally on the right side of the plate.
- Sprinkle a pinch of citric acid over the peach and 0.5 g of fresh chopped fennel over the apple. Lay a fresh basil shoot on top of the pear.
- Place the fir honey in a separate container so that the waiter can serve it in front of the diner.

Cutlery

- Tapas cutlery.

  NB: Tapas cutlery consists of a 14 x 3 cm spoon and fork.

How to eat

- First eat the small spherical burrata whole. Then break the large burrata and eat the soup, alternating each mouthful with the fir honey and the fruit-CRU.

1185

Hot passion fruit marshmallow, fresh mint coconut milk and chocolate pearls

Year
2005

Family
Pre desserts

Temperature
Hot

Season
All year round

Serves 4

For the passion fruit methyl cloud

250 g Garnier passion fruit pulp
3.5 g methylcellulose
3½ x 2 g gelatine leaves (previously rehydrated in cold water)

- Mix 200 g of passion fruit pulp with the methylcellulose in a bowl.
- Process with a stick blender until it is lump-free.
- Place in the freezer and leave there until a temperature of 3 °C is reached. Mix with a whisk every 3 minutes.
- When it has reached 3 °C, leave at room temperature until it rises to 14 °C.
- Meanwhile, dissolve the gelatine leaves in the remaining 50 g of passion fruit pulp in a pan.
- The passion fruit pulp and methylcellulose mixture should reach 14 °C at the same time as the passion fruit pulp and gelatine mixture is at 39 °C.
- Whip the methylcellulose mixture in the mixer while gradually pouring in the gelatine mixture.
- Whip at medium speed for 7 minutes until the mixture forms peaks like beaten egg whites.

For the passion fruit methyl cloud marshmallows

Passion fruit methyl cloud
(previously prepared)

- Fill a piping bag with the methyl cloud. Use a No. 8 plain nozzle.
- Pipe 3 1.5 cm tall x 1.5 cm diameter marshmallows on each of 4 x 21 cm soup plates, making sure they do not touch each other.

For the coconut milk

400 g Sicoly coconut milk

- Thaw the coconut milk and strain it through a Superbag.
- Refrigerate.

Finishing and presentation

12 x 5 mm fresh chocolate mint flowers
32 g crunchy chocolate pearls

- Place the dishes with the marshmallows under the salamander grill for 5 seconds to heat, taking care they do not change colour.
- Lean 1 fresh chocolate mint flower against each marshmallow.
- Serve 50 g of hot coconut milk in a jug and the chocolate pearls in a bowl so that the waiter can serve them in front of the diner with care so as not to break the marshmallows.

NB: Another version of this dish was made substituting the coconut milk with a hot banana and lime soup. If chocolate mint flowers are not available, substitute with small fresh chocolate mint leaves.

Cutlery

- Tapas cutlery.

NB: Tapas cutlery consists of a 14 x 3 cm spoon and fork.

How to eat

- Alternate the marshmallows with the coconut milk and the chocolate pearls. Eat the marshmallows in a single mouthful.

1186

Coulant/soufflé of granadilla with cardamom toffee

Year
2005

Family
Pre desserts

Temperature
Hot/ambient

Season
All year round

Serves 4

For the sweet granadilla juice

15 x 100 g sweet granadillas

- Cut the granadillas in half and scoop out the flesh with a teaspoon over a chinois to catch and strain the juice.
- Process the flesh and seeds with a stick blender on the lowest speed so that they release all their juice without being crushed.
- Strain the juice through a Superbag and refrigerate.

NB: The sweet granadilla, *Passiflora ligularis*, is related to the passion fruit and is native to tropical areas of South and Central America. It is a round, orange fruit with black spots and juicy seeds.

For the chilled cardamom toffee foam

175 g 35% fat single cream
150 g sugar
2 g cardamom seeds
1 x 0.5 litre ISI siphon
1 N$_2$O cartridge

- Powder the cardamom seeds in a grinder.
- Put the sugar in a small pan and heat to make a dark caramel.
- Heat the cream, add to the caramel and stir continuously to create a smooth, even mixture.
- Add the powdered cardamom and leave to infuse for 30 minutes. Strain and allow the toffee to stand in the refrigerator for 12 hours.
- Fill the siphon with the toffee.
- Close it and insert the gas cartridge.
- Refrigerate.

For the granadilla juice methylcellulose cloud

250 g granadilla juice (previously prepared)
3 g methylcellulose
3 x 2 g gelatine leaves (previously rehydrated in cold water)

- Blend 200 g granadilla juice with the methylcellulose with a stick blender until lump-free.
- Place the mixture in the freezer to reduce the temperature quickly to 3 °C.
- Drain the rehydrated gelatine sheet and heat to dissolve in 50 g granadilla juice.
- Once the granadilla and methylcellulose solution has reached 3 °C, remove from the freezer and leave in a warm place until the temperature increases to 14 °C.
- Put the solution into the mixer and begin beating at medium speed.
- When it starts to foam, add the granadilla juice and gelatine mixture, which has been heated to 39 °C.
- Beat for about 7 minutes until the mixture forms peaks like beaten egg whites.

For the toffee and granadilla coulant/soufflé

Granadilla juice methylcellulose cloud (previously prepared)
Chilled cardamom toffee foam (previously prepared)
4 x 4.5 cm round moulds, 6 cm deep and lined with parchment paper

- Put the methylcellulose cloud into a piping bag with a No.8 plain nozzle.
- Place the moulds on a flat tray lined with parchment paper.
- Pipe the methylcellulose cloud into the base of the mould to form a 1 cm layer. Continue to pipe the cloud around the walls of the mould, leaving a 1.5 cm diameter space in the middle.
- Freeze for 5 minutes until the cloud sets, then fill the space with toffee foam.
- Finish by covering the moulds with a 1 cm layer of cloud.
- Set in the freezer for 5 minutes.

For the cardamom powder

20 g cardamom pods

- Break open the cardamom pods and take out the seeds.
- Powder the seeds in a grinder.

1186

Coulant/soufflé of granadilla with cardamom toffee

Finishing and presentation

1 x 50 g passion fruit, halved

- Lift the soufflé with a spatula and place it in the middle of a 21 cm dish.
- Carefully remove the moulds without breaking the soufflé.
- Heat the soufflé under the salamander grill until hot on the outside and the inside is almost liquid.
- Sprinkle powdered cardamom over the surface of the soufflé.
- Serve the halved passion fruit open and separately so that the waiter can spoon out the passion fruit seeds around the soufflé in front of the diner.

NB: Alternatively, the soufflé could be heated in a microwave at full power for 5 seconds.

Cutlery

- Tapas cutlery.

NB: Tapas cutlery consists of a 14 x 3 cm spoon and fork.

How to eat

- Break the soufflé and eat it alternately with the passion fruit seeds.

Desserts
1187–1199

1187

Peach-CRU in amaretto with electric ice cream

Year
2005

Family
Desserts

Temperature
Frozen/cold

Season
June, July, August, September

Serves 4

For the cold white peach foam

275 g Garnier white peach purée
2¼ x 2 g gelatine leaves (previously rehydrated in cold water)
1 x 0.5 litre ISI siphon
1 N₂O cartridge

- Strain the white peach purée through a Superbag.
- You should obtain 250 g of purée.
- Dissolve the gelatine in a quarter of the hot peach purée.
- Add the remaining purée, strain and fill the siphon.
- Close and insert the gas cartridge.
- Refrigerate for 4 hours.

For the freeze-dried cold white peach foam

Cold white peach foam (previously prepared)

- Fill 4 small plastic cups with the white peach foam.
- Freeze dry for 48 hours.
- Keep in an airtight container in a cool, dry place.

For the freeze-dried cold white peach foam rocks

Freeze-dried cold white peach foam (previously prepared)

- Use a paring knife to cut out 8 x 2 cm rocks from the freeze-dried white peach foam.
- They should not have defined geometric shapes so that they resemble rocks.
- Store immediately in an airtight container in a cool, dry place.

For the yogurt ice cream

225 g water
125 g glucose
55 g dextrose
65 g Sosa Procrema stabiliser
2 g citric acid
25 g Sosa Prosorbet stabiliser
225 g Greek yogurt
225 g plain yogurt

- Mix all the ingredients and process with a stick blender until everything is well dissolved in the yogurt.
- Stand in the refrigerator for 8 hours, then process in the sorbet maker.
- Store in the freezer.

For the instant coffee caramel pieces

125 g fondant
30 g glucose
50 g Isomalt
10 g instant coffee

- Heat up the glucose and fondant.
- When it is half melted, add the Isomalt.
- Raise the temperature of the mixture to 160 °C and remove from the heat (the remaining 5 °C will be reached by its own heat).
- When the caramel stops boiling, add the instant coffee while stirring with a spatula.
- Spread over parchment paper and slice into 4 cm squares before it cools.
- When the caramel is cold, place between 2 sheets of parchment paper and crush with a rolling pin to obtain small pieces of instant coffee caramel.
- Store in an airtight container in a cool, dry place.

For the instant coffee caramel teardrops

Instant coffee caramel pieces (previously prepared)

- Spread the pieces over a baking tray lined with a Silpat.
- Melt in the oven at 175 °C for 1 minute to obtain instant coffee caramel teardrops.
- Remove them from the tray with a small spatula and store them in an airtight container in a cool, dry place.

For the bitter almond and yogurt powder

50 g bitter almonds
30 g sugar
10 g water
30 g Pral yogurt powder
2 g powdered citric acid

- Boil the sugar with the water until it reaches 117 °C.
- Remove from the heat, add the bitter almonds and stir until the almonds are coated with sugar; then leave to cool on parchment paper.
- Blend the bitter almond coated in yogurt powder and citric acid in a liquidiser.
- Store in an airtight container in a cool, dry place.

For the fresh lemon verbena water

70 g fresh lemon verbena leaves
0.6 g ascorbic acid
Water

- Blanch the leaves in water for 20 seconds.
- Drain and chill in iced water.
- Blend the blanched lemon verbena leaves with 120 g of cold cooking water and the ascorbic acid in a liquidiser.
- Strain and refrigerate in an airtight container.

1187

**Peach-CRU in amaretto
with electric ice cream**

For the lemon verbena concentrate

100 g fresh lemon verbena water
(previously prepared)

- Pour 50 g of the tarragon water into each
  of 2 centrifuge tubes and 50 g of water
  in the other 2 tubes.
- Spin in the centrifuge for 5 minutes at 100 rpm.
- When the process is complete, separate
  the water from on top of the concentrated pulp
  that has settled at the bottom of each tube.
- Transfer the concentrate to a piping bag, vacuum
  seal and refrigerate.

For the 100% syrup

25 g water
25 g sugar

- Mix both ingredients and bring to the boil.
- Refrigerate.

**For the lemon verbena concentrate
and 100% syrup**

Lemon verbena concentrate (previously prepared)
25 g 100% syrup (previously prepared)

- Blend the 100% syrup with the lemon verbena
  concentrate. The resulting texture should
  be a thick cream.
- Refrigerate.

For the peach-CRU in amaretto

2 x 300 g vineyard peaches
65 g Disaronno amaretto
105 g water

- Cut 5 mm from each end of the peaches
  to remove their irregularities. Peel the peaches
  and pit them with a pineapple corer.
- In the slicer cut them into 2 mm slices.
  It is essential to stack the slices immediately after
  they come out of the slicer so that the 2 peaches
  are reconstructed.
- Place the 2 reconstructed peaches in a vacuum
  bag with the water and amaretto.
- Vacuum seal and refrigerate for 6 hours.

For the peach-CRU in amaretto portions

2 peach-CRU in amaretto (previously prepared)

- Open the bags and drain.
- Cut the 2 peaches in half vertically.
- Slice 2 mm off each peach half.
- Remove the smallest outer slices from each
  of the peach halves (4 in total).
- You should now have 4 halves 3 cm thick
  at the centre.
- Refrigerate.

For the fresh lemon sugar

50 g sugar
Zest of ½ lemon grated with a Microplane grater
0.7 g powdered citric acid
8 g lemon juice

- Mix all the ingredients in a bowl without dissolving
  the sugar.
- Refrigerate.

For the Szechuan button crumbs

4 Szechuan button flowers

- Use a paring knife to break up the Szechuan
  button flowers into crumbs.
- Refrigerate.

  NB: The Szechuan button causes an electrical
  effect on the palate. It is the flower of the
  Spilanthes oleracea, native of Sichuan (formerly
  Szechuan) province in China. It is also found
  in Madagascar and the Amazon region. It is also
  known as jambu in certain areas of South America.

1187

**Peach-CRU in amaretto
with electric ice cream**

Finishing and presentation

4 x 5 mm fresh basil leaves
4 fresh lemon thyme leaves

- Process the yogurt ice cream in the sorbet-maker.
- Take it out of the sorbet maker and add the crumbled Szechuan buttons.
- Use a fine brush to paint an arc with the lemon verbena concentrate and syrup cream in the middle of an elongated plate.
- Place a portion of peach-CRU in amaretto over it.
- Spread a perpendicular line of bitter almond powder on top.
- Put a basil leaf on one side of the peach-CRU and a lemon thyme leaf on the other.
- Place 1 g of lemon sugar on the right side of the plate 2 cm from the peach-CRU.
- Place 2 freeze-dried white peach foam rocks on the left side of the peach-CRU.
- Make a quenelle of the yogurt ice cream with Szechuan button and place it on top of the peach-CRU.
- Finish by arranging 5 instant coffee caramel tears over the yogurt ice cream quenelle.

Cutlery

- Carving knife and fork.

How to eat

- Alternate the ice cream with the peach and other components.

1188

Mango-puzzle with frozen elderflower wedge and coconut foam

Year
2005

Family
Desserts

Temperature
Cold/frozen

Season
All year round

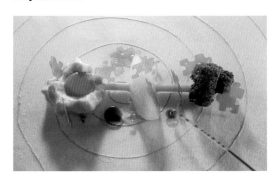

Serves 4

For the mango crisp base

150 g Garnier mango purée
45 g icing sugar
25 g Isomalt
5 g glucose

- Blend the mango purée, Isomalt, glucose and half the icing sugar in a Thermomix at 80 °C for 5 minutes.
- Strain the mixture and add the rest of the sugar, stirring with a spatula.
- Store in an airtight container.

For the dehydrated mango crisp base puzzle pieces

150 g mango crisp base (previously prepared)
1 transparent sheet the same size as the dehydrator disc making 40 puzzle pieces
1 Silpat the same diameter as the dehydrator disc

- Place the transparent sheet over the Silpat and spread the mango crisp mixture evenly over the circular holes to a depth of 1 mm
- Dry out in a dehydrator for 48 hours at 55 °C.
- Once completely dried, store the mango crisp puzzle pieces in an airtight container in a cool, dry place.

For the frozen elderflower sphere

250 g water
120 g Hafi elderflower concentrate
1 x 7 cm diameter spherical silicone mould

- Mix both ingredients in a bowl.
- Use a syringe to fill the silicone mould with the liquid.
- Freeze at -20 °C for 12 hours.

For the elderflower wedges

1 x 7 cm frozen elderflower sphere (previously prepared)

- Remove the frozen elderflower sphere from the mould.
- Use a serrated knife to cut 4 x 7 cm frozen elderflower wedges measuring 2 cm at their widest point.
- Store in the freezer.

For the 30% syrup

100 g water
30 g sugar

- Mix both ingredients in a small pan and bring to the boil.
- Refrigerate.

For the saffron syrup

125 g 30% syrup (previously prepared)
0.1 g toasted saffron threads

- Bring the syrup to the boil and add the saffron threads.
- Refrigerate for 12 hours.

For the white chocolate and passion fruit ganache

50 g white chocolate
40 g 35% fat single cream
50 g Garnier passion fruit purée
18 g butter

- Crush the chocolate and place it in a bowl.
- Bring the cream to the boil and pour over the chocolate.
- Wait for 30 seconds then mix with a spatula.
- When the mixture is at some 35 °C, add the butter in cubes at room temperature.
- Once the butter has melted completely, add the passion fruit purée and mix.
- Fill a piping bag with a No. 7 nozzle and store in a cool, dry place for 6 hours.

For the coconut milk

125 g Sicoly coconut milk

- Strain and refrigerate.

For the cold coconut milk foam

100 g strained coconut milk (previously prepared)
35 g 35% fat single cream
½ x 2 g gelatine leaf (previously rehydrated in cold water)
1 x 0.5 litre ISI siphon
1 N₂O cartridge

- Dissolve the gelatine in a third of the hot coconut milk.
- Add the rest of the coconut milk and the cream.
- Strain and fill the siphon.
- Close and insert the gas cartridge.
- Refrigerate for 6 hours.

1188

Mango-puzzle with frozen elderflower wedge and coconut foam

For the spherical mango ravioli base

125 g Garnier mango purée
125 g water
0.9 g sodium alginate
0.7 g sodium citrate

- Process the sodium citrate in the water with a stick blender.
- Add the sodium alginate and process again with the stick blender.
- Bring the mixture to the boil, stirring constantly.
- Leave to cool down at room temperature, then add the mango purée and stir.
- Store in an airtight container in a cool, dry place.

For the calcium chloride solution

6.5 g calcium chloride
1 kg water

- Dissolve the calcium chloride in the water with a whisk.
- Set aside.

For the toasted spiced bread with honey

75 g spiced bread with honey

- Cut off the crust.
- Make breadcrumbs in a liquidiser.
- Spread the crumbs over a baking tray lined with a Silpat.
- Bake at 150 °C for 35 minutes.
- It should be toasted to a golden colour as a slightly bitter taste is required.
- Store in an airtight container in a cool, dry place.

For the banana-CRU with saffron syrup

100 g saffron syrup (previously prepared)
1 x 200 g banana

- Peel the banana and cut 2 x 3 cm thick slices.
- Cut each slice vertically into 4 quarters.
- Place the banana and the saffron syrup in a bag and vacuum seal to 45% only.
- Store at room temperature for 6 hours.

1188

Mango-puzzle with frozen elderflower wedge and coconut foam

Finishing and presentation

12 fresh lemon thyme leaves
16 g Familie Engl pumpkin seed oil

- Using a 3 cm diameter hemispherical measuring spoon, make 4 x 15 g spherical mango ravioli and place them in the calcium chloride solution.
- Leave the spherical mango ravioli to 'cook' in the calcium chloride solution for 2 minutes.
- Remove from the calcium chloride solution and rinse in cold water.
- Pipe an 11 cm line of white chocolate and passion fruit ganache on a rectangular plate.
- Coat 2 pieces of the banana-CRU with saffron in the spiced bread crumbs and place them to the far right of the white chocolate and passion fruit ganache.
- Make a small mound of coconut foam to the far left.
- Place a frozen elderflower wedge in the middle of the white chocolate and passion fruit ganache line.
- Arrange 3 fresh lemon thyme leaves around the ganache.
- Place a piece of spherical mango ravioli on top of the coconut foam mound.
- Finish by arranging 4 puzzle pieces on the coconut foam and 6 more on the rest of the plate.
- Fill a pipette with the pumpkin seed oil so that the waiter can serve it in front of the diner.

Cutlery

- Tapas cutlery.

  NB: Tapas cutlery consists of a 14 x 3 cm spoon and fork.

How to eat

- Alternate the components. Eat the spherical ravioli in a single mouthful. Eat the pumpkin seed oil halfway through the dessert.

1189

Red variation

Year
2005

Family
Desserts

Temperature
Ambient

Season
June, July, August, September

Serves 4

For the starch

525 g cornflour

- Sift 525 g of cornflour over a baking tray lined with parchment paper.
- Dry in the oven at 120 °C for 1 hour.
- Sift again, this time filling a container with 450 g to a thickness of 2 cm.
- Set aside 75 g in a separate container.
- Use a mould to make 10 wells in the cornflour.
- It is essential that the walls of the wells are smooth and stable, otherwise the outer layer of the sweets will not be even.

For the gin and menthol sweets

Starch (previously prepared)
125 g sugar
42 g water
50 g gin
1 g menthol crystals
1.5 g water
20 g freeze-dried raspberry powder

- Combine the 42 g of water with the sugar in a pan and boil at 112 °C.
- Use a fine brush with water to keep the sides of the pan clean while boiling.
- Leave the syrup to cool to 85 °C.
- Carefully add the gin along the sides of the pan, then transfer the contents from one pan to another until the mixture is even. Leave to cool at room temperature.
- While the syrup is cooling, heat the 1.5 g of water in the microwave and dissolve the crushed menthol crystals in it. Strain.
- Allow the gin and syrup mixture to cool to 35 °C. Strain the menthol dissolved in water and add.
- When the temperature of the mixture reaches 25 °C, use a teaspoon to fill the wells made in the container of starch with it.
- Store in a cool, dry place for 20 minutes.
- Sift the remaining 75 g of starch over the top.
- After 5 hours, gently turn each sweet over and leave in a cool, dry place.
- After 14 hours, remove the sweets from the starch and clean them with a small brush.
- Keep in an airtight container with the freeze-dried raspberry powder.

For the raspberry water

250 g frozen raspberries
35 g sugar

- Combine both ingredients in a container, cover and heat in the microwave at full power. Remove and stir so that the sugar dissolves.
- Repeat the operation until the temperature of the liquid reaches 70 °C.
- Drain the obtained water through a strainer.
- Refrigerate.

For the cold raspberry water jelly

175 g raspberry water (previously prepared)
1 x 2 g gelatine leaf (previously rehydrated in cold water)
0.7 g powdered agar-agar

- Mix the agar-agar and the raspberry water in a pan.
- Bring to the boil while stirring continuously, then remove from the heat.
- Add the gelatine leaf and dissolve.
- Transfer to a container to a thickness of 1.5 cm and leave to set in the refrigerator for 3 hours.
- Cut into 8 x 1.5 cm cubes and refrigerate

For the freeze-dried raspberry croquant powder

125 g fondant
60 g glucose
60 g Isomalt
32 g freeze-dried raspberry powder

- Mix the fondant and glucose in a pan over a medium heat.
- Once dissolved, add the Isomalt.
- Raise the temperature to 160 °C (the remaining 5 °C will be reached by its own heat), then allow to cool to 140 °C. Add the freeze-dried raspberry powder and stir.
- Pour over parchment paper to a thickness of 1 cm. Allow to cool down at room temperature in a cool, dry place.
- Grind to a powder in a liquidiser.
- Store in an airtight container in a cool, dry place.

1189

Red variation

For the freeze-dried raspberry croquant and raspberry crisp pistachulines

Freeze-dried raspberry croquant powder
(previously prepared)
15 g freeze-dried raspberry crisp

- Sift the raspberry croquant powder over a baking tray lined with a Silpat.
- Heat the oven to 170 °C.
- When the croquant is melted, make 8 small mounds with 4 raspberry crisps over it.
- Use your fingers to stretch the croquant with the crisps to make 8 pistachulines.
- Store in an airtight container in a cool, dry place.

For the strawberry water

500 g frozen strawberries
200 g water
200 g sugar

- Combine the ingredients in a pan and place over a low heat until the mixture breaks into a boil.
- Cover and leave to stand for 10 minutes.
- Strain the water obtained and refrigerate.

For the strawberry air base

500 g strawberry water (previously prepared)
2.5 g soya lecithin powder

- Combine both ingredients in a bowl and process with a stick blender.
- Refrigerate.

For the fresh and frozen watermelon cubes

1 x 150 g piece of watermelon

- Cut the watermelon into 12 x 1.5 cm cubes.
- Store 4 cubes in an airtight container in the refrigerator, store another 4 cubes in the freezer at -10 °C and set the remaining 4 cubes aside for the following preparation.

For the watermelon-CRU cubes in amaretto

4 x 1.5 cm watermelon cubes (previously prepared)
65 g Disaronno amaretto
105 g water

- Combine the water, amaretto and watermelon cubes in a vacuum bag.
- Vacuum seal and refrigerate.

For the semi-dehydrated cherry halves and the fresh cherry halves

4 x 8.5 g cherries

- Halve and stone the cherries.
- Dehydrate 4 cherry halves at 55 °C for 2½ hours.
- Refrigerate the other 4 halves in an airtight container.
- Store the dehydrated cherry halves in an airtight container in a cool, dry place.

For the semi-dehydrated strawberry quarters and the fresh strawberry quarters

2 x 15 g strawberries

- Remove the green cap from the strawberries.
- Quarter the strawberries.
- Dehydrate 4 strawberry quarters at 55 °C for 2½ hours.
- Refrigerate the 4 fresh quarters in an airtight container.
- Store the dehydrated strawberry quarters in an airtight container in a cool, dry place.

For the semi-dehydrated raspberries and the fresh raspberries

8 x 2.5 g raspberries

- Dehydrate 4 raspberries at 55 °C for 2½ hours.
- Store the dehydrated raspberries in an airtight container in a cool, dry place and refrigerate the fresh raspberries in an airtight container.

For the pink grapefruit wedges

1 x 125 g pink grapefruit

- Peel the pink grapefruit.
- Use a knife to separate 4 segments, removing any pith or membrane.
- Cut 4 pink grapefruit segments with a thickness of 1.5 cm.
- Refrigerate.

1189

Red variation

Finishing and presentation

4 x 0.5 cm diameter redcurrants
4 x 1.5 g wild strawberries
12 elderberries
16 fresh beetroot shoots
8 purple shiso shoots
4 whole freeze-dried raspberries
4 freeze-dried strawberry slices

NB: Shiso is a kind of Asian herb similar to basil and mint. There are 2 varieties, purple and green.

- Imagining the plate as a clock face, arrange the components at the base of a soup plate as follows.
- Place 1 cube of watermelon-CRU in amaretto in the 12 o'clock position.
- Place 1 fresh wild strawberry after it.
- Follow with 1 cube of raspberry jelly, then 1 semi-dehydrated cherry half.
- Place a fresh raspberry at 3 o'clock.
- Leave a space for 1 frozen watermelon cube and another space for 1 raspberry pistachuline, which will be placed there later.
- Place 1 fresh strawberry quarter at 5 o'clock.
- Place 1 cold raspberry jelly cube at 6 o'clock.
- Place 1 pink grapefruit wedge after it.
- Follow with a semi-dehydrated strawberry quarter.
- Place 1 fresh watermelon cube at 9 o'clock.
- Place 1 semi-dehydrated raspberry after it.
- Follow with 1 gin sweet with freeze-dried raspberry powder.
- Then place 1 fresh cherry half. There should be space for 1 raspberry pistachuline before coming back to the watermelon-CRU in amaretto.
- Work the stick blender over the surface of the strawberry air base until it emulsifies and air forms.
- Place 3 elderberries along the edge of the dish.
- Place 2 purple shiso shoots, 1 at 7 o'clock and the other at 3 o'clock.
- Arrange 4 beetroot shoots, 2 at 7 o'clock and 2 at 12 o'clock.
- Place 1 freeze-dried raspberry on top of the watermelon-CRU in amaretto.
- Place 1 half of a freeze-dried strawberry slice on top of the fresh strawberry quarter.
- Now place the 2 raspberry pistachulines in the spaces left free for them.
- Finish with a spoon of strawberry air in the middle of the dish.

Cutlery

- Tapas cutlery.

  NB: Tapas cutlery consists of a 14 x 3 cm spoon and fork.

How to eat

- Drag your spoon from the middle of the plate to each of the different components of the dish.

1190

Strawberries or roses?

Year
2005

Family
Desserts

Temperature
Ambient/frozen

Season
April, May, June, July

Serves 4

For the light strawberry meringue

200 g water
6 g powdered egg white
150 g Garnier strawberry concentrate
2 x 2 g gelatine leaves (previously rehydrated in cold water)

- Put the powdered egg white in the water and leave to hydrate for 5 minutes.
- Dissolve the gelatine in a third of the hot strawberry concentrate.
- Add the rest of the concentrate and mix.
- Whip the egg white and water mixture in an electric mixer.
- When it forms peaks, add the strawberry and gelatine mixture.
- Whip for 3 more minutes then fill a piping bag with a 7 mm nozzle.
- Line a dehydrator disc with parchment paper, then pipe 8 x 6 cm diameter lattices over it.
- Dehydrate for 12 hours at 30 °C and a further 8 hours at 55 °C.
- Store in an airtight container in a cool, dry place.

For the cream cheese and Greek yogurt ice cream

120 g Philadelphia cream cheese
125 g Greek yogurt
105 g water
90 g rosemary honey
2.3 g ice cream stabiliser
1 drop red food colouring

- Combine the water and stabiliser in a pan.
- Stir over a medium heat to a temperature of 85 °C.
- Remove from the heat and add the honey.
- Stand in the refrigerator for 12 hours.
- Add the cream cheese and yogurt. Mix.
- Tint the mixture with the food colouring.
- Mix well with a whisk and refrigerate.

For the steamed sponge

4 x 65 g eggs
125 g plain flour
125 g sugar
3 g baking powder
3 drops red food colouring

- Beat 2 eggs with the sugar.
- When they are thoroughly beaten, add 1 egg, then add the other egg 5 minutes later. Continue to beat until the mixture is well whipped.
- Sift the flour and baking powder over the egg mixture, gradually folding it in with a spatula.
- Tint the mixture with the 3 drops of red food colouring.
- Spread the mixture out to a 5 mm thickness over parchment paper.
- Cook in the steamer at 90 °C for 5½ minutes.
- Cut 2 x 6 cm diameter discs, then cut them in half.
- Store in an airtight container in a cool, dry place.

For the 100% syrup

100 g water
100 g sugar

- Mix the ingredients in a small pan and bring to the boil.
- Refrigerate.

For the rose petals with syrup

1 fresh rose
150 g 100% syrup (previously prepared)
1 drop rose essential oil

- Break up the rose and separate 8 well-formed petals from the centre. Choose the smallest as they will be more tender.
- Mix the rose petals with the syrup and the rose essential oil in a bowl and refrigerate for 25 minutes.

For the caramelised rose petals

Rose petals in 100% syrup (previously prepared)

- Drain off the syrup from the rose petals and spread over a baking tray lined with a Silpat.
- Bake at 120 °C for 12 minutes.
- Store in an airtight container in a cool, dry place.

For the quark cheese and rose water cream

100 g Quark cheese, or similar
2 g rose water
1 drop red food colouring

- Mix the rose water with the cheese and tint with the red food colouring.
- Fill a piping bag with the mixture and refrigerate.

1190

Strawberries or roses?

For the strawberry water

500 g frozen strawberries
200 g sugar
200 g water

- Mix the ingredients in a pot and place over a low heat.
- When the mixture begins to simmer, remove it from the heat and cover.
- Keep covered for 30 minutes, then strain without pressing so that the strawberries release all their water.
- Refrigerate.

For the strawberry water air base

500 g strawberry water (previously prepared)
2.5 g soya lecithin powder

- Mix both ingredients cold and process with a stick blender.

For the 20% syrup

250 g water
50 g sugar

- Mix the ingredients in a small pan and bring to the boil.
- Refrigerate.

For the lychees in syrup

4 fresh lychees
200 g 20% syrup (previously prepared)

- Peel the lychees.
- Bring the syrup to the boil and add the lychees.
- Remove from the heat and refrigerate.
- When the lychees are cold, halve them and remove the pit.
- Use a sharp knife to remove the inner skin from each lychee half.
- Cover the lychee halves with their syrup and refrigerate.

For the Parmesan water

125 g grated Parmesan cheese
110 g water

- Bring the water to a boil in a pan and add the grated cheese.
- Stir until the cheese dissolves.
- Remove from the heat and leave to infuse for 1 hour.
- Strain the resulting paste through a Superbag to release all the water. Discard the paste.
- Refrigerate the Parmesan water for 12 hours.

For the Parmesan shavings

1 x 100 g piece of Parmesan cheese
100 g Parmesan water
(previously prepared)

- Stand the ingredients out of the refrigerator for 3 hours.
- Make 4 well-formed Parmesan shavings with a peeler.
- Soak the shavings in the Parmesan water for 5 minutes before finishing and presentation.

For the strawberries

4 x 5 g strawberries

- Remove the cap from the strawberries and clean them.
- Refrigerate in an airtight container.

1190

Strawberries or roses?

Finishing and presentation

4 freeze-dried strawberry slices
50 g Disaronno amaretto

- Process the cream cheese and yogurt ice cream in the sorbet-maker.
- Brush 2 steamed sponge pieces with the amaretto until soaked and cut them in half.
- Work the stick blender over the surface of the strawberry air base until it emulsifies and the air forms.
- Pipe 2 lines of quark and rose water cream over the base of an O! LUNA large eclipse plate.
- Place 1 light strawberry meringue in the middle of the plate over the cream.
- Place a piece of steamed sponge on top of it.
- Place 2 lychee halves, 1 strawberry quarter and 1 freeze-dried strawberry slice on top of the sponge.
- Lean 1 quenelle of cream cheese and yogurt ice cream against the meringue. Place a Parmesan shaving over it.
- Cover everything with another light strawberry meringue.
- Finish the dish by piercing the cream cheese and yogurt ice cream quenelle with a rose petal and placing a spoon of strawberry water air behind it.

Cutlery

- Tapas cutlery.

  NB: Tapas cutlery consists of a 14 x 3 cm spoon and fork.

How to eat

- Alternate the components.

1191

Mont Blanc

Year
2005

Family
Desserts

Temperature
Cold/frozen

Season
All year round

Serves 4

For the vanilla-infused cream

250 g 35% fat single cream
¾ x 4 g vanilla pod
½ x 2 g gelatine leaf (previously rehydrated in cold water)

- Split open the vanilla pod lengthways and place in a pan with the cream.
- Bring to the boil and cover.
- Leave to infuse for 20 minutes, then strain.
- Dissolve the gelatine in the cream while still hot.
- Refrigerate for 12 hours in an airtight container.

For the whipped vanilla-infused cream

Vanilla-infused cream (previously prepared)

- Whip the cream in an electric mixer and fill a piping bag with a No. 8 nozzle.
- Pipe 4 6 x 6 cm mounds of cream.
- Freeze for 2 hours.

For the chestnut in syrup discs

4 chestnuts in syrup

- Leave the chestnuts to drain for 2 hours outside the refrigerator.
- Place 1 chestnut in syrup between 2 sheets of clingfilm.
- Use a rolling pin to flatten it into a disc with a thickness of 1 mm.
- Set aside.

For the Mont Blancs

4 frozen vanilla-infused cream mounds (previously prepared)
4 chestnut in syrup discs (previously prepared)

- Cover each cream mound with a chestnut in syrup disc.
- It is essential that the disc fits the shape of the cream mound perfectly.
- Freeze for 2 hours.
- After 2 hours, carefully remove the sheets of clingfilm.
- Refrigerate 3 hours before use so that the cream can thaw completely.

For the coffee and coffee liqueur water ice

125 g espresso coffee
25 g coffee liqueur
10 g sugar

- Dissolve the sugar in the hot espresso coffee.
- Add the coffee liqueur.
- Freeze.
- When frozen, scrape the ice with a spatula to obtain frozen shavings.
- Store in the freezer.

For the sponge discs

100 g egg yolk
100 g sugar
5 egg whites
25 g sugar
100 g plain flour
25 g cornflour

- Beat the egg yolks with the 100 g of sugar.
- Beat the egg whites with the 25 g of sugar.
- Combine both beaten mixtures in a bowl, then sift the corn starch over while folding in gradually with a spatula.
- Spread out over baking trays lined with a Silpat and bake at 210 °C for 7 minutes.
- When cold, cut into 4 cm diameter discs with a pastry-cutter.
- Refrigerate in an airtight container.

For the 100% syrup

100 g sugar
100 g water

- Mix both ingredients and bring to the boil.
- Set aside.

For the cold lime juice jelly

100 g 100% syrup (previously prepared)
50 g lime juice grated zest of 1 lime
1 x 2 g gelatine leaf (previously rehydrated in cold water)

- Heat half of the syrup and dissolve the gelatine in it.
- Remove from the heat and mix with the rest of the syrup and the lime juice.
- Leave to set in the refrigerator for 3 hours.
- When set, mix with the lime zest.
- Refrigerate.

For the dehydrated mint

4 fresh mint leaves

- Put in the dehydrator for 2 hours at 60 °C until completely crisp.
- Store in an airtight container in a cool, dry place.

1191

Mont Blanc

Finishing and presentation

Coconut milk powder
1 lime
1 Microplane grater
75 g cold espresso coffee

- Sprinkle the Mont Blanc with the coconut milk powder.
- Place a broken-up dehydrated mint leaf with a little grated lime zest at the bottom of the Mont Blanc.
- Place a sponge disc lightly soaked in espresso coffee in the middle of an O! LUNA small eclipse plate.
- Place 20 g of lime jelly on the upper part of the dish in such a way that the thinnest part ends at the centre of the dish.
- Place 10 g of coffee ice water on top of the sponge disc.
- Finish by placing the Mont Blanc on top of sponge and water ice.

Cutlery

- Tapas cutlery.

  NB: Tapas cutlery consists of a 14 x 3 cm spoon and fork.

How to eat

- Gradually eat the Mont Blanc alternating each mouthful with the lime jelly to refresh the palate.

1192

Pea jelly with banana and lime ice cream

Year
2005

Family
Desserts

Temperature
Frozen/cold

Season
All year round

Serves 4

For the 100% syrup

50 g sugar
50 g water

- Mix the ingredients in a small pan and bring to the boil.
- Refrigerate.

For the water and pea pulp

200 g frozen petits pois
200 g water
100 g 100% syrup (previously prepared)

- Combine the ingredients in a liquidiser and blend for 1 minute.
- Transfer to a strainer and leave to drain in the refrigerator for 12 hours.
- Set aside both the pea water and the pea pulp from the strainer separately.
- Refrigerate.

For the pea crisp base

150 g pea water (previously prepared)
20 g icing sugar
25 g Isomalt
5 g glucose

- Mix all the ingredients in the Thermomix and process at 80 °C for 4 minutes.
- Refrigerate.

For the pea crisps

Pea crisp base
(previously prepared)
12 x 3 cm banana-shaped PVC mould

- Spread the crisp base in the PVC mould over a circular Silpat the size of the dehydrator disc.
- Lay out 4 bananas.
- Put in the dehydrator for 48 hours at 55 °C.
- Heat the crisps in the oven at 150 °C for 5 seconds and bend them while still hot to create a hollow space in the middle for an ice cream quenelle during finishing and presentation.
- Bend the crisp at the narrowest part leaving the widest part straight.

For the plates with cold pea water jelly

150 g pea water (previously prepared)
1 x 2 g gelatine leaf (previously rehydrated in cold water)

- Dissolve the gelatine in a quarter of the hot pea water.
- Add the cold remaining pea water and mix.
- Place 30 g of pea water jelly in each O! LUNA deep lunar plate.
- Refrigerate for 3 hours.

For the lime ice cream

225 g milk
30 g 35% fat single cream
6 g powdered milk
9 g dextrose
30 g sugar
1.2 g ice cream stabiliser
85 g lime juice
2 limes
1 Microplane grater

- Mix the cream with the milk in a pan and heat to 50 °C.
- Mix the powdered milk, sugar, stabiliser and dextrose and add to the milk and cream mixture. Whisk until the mixture reaches 85 °C.
- Leave to stand in the refrigerator for 8 hours.
- Add the juice of the 2 limes and their grated zest while mixing with a whisk.
- Leave to stand for 5 minutes, then strain.

For the dark syrup

100 g sugar
125 g water

- Caramelise the sugar in a pan. Remove it from the heat when it turns dark.
- Add the warm water and mix. If necessary, heat lightly so that the syrup will be even.
- Refrigerate.

For the banana marinated in dark syrup

2 ripe bananas
200 g dark syrup (previously prepared)

- Peel the banana and cut into 5 cm lengths.
- Trim both sides to leave the pieces with a thickness of 1.7 cm.
- Use a pointed knife to make a diagonal incision in the middle of one of the trimmed sides.
- Place the banana in a container and cover them with dark syrup.
- Store at room temperature for 24 hours.

1192

Pea jelly with banana and lime ice cream

For the 60% syrup

60 g sugar
100 g water

- Mix the ingredients in a small pan and bring to the boil.
- Refrigerate.

For the pineapple-CRU in aniseed liqueur

1 x 150 g piece pineapple
100 g 60% syrup (previously prepared)
30 g dry aniseed liqueur

- Cut the pineapple into 4 x 2 cm cubes.
- Vacuum seal with the syrup and the aniseed liqueur.
- Refrigerate for 4 hours.

For the cold Greek yogurt jelly

1 x 125 g tub Greek yogurt
75 g water
½ x 2 g gelatine leaf (previously rehydrated in cold water)
0.5 g powdered agar-agar

- Combine the water and agar-agar in a pan.
- Bring to the boil stirring constantly with a whisk, then remove from the heat.
- Add the gelatine leaf and mix with the Greek yogurt.
- Pour into a container to a thickness of 2 cm.
- Leave to set in the refrigerator for 3 hours.
- Cut 4 x 2 cm cubes.
- Refrigerate.

Finishing and presentation

12 fresh fennel shoots
Pral yogurt powder
The seeds of 1 passion fruit

- Process the lime ice cream in the sorbet maker. In the meantime, drain the marinated banana and the pineapple in aniseed liqueur.
- Place the pineapple cube on the upper left of the plate.
- Place a piece of marinated banana in the middle, forming a diagonal with the pineapple cube.
- Arrange 3 passion fruit seeds and 3 fresh fennel shoots around it.
- Place a cold yogurt jelly cube on the lower right.
- The pineapple, banana and yogurt gelatine cubes should be in a straight line.
- Place a fresh fennel shoot on top of the yogurt cube.
- Sprinkle yogurt powder over the incision in the banana.
- Make a quenelle with the lime ice cream and place it diagonally on top of the banana cube.
- Finish the dish by placing the pea crisp around the quenelle.

Cutlery

- Tapas cutlery.

  NB: Tapas cutlery consists of a 14 x 3 cm spoon and fork.

How to eat

- Alternate the components, leaving the pineapple cube at one end of the dish until last.

1193

Thai ice cream nigiri with lime marshmallow

Year
2005

Family
Desserts

Temperature
Frozen/warm

Season
All year round

Serves 4

For the Thai ice cream

250 g water
112 g glucose
65 g sugar
2.3 g ice cream stabiliser
200 g tinned coconut milk
90 g coconut milk powder
50 g fresh coriander
50 fresh basil
75 g peeled fresh ginger
6 fresh kaffir lime leaves
2.5 stalks lime grass

- Mix the water and glucose on a medium heat.
- Mix the stabiliser and sugar and add them when the temperature of the glucose mixture reaches 50 °C.
- Heat to 85 °C, stirring constantly.
- Combine the coconut milk with the coconut milk powder in a bowl and process with a stick blender.
- Add the stabiliser base while continuing to process with the stick blender.
- Set aside two thirds of the coconut and stabiliser mixture.
- Blanch and cool the coriander and basil leaves and combine with the remaining third of the mixture.
- Blend in a liquidiser.
- Without straining, add the crushed lemon grass, peeled and chopped fresh ginger and broken up kaffir lime leaves.
- Heat to 50 °C, then cover. Leave to infuse for 20 minutes.
- Strain through a Superbag, then mix with the two thirds of the mixture that was previously set aside.
- Refrigerate.

For the icing sugar with cornflour

95 g icing sugar
5 g cornflour

- Mix both ingredients in a bowl.
- Store in an airtight container in a cool, dry place.

For the lime juice marshmallow

90 g lime juice
5 x 2 g gelatine leaves (previously rehydrated in cold water)
250 g sugar
120 g water
10 g glucose
40 g egg white
Grated zest of 1 lime
1 Microplane grater
Icing sugar with cornflour (previously prepared)

- Boil the sugar with the water in a pan until the temperature reaches 117 °C.
- Remove from the heat and leave to cool to 85 °C.
- In the meantime, dissolve the gelatine leaves in a third of the lime juice.
- When they are dissolved, remove from the heat and add the remaining juice while mixing with a whisk. It is essential that the caramel is at 85 °C when the gelatine is at about 35 °C.
- Whip the egg whites in the electric mixer. When they are close to forming peaks, gradually pour in the syrup at 85 °C.
- Alternate the syrup with the gelatine and lime juice mixture. The egg whites must remain spongy.
- When the marshmallow mixture is thoroughly whipped, add the grated zest of 1 lime.
- While at room temperature, spread the marshmallow mixture over a transparent sheet previously sprinkled with the icing sugar and cornflour to a thickness of 1 cm.
- Sift the icing sugar and cornflour over it.
- Leave to stand at room temperature for 2 hours, then cut 4 7.2 x 2.5 cm rectangles.
- Store in an airtight container in a cool, dry place.

For the toasted Japanese white sesame seed *gomashio*

50 g toasted Japanese white sesame seeds
15 g muscovado sugar
0.3 g salt

- Blend the ingredients in a liquidiser to obtain a coarse powder.
- Store in an airtight container in a cool, dry place.

NB: *Gomashio* is the name given to a Japanese condiment made from sesame seeds and salt used for seasoning.

1193

Thai ice cream nigiri with lime marshmallow

For the macerated grated coconut

¼ fresh coconut
25 g strained Sicoly coconut milk

- Split open the coconut and separate the shell from the pulp.
- Peel the pulp and grate.
- Mix 35 g of grated coconut with the strained coconut milk.
- Refrigerate in an airtight container.

For the Thai grapefruit segment granules

1 segment Thai grapefruit

- Peel the segment and separate the pulp granules without breaking them.
- Refrigerate in an airtight container.

For the of glazed ginger slices

1 piece glazed ginger

- Cut 12 x 0.1 g slices.
- Store in an airtight container.

Finishing and presentation

12 x 0.5 cm fresh basil leaves
20 g tamarind paste in a piping bag
Madras curry powder
20 coriander shoots
1 lime
1 Microplane grater

- Pipe 5 g of tamarind paste on the lower right part of a round flat plate.
- Use a spatula to spread it upwards making it resemble a brushstroke.
- Put 3 pieces of glazed ginger on the far right of the brushstroke.
- Place 0.5 g of gomashio above the brushstroke and 2 g below it.
- Sprinkle the Thai grapefruit granules over the rest of the plate without touching the tamarind paste.
- Arrange 3 basil leaves and 5 coriander shoots over them.
- Make a small mound of marinated coconut on the far left.
- Sprinkle a little curry powder over the coconut.
- Make a quenelle of Thai ice cream and place it over the gomashio above the tamarind paste.
- Place a rectangle of lime marshmallow over the quenelle with the side with more sugar facing downward.
- Use a blow torch to caramelise the top of the marshmallow.
- Finish by sprinkling a little grated lime zest over the marshmallow.

Cutlery

- Tapas cutlery.

  NB: Tapas cutlery consists of a 14 x 3 cm spoon and fork.

How to eat

- Alternate the components in different combinations.

1194

Figs with light rose and white chocolate meringue powder

Year
2005

Family
Desserts

Temperature
Cold/frozen

Season
June, July, August

Serves 4

For the fig sorbet

8 x 65 g figs

- Clean the figs without peeling them. Place them in a Pacojet beaker and press them down.
- Freeze at -20 °C.

For the 100% syrup

25 g water
25 g sugar

- Mix both ingredients and bring to the boil.
- Refrigerate.

For the light rose meringue powder

225 g water
6 g powdered egg white
40 g 100% syrup
1½ x 2 g gelatine leaves (previously rehydrated in cold water)
25 g rose water

- Place the water and powdered egg white in the cream whipping machine bowl and leave for 5 minutes to rehydrate.
- In the meantime, mix the syrup with the gelatine in a bowl.
- Dissolve at 40 °C.
- Whip the egg white until it forms peaks, then gradually add the gelatine when it is at about 35 °C.
- Whip for 30 seconds, then add the cold rose water.
- Whip for a further 20 seconds, then spread the mixture over a Silpat for the dehydrator.
- Dehydrate at 30 °C for 12 hours, and at 55 °C for 12 more hours.
- Place the meringue inside a bag and crush it to obtain a fine light rose meringue powder.
- Store in an airtight container in a cool, dry place.

For the white chocolate powder

100 g white chocolate

- Chop the chocolate into even pieces and freeze them for at least 1 hour.
- Grind to a coarse powder in a liquidiser.

For the toasted spiced bread with honey

75 g spiced bread with honey

- Cut off the crust.
- Make breadcrumbs in a liquidiser.
- Spread the crumbs over a baking tray lined with a Silpat.
- Bake at 150 °C for 35 minutes.
- It should be toasted to a golden colour as a slightly bitter taste is required.
- Store in an airtight container in a cool, dry place.

For the semi-dehydrated figs

2 x 60 g figs

- Halve the figs horizontally.
- Cut the wider part into 4 equal quarters.
- Dehydrate for 4 hours.
- Store in an airtight container in a cool, dry place.

1194

Figs with light rose and white chocolate meringue powder

For the dark syrup

200 g sugar
250 g water

- Caramelise the sugar in a pan. Remove it from the heat when it turns dark.
- Add the warm water and mix. If necessary, heat lightly so that the syrup will be even.
- Refrigerate.

For the cold dark syrup jelly

250 g dark syrup (previously prepared)
12.5 g Sosa powdered plant-based gelling agent

- Combine the dark syrup and the gelling agent in a pan.
- Bring to the boil, stirring constantly.
- Keep hot until the following step.

For the figs bathed in cold dark syrup jelly

2 x 60 g figs
Cold dark syrup jelly (previously prepared)

- Peel and halve the figs.
- Trim a little off the base of each fig so that they will be steady.
- Bathe 1 fig half at a time in the hot jelly and lay them over a tray lined with parchment paper.
- Repeat the operation until all the fig halves have 2 coatings of dark syrup jelly.

For the glazed ginger

1 piece glazed ginger

- Cut 4 x 5 mm cubes.
- Store in an airtight container in a cool, dry place.

Finishing and presentation

8 fresh lavender flowers
8 g freeze-dried passion fruit crisps
125 g Greek yogurt in a squeeze bottle.
Pacojet

- Process the fig sorbet with a Pacojet.
- Place 2.5 g of toasted spiced bread in the middle of an O! LUNA small eclipse plate.
- Place 2 glazed ginger cubes on top.
- Spread a curved tear of white chocolate powder on the left.
- Continuing from the white chocolate, pipe 15 g of Greek yogurt in a line around the spiced bread.
- Cover the Greek yogurt completely with light rose meringue powder.
- Arrange two lavender flowers over the meringue powder, alternating with two freeze-dried passion fruit crisps.
- Place 10 g of fig sorbet over the spiced bread.
- Place 1 fig half bathed in cold dark syrup jelly on top of the sorbet.
- Finish with 1 semi-dehydrated fig quarter on top of the bathed fig.

Cutlery

- Tapas cutlery.

  NB: Tapas cutlery consists of a 14 x 3 cm spoon and fork.

How to eat

- Start with the figs (sorbet, bathed) mixing them with the white chocolate. Finish with the meringue powder and yogurt.

1195

Light honey meringue with apple-CRU and rosemary and cinnamon ice cream

Year
2005

Family
Desserts

Temperature
Ambient/frozen

Season
All year round

Serves 4

For the rosemary and cinnamon ice cream

270 g milk
30 g 35% fat single cream
60 g egg yolk
45 g sugar
30 g glucose
3 g fresh rosemary
3 g cinnamon stick
1.3 g ice cream stabiliser

- Combine the milk, cream, glucose, rosemary and cinnamon in a pan and bring to the boil.
- Remove from the heat and cover.
- Leave to infuse for 7 minutes.
- Strain. Set the cinnamon stick aside.
- Mix the egg yolk with the sugar and stabiliser in a bowl with a whisk.
- Blanch the mixture in the strained infusion.
- Transfer to a pan and heat, stirring constantly with a spatula until it reaches 85 °C.
- Strain and add the cinnamon stick.
- Leave to stand in the refrigerator for 12 hours.
- Strain.

For the 30% syrup

150 g water
45 g sugar

- Mix both ingredients and bring to the boil.
- Refrigerate.

For the 30% syrup with ascorbic acid

150 g 30% syrup (previously prepared)
1.6 g ascorbic acid

- Pour the syrup into a bowl and add the ascorbic acid.
- Dissolve the ascorbic acid in the syrup with a whisk.
- Refrigerate in an airtight container.

For the apple-CRU wedges

1 x 150 g Granny Smith apple
150 g 30% syrup with ascorbic acid
(previously prepared)

- Peel the apple with a peeler.
- Cut 8 vertical wedges measuring 6 cm in length and 1.5 cm at their widest point.
- Immerse them immediately in the 30% syrup with ascorbic acid and vacuum seal.
- Refrigerate for 24 hours.

For the rosemary honey water

50 g rosemary honey
Water

- Bring the rosemary honey to the boil in a pan.
- Add a little water, then place on the scales to weigh.
- Gradually add water until the water and honey mixture reaches 125 g.
- Refrigerate.

For the light rosemary honey meringue

125 g rosemary honey water (previously prepared)
125 g pasteurised liquid egg white

- Combine both cold ingredients in the electric mixer.
- Whip on a fast speed for 10 minutes.
- Use 2 spoons to make 12 small mounds of honey meringue on a baking tray lined with a Silpat.
- Make 8 x 8 cm long mounds and another 4 x 6 cm mounds.
- Bake at 100 °C for 40 minutes.
- Raise the temperature to 120 °C without taking the meringues out of the oven and bake for a further 40 minutes.
- When ready, they will have a light golden colour and the base of each meringue will be caramelised.
- Store in an airtight container in a cool, dry place.

1195

**Light honey meringue
with apple-CRU and rosemary
and cinnamon ice cream**

Finishing and presentation

100 g fresh *mató* curd cheese
1 lemon
12 fresh rosemary flowers
1 Microplane grater

- Process the rosemary and cinnamon ice cream in the sorbet-maker.
- Arrange 5 x 5 g pieces of *mató* cheese in the base of an O! LUNA large eclipse plate.
- Open the vacuum bag containing the apple wedges and drain.
- Place 2 apple wedges among the *mató* pieces and place 1 rosemary flower at one end of each wedge.
- Great a little lemon zest over the *mató*.
- Arrange 2 long and 1 short dry honey meringues in the middle of the plate, allowing the apple-CRU wedges to be seen.
- Place a quenelle of rosemary and cinnamon ice cream in the centre of the 3 meringues so it is equally held up by the meringues.
- Finish the dish with a rosemary flower at the wider end of the quenelle.

Cutlery

- Tapas cutlery.

  NB: Tapas cutlery consists of a 14 x 3 cm spoon and fork.

How to eat

- Mix a little ice cream with the meringue and then with the other components.

1196

Chocolate air-LYO with crisp raspberry sorbet and eucalyptus water ice

Year
2005

Family
Desserts

Temperature
Frozen/ambient

Season
All year round

Serves 4

For the chocolate and hazelnut praline air base

1 kg water
400 g chocolate
50 g Piedmont hazelnut praline
5 g soya lecithin powder

- Crush the chocolate and place it in a bowl.
- Add the praline and lecithin.
- Heat the water to 90 °C and add the chocolate, praline and soya lecithin powder solution.
- Allow to stand for 1 minute, then process with a stick blender.
- Maintain the temperature at 50 °C.

For the frozen chocolate and hazelnut praline air

Chocolate and hazelnut praline air base
(previously prepared)
2 containers, 10 x 20 x 5 cm

- Work the stick blender over the top of the chocolate and praline mixture until it emulsifies and the air forms on top of the liquid.
- Fill the 2 containers with this air and freeze immediately.
- Leave in the freezer for 2 hours with an airtight lid to prevent the frozen air from absorbing other flavours.

For the freeze-dried chocolate and hazelnut praline air

Frozen chocolate and hazelnut praline air
(previously prepared)

- Place in the freeze-dryer for 48 hours.
- Once the freeze-drying process is complete, store in an airtight container in a cool, dry place.

For the 100% syrup

50 g sugar
50 g water

- Mix the ingredients in a small pan and bring to the boil.
- Refrigerate.

For the raspberry sorbet

200 g raspberries
50 g 100% syrup (previously prepared)
1 g sorbet stabilizer
25 g glucose
Pacojet

- Combine the glucose and 100% syrup in a pan at a medium heat.
- When the temperature reaches 40 °C, add the powdered stabiliser and turn the heat up to 85 °C.
- At the same time, purée the raspberries in the liquidiser.
- When the base containing the stabilizer is warm, add the raspberry purée and strain.
- Mix and then allow to stand in the refrigerator for 8 hours.
- Transfer to a Pacojet beaker and freeze at -20 °C.

For the eucalyptus leaf infusion

500 g water
65 g sugar
25 g young eucalyptus leaves

- Combine the water and sugar in a small pan and bring to the boil.
- Chop the eucalyptus leaves and add to the pan.
- Cover and infuse for 5 minutes.
- Strain.

For the eucalyptus leaf water ice

300 g eucalyptus leaf infusion (previously prepared)
½ x 2 g gelatine leaf (previously rehydrated in cold water)

- Dissolve the gelatine in a quarter of the eucalyptus infusion.
- Add the remaining infusion and freeze in a shallow container to a depth of 1 cm.
- Freeze at -10 °C.

For the kataifi pastry skein

15 g kataifi pastry

- Shape 4 x 1 g skeins from the kataifi pastry.
- Bake at 210 °C for 5 minutes.
- Store in an airtight container in a cool, dry place.

For the chocolate-sprayed kataifi skeins

150 g chocolate
50 g cocoa butter
4 kataifi skeins (previously prepared)

- Melt the chocolate in a microwave on medium power.
- Add the cocoa butter and let it dissolve. The mixture should be kept at 35 °C.
- When it is free of lumps and the cocoa butter is well melted, fill a chocolate spray gun.
- Spray the kataifi skeins with chocolate and place in the freezer for 20 seconds.
- Repeat this step twice.
- When complete, store in an airtight container in a cool, dry place.

1196

Chocolate air-LYO with crisp raspberry sorbet and eucalyptus water ice

For the chocolate-sprayed raspberries

4 x 2.5 g raspberries
150 g chocolate
50 g cocoa butter

- Melt the chocolate in a microwave.
- Add the cocoa butter and let it dissolve. The chocolate and cocoa butter mixture should be kept at 35 °C.
- When the mixture is lump-free and the cocoa butter is melted, fill a chocolate spray gun.
- Place the 4 raspberries on a tray in the freezer for 3 minutes.
- Spray until evenly coated.
- Refrigerate in an airtight container.

Finishing and presentation

20 g freeze-dried raspberry crisp

- Process the raspberry sorbet with a Pacojet and store in the freezer.
- Scrape the eucalyptus water ice with a spatula to obtain frozen shavings and store them in the freezer.
- Place in a little freeze-dried chocolate air in the middle of an O! LUNA deep lunar plate.
- Mix 7.5 g raspberry sorbet with 1 g freeze-dried raspberry crisp.
- Place in the middle of the dish.
- Imagining the plate as a clock face, place a skein of chocolate-sprayed kataifi pastry at 11 o'clock.
- Place 20 g eucalyptus water ice shavings from 10 o'clock to 5 o'clock.
- Spread 1 g freeze-dried raspberry crisp along the edge of the water ice, bordering the freeze-dried chocolate air.
- Scatter 5.5 g freeze-dried frozen chocolate air over the part of the dish that is not covered by the water ice.
- Place a chocolate-sprayed raspberry opposite the kataifi pastry, where the freeze-dried chocolate air meets the eucalyptus water ice.

Cutlery

- Tapas cutlery.

  NB: Tapas cutlery consists of a 14 x 3 cm spoon and fork.

How to eat

- Eat each element separately and alternately.

1197

Apricot palet with milk chocolate and passion fruit ice cream

Year
2005

Family
Desserts

Temperature
Cold/frozen

Season
All year round

Serves 4

For the 100% syrup

25 g water
25 g sugar

- Mix both ingredients and bring to the boil.
- Refrigerate.

For the cold apricot purée jelly

200 g Garnier apricot purée
25 g water
25 g 100% syrup (previously prepared)
0.6 g powdered agar-agar
1¼ x 2 g gelatine leaf
(previously rehydrated in cold water)

- Combine 75 g of apricot purée with the water and syrup in a pan.
- Add the agar-agar and bring to the boil on a medium heat while stirring constantly.
- Remove from the heat and dissolve the gelatine in the mixture.
- Add the remaining apricot purée and mix.
- Spread the mixture out in a container to a thickness of 8 mm.
- Refrigerate for 3 hours.

For the cold apricot purée jelly squares

Cold apricot purée jelly (previously prepared)

- Cut the jelly into 4 x 5.5 cm squares.
- Place on a Silpat and refrigerate.

For the white chocolate and cocoa butter coating

70 g white chocolate
30 g cocoa butter

- Crush the chocolate and melt.
- Add the cocoa butter and mix with a spatula until the cocoa butter is completely melted.
- Keep at 32 °C.

For the apricot palets

4 cold apricot purée jelly squares
(previously prepared)
White chocolate coating (previously prepared)

- Place the jelly in the freezer for 1 minute before coating.
- Use a spray gun to apply the coating to one side of the jelly squares.
- Return to the freezer for 1 minute, then turn them over.
- Finish coating the remaining side, then refrigerate until needed.

For the milk chocolate and passion fruit ice cream

420 g water
32 g sugar
105 g invert sugar
40 g skimmed milk powder
6 g ice cream stabiliser
200 g milk chocolate
200 g Garnier passion fruit purée

- Mix the powder ingredients in a bowl. Combine the water and sugar in a pan and heat. When the temperature reaches 40 °C, add the powdered ingredients.
- Stir constantly until the temperature rises to 85 °C.
- Pour the crushed milk chocolate over it.
- Leave to stand for 1 minute, then mix well with a whisk.
- When it is cold, add the passion fruit purée.
- Mix and then allow to stand in the refrigerator for 8 hours.
- Given the acidity and sweetness of the mixture, process the sorbet 3 hours before use to achieve the desired texture.

For the yogurt and white chocolate sauce

85 g Greek yogurt
70 g 35% fat single cream
105 g white chocolate

- Bring the cream to the boil, then pour the chopped white chocolate over it.
- Leave the mixture to stand for 30 seconds, then mix with a spatula.
- When it is cold, add the Greek yogurt and mix thoroughly.
- Fill a squeeze bottle and refrigerate.

For the feuillantine with hazelnut praline

20 g feuillantine wafer
50 g Piedmont hazelnut praline

- Mix both ingredients in a bowl and store in an airtight container in a cool, dry place.

1197

Apricot palet with milk chocolate and passion fruit ice cream

For the fresh lemon sugar

50 g sugar
Zest of ½ lemon grated with a Microplane grater
0.7 g powdered citric acid
8 g lemon juice

- Mix all the ingredients in a bowl without dissolving the sugar.
- Refrigerate.

For the glazed ginger rectangles

1 piece glazed ginger

- Cut the ginger into 4 rectangles, 10 x 2 mm.
- Store in an airtight container in a cool, dry place.

Finishing and presentation

24 fresh peppermint leaves
4 small fresh lemon verbena leaves
4 leaves fresh small-leaved basil
8 passion fruit seeds
1 g toasted saffron powder
5 g Pral yogurt powder

- Scatter 10 g of feuillantine with praline over the middle of the base of an O! LUNA deep solar plate.
- Make small mounds with 0.8 g of fresh lemon sugar at both ends of the plate.
- Arrange 3 peppermint leaves on top of each mound of lemon sugar.
- Starting at the feuillantine, trace 2 parallel lines in yogurt and white chocolate sauce towards each of the 2 mounds.
- Place the apricot palet on top of the feuillantine.
- Place the different components on top of the palet in the following order:
  - Place a glazed ginger rectangle at the centre with a fresh lemon verbena leaf on top.
  - Place on passion fruit seed in the top right-hand and lower left-hand corners.
  - Arrange 3 basil leaves on top of 1 of the seeds.
  - Place a pinch of toasted saffron powder in the lower right-hand corner.
  - Place a little yogurt powder in the top left-hand corner.
- Finish the dish by laying a quenelle of milk chocolate and passion fruit ice cream over the yogurt powder.

Cutlery

- Tapas cutlery.

  NB: Tapas cutlery consists of a 14 x 3 cm spoon and fork.

How to eat

- Alternate the components.

1198

Frozen chocolate and hazelnut praline crumbs with passion fruit caramel

Year
2005

Family
Desserts

Temperature
Frozen

Season
All year round

Serves 4

For the chocolate and hazelnut praline air base

1 kg water
400 g chocolate
50 g Piedmont hazelnut praline
5 g soya lecithin powder

- Crush the chocolate and place in a bowl.
- Add the praline and soya lecithin.
- Heat the water to 90 °C and pour it over the chocolate.
- Allow to stand for 1 minute, then process with a stick blender.
- Keep at 50 °C.

For the frozen chocolate and hazelnut praline air

Hot chocolate and hazelnut praline air base (previously prepared)
2 containers, 10 x 20 x 5 cm

- Work the stick blender over the top of the chocolate and praline mixture until it emulsifies and the air forms on top of the liquid.
- Fill the 2 containers with this air and freeze immediately.
- Leave in the freezer for 2 hours with an airtight lid to prevent the frozen air from absorbing other flavours.

For the frozen chocolate powder

80 g chocolate
30 g cocoa powder
30 g sugar
100 g 35% fat single cream
300 g water
Pacojet

- Mix the cream, water, sugar and cocoa powder and bring to the boil.
- Pour the chopped chocolate over and stir until all the ingredients are thoroughly dissolved.
- Transfer to a Pacojet beaker and freeze for 24 hours.
- Process the beaker contents with the Pacojet.
- Count 10 seconds from the moment the Pacojet blade touches the chocolate in the beaker and then stop the process so that the blade returns to its starting point.
- A frozen chocolate powder will have formed at the top of the beaker.
- Freeze for 5 minutes to stabilise the powder, then transfer to a frozen, empty bowl.
- Repeat the operation 4 times.

For the 100% syrup

50 g sugar
50 g water

- Mix both ingredients in a small pan and bring to the boil.
- Refrigerate.

For the pear-CRU wedges in coffee

1 x 120 g ripe Conference pear
60 g espresso coffee
30 g 100% syrup (previously prepared)

- Peel and halve the pear.
- Remove the core and cut into 1 cm wide vertical wedges.
- Place the pear wedges with the coffee and 100% syrup in a vacuum bag and vacuum seal to 95%.
- Refrigerate for 12 hours.

For the pieces of pear-CRU wedges in coffee

Pear-CRU wedges in coffee (previously prepared)

- Cut the pear-CRU wedges into 2 x 2 cm pieces.
- Refrigerate in an airtight container.

For the freeze-dried passion fruit caramel powder

65 g freeze-dried passion fruit powder
250 g fondant
125 g glucose
125 g Isomalt

- Mix the fondant and glucose in a pan and place over a medium heat.
- Once dissolved, add the Isomalt.
- Raise the temperature to 160 °C (the remaining 5 °C will be reached by its own heat), then allow to cool to 140 °C. Add the freeze-dried passion fruit powder and stir.
- Pour over parchment paper to a thickness of 1 cm. Leave to cool down at room temperature in a cool, dry place.
- Grind to a powder in a liquidiser.
- Store in an airtight container in a cool, dry place.

1198

Frozen chocolate and hazelnut praline crumbs with passion fruit caramel

For the toasted, broken and fried hazelnuts

30 g toasted hazelnuts
80 g olive oil
Salt

- Place the hazelnuts between 2 sheets of parchment paper and use a rolling pin to crush them lightly.
- Shake them in a sieve to remove the powder.
- Combine the broken hazelnuts with the oil in a pan from cold and place over a medium heat.
- When the hazelnuts begin to fry, watch them carefully so they do not burn.
- Drain off the oil and season with salt while still hot.
- Store in an airtight container in a cool, dry place.

For the freeze-dried passion fruit and fried hazelnut caramel scarves

Freeze-dried passion fruit caramel powder
(previously prepared)
Toasted, broken and fried hazelnuts
(previously prepared)

- Use a well-dried sieve to sprinkle the passion fruit caramel powder over a baking tray lined with a Silpat.
- Sprinkle the fried hazelnut over it and bake at 175 °C for 1 minute.
- Remove from the oven and cover with another Silpat.
- Crush with a rolling pin, then remove the top Silpat.
- Return to the oven for 30 seconds.
- Make 12 passion fruit and hazelnut scarves.
- Store in an airtight container in a cool, dry place.

For the hazelnut praline cream

85 g Piedmont hazelnut praline
110 g 35% fat single cream

- Weigh the praline in a bowl.
- Add the newly boiled cream while mixing with a spatula.
- When the cream is thoroughly mixed, leave to cool in the refrigerator.
- When cold, fill a piping bag and refrigerate.

Finishing and presentation

20 g cocoa nibs

- Place 2 spoons of frozen chocolate powder in the middle of a deep round plate.
- Arrange 4 pieces of pear-CRU in coffee on top.
- Scatter 3 cocoa nibs over the dish.
- Pipe the hazelnut praline cream over the pear pieces and the frozen chocolate powder.
- Use a spoon to scrape 5 crumbs of frozen chocolate and praline air and arrange them on top.
- Finish the dish with 3 passion fruit caramel scarves.

Cutlery

- Tapas cutlery.

  NB: Tapas cutlery consists of a 14 x 3 cm spoon and fork.

How to eat

- Eat the dish from the top down to take all the components.

1199

Des/sert

Year
2005

Family
Desserts

Temperature
Ambient/frozen

Season
All year round

Serves 4

For the light coffee meringue powder and rocks

125 g water
125 g pasteurised liquid egg white
7.5 g powdered egg white
25 g sugar
5 g instant coffee

- Mix all the ingredients together while cold and beat in the electric mixer for 5 minutes.
- Leave to stand for 2 minutes with the mixer switched off.
- Beat for 10 more minutes and spread over a baking tray lined with a Silpat to a depth of 1 cm.
- Dry in the oven at 100 °C for 1½ hours.
- When it is dry, break up into 4 x 3.5 cm diameter rocks.
- Put the rest of the meringue in a bag and crush to a powder.
- Store the meringue rocks and powder in separate airtight containers in a cool, dry place.

For the light liquorice paste meringue powder

125 g water
125 g pasteurised liquid egg white
7.5 g powdered egg white
25 g sugar
35 g liquorice paste

- Mix all the ingredients together while cold and beat in the electric mixer for 5 minutes.
- Leave to stand for 2 minutes with the mixer switched off.
- Beat for 10 more minutes, then spread over a baking tray lined with a Silpat to a thickness of 1 cm.
- Dry in the oven at 100 °C for 40 minutes.
- Raise the oven temperature to 120 °C and leave for a further 40 minutes.
- When dry, place in a bag and crush to a powder.
- Store in an airtight container in a cool, dry place.

For the caramelised cinnamon ice cream

90 g sugar
1 cinnamon stick
380 g milk
85 g cream
30 g sugar
40 g egg yolk
2 g ice cream stabiliser
26 g powdered milk
8 g dextrose
8 g invert sugar

- Make a dark caramel in a pan with the 90 g of sugar and the cinnamon stick.
- Add the hot milk and cream.
- Beat the egg yolk with the 30 g of sugar and add to the caramel mixture.
- Add the ice cream stabiliser, powdered milk, dextrose and invert sugar and raise the temperature to 85 °C.
- Strain and leave to stand in the refrigerator for 8 hours.

For the 60% syrup

30 g sugar
50 g water

- Mix both ingredients in a small pan and bring to the boil.
- Refrigerate.

For the raspberry juice

100 g raspberries
25 g sugar
25 g 60% syrup (previously prepared)

- Blend all the ingredients in a liquidiser and strain through a Superbag.
- Refrigerate.

For the cold raspberry juice jelly

85 g raspberry juice (previously prepared)
½ x 2 g gelatine leaf (previously rehydrated in cold water)

- Dissolve the gelatine in a third of the hot raspberry juice.
- Add the remaining cold juice, mix and pour into a container to a thickness of 1 cm.
- Refrigerate for 2 hours.

For the toasted spiced bread with honey

75 g spiced bread with honey

- Cut off the crust.
- Make breadcrumbs in a liquidiser.
- Spread the crumbs over a baking tray lined with a Silpat.
- Bake at 150 °C for 35 minutes.
- It should be toasted to a golden colour as a slightly bitter taste is required.
- Store in an airtight container in a cool, dry place.

1199

Des/sert

For the cinnamon sugar powder

50 g icing sugar
25 g freshly ground cinnamon stick

- Mix both ingredients and store in an airtight container in a cool, dry place.

For the kataifi pastry skein

25 g kataifi pastry
Cinnamon sugar powder (previously prepared)

- Shape 4 x 0.5 g skeins from the kataifi pastry.
- Bake at 210 °C for 5 minutes. They should turn a nice golden colour.
- Store in the container with the cinnamon sugar.

For the chocolate trees

150 g tempered chocolate
Light liquorice paste meringue powder
(previously prepared)

- Put the chocolate in a piping bag.
- Pipe 4 chocolate trees over the meringue powder.
- Cover with more meringue.
- Set aside in a cool, dry place for 1 hour.
- Transfer the trees to an airtight container and store in a cool, dry place.

Finishing and presentation

100 g Greek yogurt
8 g freeze-dried raspberry crisp

- Place 15 g of Greek yogurt at the base an O! LUNA large eclipse plate.
- Place 10 g of cold raspberry jelly next to the yogurt.
- Place 3 g of toasted spiced bread next to the jelly and yogurt.
- Sprinkle raspberry crisp over the jelly.
- Place a layer of caramelised cinnamon ice cream over the spiced bread.
- Sprinkle with liquorice meringue powder to cover the whole dish.
- Arrange a light liquorice meringue rock and a kataifi pastry skein in the middle.
- Make 3 lines of light coffee meringue powder over the liquorice powder.
- Finish by standing a chocolate tree between the kataifi pastry skein and the light coffee meringue rock.

Cutlery

- Tapas cutlery.

  NB: Tapas cutlery consists of a 14 x 3 cm spoon and fork.

How to eat

- Eat from the bottom up.

Morphings
1200–1214

1200

Pineapple/fennel

Year
2005

Family
Morphings

Temperature
Cold

Season
All year round

Serves 10

For the pineapple batons

1 x 650 g pineapple

- Slice off both ends of the pineapple and cut off the skin.
- Cut into 40 batons, 5 x 1.2 cm.
- Refrigerate.

For the pineapple infused with fennel and star anise

40 pineapple batons (previously prepared)
1 handful fresh fennel fronds
5 star anise seeds

- Wash the fennel thoroughly in cold water.
- Put the fennel and star anise in a container.
- Place the pineapple batons over the fennel and star anise, leaving space between them so that they will be completely infused with the aroma. Then cover the pineapple with another layer of fennel and star anise.
- Cover the container with an airtight lid and refrigerate for 7 hours.

Finishing and presentation

- Just before serving, open the container and separate the pineapple batons.
- Take some fennel sprigs from the container and fill 10 black bowls.
- Arrange 4 pineapple batons in each bowl so that they nestle among the fennel and do not touch one another.
- Finish by placing 3 star anise seeds between the fennel and the pineapple.
- Serve on a slate accompanied by silver tweezers.

  NB: There is another version of this dish using peach instead of pineapple and fresh lavender instead of fresh fennel.

Cutlery

- Silver tweezers.

How to eat

- Eat the pineapple batons.

1201

Spherical-I cherries with yogurt and elderflower

Year
2005

Family
Morphings

Temperature
Cold

Season
May, June, July

Serves 10

For the sodium alginate and elderflower solution 1.35 kg water 135 g Hafi elderflower concentrate 7.5 g sodium alginate	• Mix the elderflower concentrate and the sodium alginate with a stick blender until lump-free. • Add the water and blend gently until the sodium alginate is completely dissolved. • Leave it to stand in the refrigerator for 24 hours until the air bubbles disappear and the sodium alginate is completely rehydrated.
For the cherry halves with stalks 10 x 10 g cherries	• Cut each cherry in half horizontally with a paring knife. • Remove the pit. Keep the top half of each cherry with its stalk still attached. • Refrigerate.
For the sugared yogurt 150 g plain yogurt 15 g sugar	• Mix both ingredients in a bowl until the sugar dissolves. • Refrigerate.
For the elderflower mixture 500 g water 300 g Hafi elderflower concentrate	• Mix both ingredients in a container and refrigerate. • Set aside 200 g in the freezer for finishing and presentation.
For the spherical-I cherries with yogurt and elderflower 10 cherry halves with stalks 150 g sugared yogurt (previously prepared) Sodium alginate and elderflower solution (previously prepared) Elderflower mixture (previously prepared)	• Dip each cherry half into the sugared yogurt. • Drain and place in a 3 cm hemispherical measuring spoon. • Fill the spoon while covering the cherry at the same time. • Empty the contents of the spoon into the sodium alginate and elderflower solution with one hand while holding the cherry stalk with the other so that it is not immersed. • Repeat the operation with each of the cherry halves. Do not to allow the cherries to touch one another, as they may stick. • Carefully move each cherry in the sodium alginate solution every 30 minutes. • Repeat this operation 3 more times to make a total of 2 hours. • Gently drain the cherry halves and rinse well. • Store in a container with the elderflower mixture until required.
For the elderflowers 1 elderflower cluster	• Carefully separate the cluster into individual flowers. • Keep the flowers covered with a damp paper towel in the refrigerator.
Finishing and presentation	• Use a slotted spoon to arrange the cherries in 3 glass bowls. • Cover with the elderflower mixture from the freezer. • Scatter the elderflowers over the surface of the elderflower coating and the cherries. • When the diner picks up a cherry, the flowers will stick to it. NB: Different varieties of flowers can be used depending on the season.
Cutlery	• None.
How to eat	• Pick up each cherry by its stalk and eat in a single mouthful. Do not eat the stalk.

1202

Daiquiri, coffee and caramel nigiri

Year
2005

Family
Morphings

Temperature
Cold

Season
All year round

Serves 10

For the 100 % syrup

125 g water
125 g sugar

- Mix both ingredients and bring to the boil.
- Refrigerate.

For the frozen sheets of cold daiquiri jelly

95 g water
100 g lemon juice
65 g 100% syrup (previously prepared)
35 g white rum
1.7 g powdered agar-agar
1½ x 2 g gelatine leaves (previously rehydrated in cold water)
Grated zest of ½ lemon

- Dissolve the agar-agar in the water and bring to the boil while stirring constantly with a whisk.
- Add the gelatine and mix with the rest of the ingredients.
- Spread over 2 transparent sheets, 7 x 15 cm, to a 3 mm thickness and leave to set.
- Before it sets, sprinkle the grated lemon zest over the jelly.
- Leave to set at room temperature, then freeze.

For the lemon cloud

175 g water
25 g lemon juice
2¼ x 2 g gelatine leaves (previously rehydrated in cold water)
Grated zest of ¾ lemon

- Freeze two thirds of the water.
- Dissolve the gelatine in a third of the water and leave to set at room temperature.
- Place the water with the gelatine in the electric mixer and whip. When it begins to form froth, gradually add the two thirds of the water at 0 °C.
- Continue to whip for 7 minutes. When the mixture is well whipped, add the lemon juice and the grated lemon zest.
- Mix for 20 seconds, then switch off the mixer.
- Refrigerate for 2 minutes to stabilise. Make the frozen daiquiri bar immediately afterwards (following preparation).

For the frozen daiquiri bar

Frozen sheets of cold daiquiri jelly (previously prepared)
Lemon cloud (previously prepared)

- Spread the cloud over a sheet of frozen daiquiri jelly to a total thickness of 1 cm.
- Freeze.
- Cut into 4.5 x 1.7 cm bars and set aside in the freezer.

For the cold coffee jelly strips

200 g espresso coffee
100 g 100% syrup (previously prepared)
4.5 g powdered agar-agar
2¼ x 2 g gelatine leaves (previously rehydrated in cold water)

- Mix the water, base syrup, espresso coffee and powdered agar-agar in a pan.
- Bring to the boil, stirring constantly with a whisk.
- Remove from the heat and add the gelatine. Mix.
- Spread to a 1 mm thickness over a 60 x 40 cm tray.
- Refrigerate for 10 minutes.
- Then cut into 10 strips, 9.5 x 1 cm.
- Refrigerate until required.

Finishing and presentation

10 Japanese sweets

NB: We give the name 'Japanese sweets' to a tube-like confectionery that is only made in Japan during the driest months according to a secret recipe.

- Lay 10 cold espresso coffee jelly strips out on a plastic tray.
- Place 1 Japanese sweet on each one perpendicular to it.
- Place 1 daiquiri bar on top of the Japanese sweet.
- Using a small spatula, enclose the components inside the cold coffee jelly strip.
- Serve on a frozen slate.

Cutlery

- None.

How to eat

- In two mouthfuls.

1203

Yogurt and raspberry/passion fruit and liquorice/coffee and soursop *mochi*

Year
2005

Family
Morphings

Temperature
Cold

Season
All year round

Serves 10

Yogurt and raspberry *mochi*

For the *mochi* dough

NB: elBulli cannot reveal the *mochi* dough recipe because of a confidentiality agreement with Mr Sakai, who taught the chefs how to make it.

For the *mochi* discs

Mochi dough (previously prepared)
200 g potato starch

- Store the *mochi* dough at room temperature for 1 hour before rolling it out.
- Roll out the *mochi* dough between 2 sheets of parchment paper. Sprinkle potato starch over it so that it does not stick.
- Roll out to a thickness of 2 mm.
- Put in the freezer for 30 minutes.
- Cut out 10 x 11 cm *mochi* discs.
- Refrigerate the *mochi* discs in an airtight container with parchment paper between them to prevent sticking.

NB: As this dough is very elastic, care must be taken when rolling.

For the cold yogurt mousse

140 g plain yogurt
140 g Greek yogurt
120 g 35% fat single cream
60 g sugar
0.5 g citric acid
1¾ x 2 g gelatine leaves (previously rehydrated in cold water)

- Put a quarter of the plain yogurt, half of the sugar and the citric acid in a pan and heat gently.
- Dissolve the gelatine in this mixture, then add the remaining plain yogurt.
- Mix with the Greek yogurt and leave to set in the refrigerator.
- Meanwhile, semi-whip the cream with the rest of the sugar.
- When the yogurt jelly is half set, fold in the semi-whipped cream.
- When it is evenly mixed, pour the mixture into an airtight container.
- Refrigerate for 3 hours.

For the *matcha* tea syrup

25 g x 100% syrup (previously prepared)
5 g *matcha* tea

- Mix both ingredients and keep in the refrigerator.

Passion fruit and liquorice *mochi*

For the passion fruit *mochi* dough

NB: elBulli cannot reveal the *mochi* dough recipe because of a confidentiality agreement with Mr Sakai, who taught the chefs how to make it.

1203

Yogurt and raspberry/passion fruit and liquorice/coffee and soursop *mochi*

For the passion fruit *mochi* discs

Passion fruit *mochi* dough (previously prepared)
200 g potato starch

- Store the *mochi* dough at room temperature for 1 hour before rolling it out.
- Roll out the *mochi* dough between 2 sheets of parchment paper. Sprinkle potato starch over it so that it does not stick.
- Roll out to a thickness of 2 mm.
- Put in the freezer for 30 minutes.
- Cut out 10 x 11 cm *mochi* discs.
- Refrigerate the *mochi* discs in an airtight container with parchment paper between them to prevent sticking.

For the whipped cream

250 g 35% fat single cream
25 g sugar

- Combine both ingredients in the electric mixer and whip.
- Set aside in a piping bag with a No.13 nozzle.

Coffee and soursop *mochi*

For the coffee *mochi* dough

NB: elBulli cannot reveal the *mochi* dough recipe because of a confidentiality agreement with Mr Sakai, who taught the chefs how to make it.

For the coffee *mochi* discs

Coffee *mochi* dough (previously prepared)
200 g potato starch

- Store the *mochi* dough at room temperature for 1 hour before rolling it out.
- Roll out the *mochi* dough between 2 sheets of parchment paper. Sprinkle potato starch over it so that it does not stick.
- Roll out to a thickness of 2 mm.
- Put in the freezer for 30 minutes.
- Cut out 10 x 11 cm *mochi* discs.
- Refrigerate the *mochi* discs in an airtight container with parchment paper between them to prevent sticking.

NB: As this dough is very elastic, care must be taken when rolling.

For the 60% syrup

100 g sugar
60 g water

- Mix both ingredients and bring to the boil.
- Refrigerate.

For the cold soursop foam

300 g strained soursop pulp
75 g 60% syrup (previously prepared)
125 g 35% fat single cream
2 x 2 g gelatine leaves (previously rehydrated in cold water)
1 x 0.5 litre ISI siphon
1 N$_2$O cartridge

- Dissolve the gelatine in the 60% syrup in a pan.
- Add the cream and soursop pulp.
- Mix, strain and fill the siphon.
- Close it and insert the gas cartridge.
- Refrigerate for 4 hours.

NB: The soursop comes from the custard apple family and has a very similar taste and texture. elBulli uses frozen soursop pulp because its ripeness and flavour are more reliable.

1203

Yogurt and raspberry/passion fruit and liquorice/coffee and soursop *mochi*

Yogurt and raspberry *mochi*

Finishing and presentation

10 raspberries
10 rosemary flowers

- Lay out the *mochi* discs on a table.
- When they are at room temperature, put each one in a small bowl to create a better shape.
- Using a piping bag, pipe 15 g of yogurt mousse in the middle of the *mochi* disc.
- Place a fresh raspberry in the middle and pipe another 15 g more of yogurt mousse.
- Carefully close the *mochi*.
- Once you have the folded up edges in your hand, seal carefully without tearing the dough.
- Turn the *mochi* over and brush off the excess potato starch.
- Place on a square of paper.
- Using a fine brush, apply a teardrop of *matcha* tea syrup to the top of the *mochi* and put a fresh rosemary flower on top.

Cutlery

- None.

How to eat

- Hold the *mochi* with the paper and eat in two mouthfuls.

Passion fruit and liquorice *mochi*

Finishing and presentation

10 passion fruit seeds
10 fresh small-leaved basil leaves
25 g liquorice paste in a piping bag

- Lay out the *mochi* discs on a table.
- When they are at room temperature, place in a small bowl so that they obtain a better shape.
- Start to fill them: pipe 10 g of whipped cream in the middle of the *mochi* disc.
- Pipe 1 g of liquorice paste followed by 10 g more of whipped cream.
- Carefully close the *mochi*.
- Once you have the folded up edges in your hand, close carefully without tearing the dough.
- Turn the *mochi* over and brush off the excess potato starch.
- Place over a paper square.
- Finish with a passion fruit seed and a fresh basil leaf.

Cutlery

- None.

How to eat

- Hold the *mochi* with the paper and eat in two mouthfuls.

Coffee and soursop *mochi*

Finishing and presentation

30 passion fruit seeds

- Lay out the *mochi* discs on a table.
- When they are at room temperature, place in a small bowl so that they obtain a better shape.
- Start to fill them: pipe 10 g of soursop foam in the middle.
- Once you have the folded up edges in your hand, close carefully without tearing the dough.
- Turn the *mochi* over and brush off the excess potato starch.
- Place over a paper square.
- Finish with a passion fruit seed and a fresh basil leaf over each *mochi*.

Cutlery

- None.

How to eat

- Hold the *mochi* with the paper and eat in two mouthfuls.

1204

Light coffee and chocolate meringue slice

Year
2005

Family
Morphings

Temperature
Ambient

Season
All year round

Serves 10

For the light coffee meringue squares

125 g water
125 g pasteurised liquid egg white
7.5 g powdered egg white
25 g sugar
5 g instant coffee

- Mix all the ingredients together while cold and leave to stand for 5 minutes.
- Whip in the electric mixer for 5 minutes.
- Leave to stand for 2 minutes with the mixer switched off.
- Beat for 10 more minutes and spread over a baking tray lined with a Silpat to a depth of 1 cm.
- Dry in the oven at 100 °C for 1½ hours.
- Cut into 20 x 4.3 cm squares.
- Store in an airtight container in a cool, dry place.

For the chocolate and coffee ganache

90 g chocolate
85 g 35% fat single cream
10 g water
8 g instant coffee

- Crush the chocolate in a bowl.
- Mix the cream with the water and the instant coffee and heat to 90 °C.
- Pour the chocolate over it and wait for 30 seconds.
- Fold in the chocolate and mix the ganache thoroughly with a spatula.
- Set aside in a piping bag at room temperature.

Finishing and presentation

- Pipe a little ganache on a meringue square and place another square on top.
- Serve.

Cutlery

- None.

How to eat

- In two mouthfuls.

1205

Honey Filipino biscuits

Year
2005

Family
Morphings

Temperature
Cold/frozen

Season
All year round

Serves 10

For the rosemary honey water

50 g rosemary honey
Water

- Put the rosemary honey in a pan and bring to the boil.
- Add a little water, then place on the scales to weigh.
- Gradually add water until the water and honey mixture reaches 125 g.
- Refrigerate.

For the Filipino biscuits made from light rosemary honey meringue

125 g rosemary honey water (previously prepared)
125 g pasteurised liquid egg white

- Combine both cold ingredients in the electric mixer.
- Whip on a fast speed for 10 minutes.
- Fill a piping bag and attach a nozzle for making doughnuts.
- Pipe 10 meringue circles over a baking tray lined with a Silpat.
- Bake at 100 °C for 40 minutes.
- Raise the temperature to 120 °C and bake for a further 40 minutes.
- When they are done, they will have a light golden colour and the base of each Filipino biscuit will be caramelised.
- Store in an airtight container in a cool, dry place.

  NB: The biscuits will be soft when they come out of the oven, but the outside will become perfectly crisp after 15 seconds.

Finishing and presentation

Smoked rosemary honey
1 lemon
1 Microplane grater
200 g icing sugar

- Pipe rosemary honey over the biscuit.
- Sprinkle grated lemon zest over the honey.
- Dust the biscuit with icing sugar.
- Arrange on slates and serve.

Cutlery

- None.

How to eat

- In two mouthfuls so as to appreciate the texture.

1206

Chestnut *ningyo-yaki*

Year
2005

Family
Morphings

Temperature
Warm

Season
All year round

Serves 10

For the *ningyo-yaki* batter

2 x 65 g eggs
70 g sugar
1.5 g bicarbonate of soda
145 g plain flour
8 g rosemary honey
53 g water

- Mix all the ingredients together in a bowl while cold and refrigerate.

For the frozen chestnut purée and vanilla balls

200 g chestnut purée
35 g icing sugar
40 g Piedmont hazelnut praline
1 x 4 g vanilla pod

- Scrape out the pulp from inside the vanilla pod.
- Mix the 4 ingredients in a bowl.
- Fill a piping bag.
- Pipe 10 x 5 g balls over parchment paper.
- Freeze.
- When they are frozen, trim to make them as spherical as possible.

Finishing and presentation

250 g olive oil
100 g icing sugar

- Heat the oil to 180 °C.
- Coat the frozen chestnut purée balls in the *ningyo-yaki* batter.
- Fry them in the oil until they turn a nice golden colour.
- Take them out with a spider skimmer and drain the excess oil on paper towel.
- Sprinkle them with plenty of icing sugar and serve them on a slate with holes.

Cutlery

- None.

How to eat

- In a single mouthful.

1207

Passion fruit tree

Year
2005

Family
Morphings

Temperature
Ambient

Season
All year round

Serves 10

For the freeze-dried passion fruit powder

25 g freeze-dried passion fruit crisp

- Grind the passion fruit crisp into a fine powder.
- Store in an airtight container in a cool, dry place.

For the trees

3 attractive branches without leaves
3 flowerpots
1 kg Demerara sugar

- Fill the flowerpots with sugar and stick a branch in each of one so that they look like little trees without leaves.

Finishing and presentation

50 g sugar

- Put 8 g sugar into the candyfloss machine and carefully remove the resulting floss.
- Sprinkle the candyfloss with the powdered freeze-dried passion fruit crisp.
- Carefully shape into 6 cm balls.
- Put the balls onto the branches of all 3 trees, taking care not to crush them.

  NB: This morphing cannot be served if the atmospheric humidity is over 60%.

Cutlery

- None.

How to eat

- Pick the floss with your fingers without crushing it, and eat in several mouthfuls.

1208

After Eight marshmallow

Year
2005

Family
Morphings

Temperature
Cold

Season
All year round

Serves 10

For the pressed chocolate mint water

4 chocolate mint plants growing in pots
4 g ascorbic acid
1 Green Star juice extractor

- Pluck the leaves from the plants.
- Blanch the leaves in boiling water for 10 seconds.
- Chill in iced water.
- Drain them and introduce into the juice extractor.
- Strain over a container containing the ascorbic acid.
- Make 100 g of pressed mint juice.
- Refrigerate in an airtight container.

NB: We use ascorbic acid for its antioxidant properties.

For the cold chocolate mint marshmallows

100 g pressed chocolate mint water
(previously prepared)
175 g milk
4½ x 2 g gelatine leaves (previously rehydrated
in cold water)
35 g sugar

- Place 125 g milk in the freezer until it cools to 3 °C.
- Dissolve the sugar in 50 g of milk in a pan.
- Then dissolve the gelatine in the mixture.
- When it reaches a temperature of 35 °C, place in the electric mixer and whip.
- When it starts to foam, add the 125 g of milk at 3 °C.
- When it is half whipped, add the chocolate mint water at a temperature of 3 °C.
- When the mixture has formed peaks, fill a piping bag with a No. 13 nozzle and pipe 10 marshmallows over a tray lined with parchment paper.
- Refrigerate for 1 hour.

For the chocolate-sprayed cold chocolate mint marshmallows

10 cold chocolate mint marshmallows
(previously prepared)
75 g chocolate
25 g cocoa butter

- Place the marshmallows in the freezer 2 minutes before spraying so that they are very cold.
- Melt the chocolate in a microwave on medium power.
- Add the cocoa butter and let it dissolve. The mixture should be at 35 °C.
- When the mixture is lump-free and the cocoa butter is melted, fill a chocolate spray gun.
- Spray the marshmallows until coated.
- Leave them to cool, then turn the marshmallows over on to a mould that has circular dents and will keep the marshmallows upright and finish spraying them.
- Refrigerate.

Finishing and presentation

- Serve the After Eight marshmallows on frozen slates so that the chocolate coating does not melt.

Cutlery

- None.

How to eat

- In two mouthfuls.

1209

Palet-croquant: passion fruit, chocolate and hazelnut/white chocolate and macadamia nut

Year
2005

Family
Morphings

Temperature
Ambient

Season
All year round

Serves 10

Passion fruit, chocolate and hazelnut palet-croquant

For the freeze-dried passion fruit caramel powder

250 g fondant
125 g glucose
125 g Isomalt
65 g freeze-dried passion fruit powder

- Mix the fondant and glucose in a pan and place over a medium heat.
- Once the glucose is dissolved, add the Isomalt.
- Raise the temperature to 160 °C (the remaining 5 °C will be reached by its own heat), then leave to cool to 140 °C. Add the freeze-dried passion fruit powder and stir.
- Pour over parchment paper to a thickness of 1 cm. Leave to cool to room temperature in a cool, dry place.
- Grind to a powder in a liquidiser.
- Store in an airtight container in a cool, dry place.

For the chocolate gianduja

100 g melted chocolate
80 g Piedmont hazelnut praline

- Add the hazelnut praline to the melted chocolate.
- Mix until smooth.
- Set aside in a piping bag at room temperature.

For the freeze-dried passion fruit caramel powder discs

Freeze-dried passion fruit caramel powder (previously prepared)
1 x Flexipan disc mould, 35 mm diameter x 5 mm deep

- Sift the freeze-dried passion fruit caramel powder over 10 discs of the Flexipan mould.
- Heat in the oven at 170 °C for 2 minutes.
- Keep in a cool, dry place to cool for 2 minutes.

For the chocolate and hazelnut palet-croquant

Freeze-dried passion fruit caramel powder discs (previously prepared)
Piedmont hazelnut praline in a piping bag
Dark chocolate gianduja in a piping bag (previously prepared)

- Fill the centres of the passion fruit caramel discs with 1.5 g of hazelnut praline.
- Surround the praline, then cover completely with the gianduja.
- Store in a cool, dry place for 6 hours to allow the gianduja to crystallise.
- Remove from the mould and keep in an airtight container in a cool, dry place.

White chocolate and macadamia nut palet-croquant

For the yogurt caramel powder

250 g fondant
125 g glucose
125 g Isomalt
100 yogurt powder

- Mix the fondant and glucose in a pan and place over a medium heat.
- Once dissolved, add the Isomalt.
- Raise the temperature to 160 °C (the remaining 5 °C will be reached by its own heat), then allow to cool to 140 °C. Add the yogurt powder and stir.
- Pour over parchment paper to a thickness of 1 cm. Leave to cool at room temperature in a cool, dry place.
- Grind to a powder in a liquidiser.
- Store in an airtight container in a cool, dry place.

For the tempered white chocolate

200 g white chocolate

- Temper the white chocolate.
- Fill a piping bag and set aside at room temperature.

For the yogurt caramel powder discs

Yogurt caramel powder (previously prepared)
1 x Flexipan disc mould, 35 mm diameter x 5 mm deep

- Sift the yogurt caramel powder over 10 discs of the Flexipan mould.
- Heat in the oven at 170 °C for 2 minutes.
- Keep in a cool, dry place to cool for 2 minutes.

1209

Palet-croquant: passion fruit, chocolate and hazelnut/white chocolate and macadamia nut

For the white choclate and macadamia nut palet-croquant

Yogurt caramel powder discs (previously prepared)
1.5 g macadamia nut paste in a piping bag
Tempered white chocolate in a piping bag
(previously prepared)

- Fill the centre of the yogurt caramel discs with 1.5 g of macadamia nut paste.
- Then surround and cover the macadamia nut paste with the tempered white chocolate.
- Store in a cool, dry place for 6 hours to allow the white chocolate to crystallise.
- Remove from the mould and keep in an airtight container in a cool, dry place.

Finishing and presentation

For the passion fruit, chocolate and hazelnut palet-croquant

- Arrange on a black slate and serve.

For the white chocolate and macadamia nut palet-croquant

- Arrange on a black slate and serve.

Cutlery

- None.

How to eat

- In two mouthfuls.

1210

**Strawberry iced lolly
with eucalyptus Peta Zetas**

Year
2005

Family
Morphings

Temperature
Frozen/ambient

Season
**April, May, June, July,
August, September**

Serves 10

For the strained strawberry concentrate	• Strain and refrigerate.
100 g Garnier strawberry concentrate	

For the 100% syrup

50 g water
50 g sugar

- Mix both ingredients in a pan and bring to the boil.
- Refrigerate.

For the strawberry iced lolly base

120 g strawberries
25 g strained strawberry concentrate
(previously prepared)
17 g 100% syrup (previously prepared)
½ lemon

- Use a paring knife to remove the cap and stem of the strawberries.
- Combine the strawberries with the syrup and 5 drops of lemon juice in a liquidiser.
- Blend and mix with the strained strawberry concentrate.
- Strain and refrigerate.

For the strawberry iced lollies

Strawberry iced lolly base (previously prepared)
10 x 20 ml iced lolly moulds 2 cm in diameter

- Use a syringe to fill each of 10 iced lolly moulds with 15 ml of the strawberry base.
- Freeze for 15 minutes.
- Insert a skewer in each and freeze for 4 hours.
- Remove from the moulds and keep in a container in the freezer.

For the chocolate-sprayed strawberry iced lollies

150 g chocolate
50 g cocoa butter

- Melt the chocolate in a microwave.
- Add the cocoa butter and dissolve. The mixture should be at 35 °C.
- When the mixture is lump-free and the cocoa butter is totally melted, fill the chocolate spray gun.
- Spray each strawberry iced lolly one at a time with the chocolate coating.
- Store in the freezer.

Finishing and presentation

50 g neutral Peta Zetas granules
10 drops eucalyptus essential oil

- Fill each of 10 medicine spoons with 4 g of Peta Zetas.
- Position each spoon at one end of a black slate.
- Place 1 shot glass at the other end.
- Stand 1 chocolate-coated strawberry iced lolly in each shot glass.
- Finish with 1 drop of eucalyptus oil over each spoon of Peta Zetas.

Cutlery

- None.

How to eat

- Alternate the components. Leave the Peta Zetas in your mouth for a few seconds without swallowing so they produce the desired effect.

1211

Frozen truffles: raspberry/passion fruit

Year
2005

Family
Morphings

Temperature
Frozen

Season
All year round

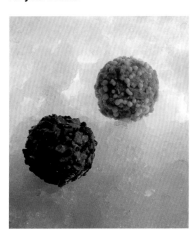

Serves 10

For the 100% syrup

50 g sugar
50 g water

- Mix the ingredients in a small pan and bring to the boil.
- Refrigerate.

For the raspberry sorbet

200 g raspberries
50 g 100% syrup (previously prepared)
1 g sorbet stabiliser
25 g glucose

- Combine the glucose and 100% syrup in a pan at a medium heat.
- When the temperature reaches 40 °C, add the powdered stabiliser and turn the heat up to 85 °C.
- At the same time, purée the raspberries in the liquidiser.
- When the base containing the stabilizer is warm, add the raspberry purée and strain.
- Mix and then allow to stand in the refrigerator for 8 hours.
- Transfer to a Pacojet beaker and freeze at -20 °C.

For the milk chocolate and passion fruit ice cream

420 g water
32 g sugar
105 g invert sugar
40 g skimmed milk powder
6 g ice cream stabiliser
200 g milk chocolate
200 g Garnier passion fruit purée

- Mix the powder ingredients in a bowl.
- Combine the water and sugar in a pan and heat. When the temperature reaches 40 °C, add the powdered ingredients.
- Stir continuously until the temperature rises to 85 °C.
- Pour the crushed milk chocolate over it.
- Allow to stand for 1 minute, then mix well with a whisk.
- When it is cold, add the passion fruit purée.
- Mix and then allow to stand in the refrigerator for 8 hours.
- Given the acidity and sweetness of the mixture, process the sorbet 3 hours before use to achieve the desired texture.

For the chocolate with cocoa butter

75 g chocolate
25 g cocoa butter

- Crush the chocolate and melt.
- Add the cocoa butter and mix with a spatula until the cocoa butter is completely melted.
- Keep at room temperature.

For the chocolate nitro-pearls

Chocolate with cocoa butter (previously prepared)
500 g liquid nitrogen

- Pour the 500 g of liquid nitrogen into the bowl for the nitrogen.
- Pipe the melted chocolate with cocoa butter into the liquid nitrogen.
- Drain the chocolate and set aside the obtained nitro-pearls.

For the white chocolate with cocoa butter

70 g white chocolate
30 g cocoa butter

- Crush the white chocolate and melt.
- Add the cocoa butter and mix with a spatula until the cocoa butter is completely melted.
- Keep at room temperature.

For the white chocolate nitro-pearls

White chocolate with cocoa butter
(previously prepared)
500 g liquid nitrogen

- Add the 500 g of liquid nitrogen into the bowl for the nitrogen.
- Pipe the melted white chocolate with cocoa butter into the liquid nitrogen.
- Drain the chocolate and set aside the obtained nitro-pearls.

For the crushed ice moulds

2 kg crushed ice
10 x 10 cm frozen slates

- Make a small mound of crushed ice on each of the slates, levelling it out to the sides of the slate.
- Make 2 wells in each mould where the frozen truffles will be placed.

1211

Frozen truffles: raspberry/ passion fruit

Finishing and presentation

20 g freeze-dried passion fruit
20 g freeze-dried raspberry crisp
1 x 5 ml melon baller
Pacojet

- Process the raspberry sorbet and the milk chocolate and passion fruit ice cream with the Pacojet.
- Make 10 x 5 ml balls of each with the melon baller and set aside in the freezer.
- Coat half of each raspberry sorbet ball with the chocolate nitro-pearls.
- Repeat the operation with the milk chocolate and passion fruit ice cream balls and the white chocolate nitro-pearls.
- Coat the other half of the raspberry sorbet balls with raspberry crisp.
- Repeat the operation with the milk chocolate and passion fruit ice cream balls and the passion fruit crisp.
- Serve 1 raspberry truffle and 1 milk chocolate and passion fruit truffle in each ice mould.

Cutlery

- None.

How to eat

- Eat each truffle in two mouthfuls.

1212

Chocolate coral

Year
2005

Family
Morphings

Temperature
Frozen

Season
All year round

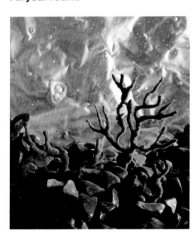

Serves 10

For the chocolate coral

500 g tempered chocolate
250 g freeze-dried raspberry powder

- Fill a piping bag with the tempered chocolate.
- Divide the freeze-dried raspberry powder into 2 airtight containers, forming mounds in each.
- Pipe chocolate over the freeze-dried raspberry powder. Try to reproduce natural coral as faithfully as possible.
- Every time you finish one, sprinkle freeze-dried raspberry powder over it so that it sticks.
- Make 5 corals with a diameter of about 7-8 cm.
- Set aside in a cool, dry place.
- After 3 hours, take out the coral without breaking them.
- Store in an airtight container in a cool, dry place.

Finishing and presentation

- Arrange some pretty stones on slates and position the corals among the stones to recreate a reef.

Cutlery

- None.

How to eat

- In several mouthfuls.

1213

Fruit crisp-LYO in chocolate

Year
2005

Family
Morphings

Temperature
Ambient

Season
All year round

Serves 10

Raspberry and chocolate

For the freeze-dried raspberry crisps with chocolate

50 freeze-dried raspberry crisps
250 g tempered chocolate

- Place the freeze-dried raspberry crisps in a bowl with the chocolate and use a long-pronged fork to remove the crisps and lay them over parchment paper.
- Make small rocks with groups of 4-5 crisps.
- Leave in a cool, dry place for 30 minutes.
- Dip each rock into the tempered chocolate with a long-pronged fork.

Passion fruit with white chocolate

For the freeze-dried raspberry crisps with chocolate

50 g freeze-dried passion fruit crisps
250 g tempered white chocolate

- Place the freeze-dried passion fruit crisps in a bowl with the white chocolate and use a long-pronged fork to remove the crisps and lay them over parchment paper.
- Make small rocks with groups of 4-5 crisps.
- Leave in a cool, dry place for 30 minutes.
- Dip each rock into the tempered chocolate with a long-pronged fork.

Finishing and presentation
- Serve in a suitable dish.

Cutlery
- None.

How to eat
- Alternate.

1214

Fruit-LYO in chocolate

Year
2005

Family
Morphings

Temperature
Frozen

Season
All year round

Serves 10

Freeze-dried raspberries dipped in chocolate

For the freeze-dried raspberries dipped in chocolate

10 freeze-dried raspberries
250 g tempered chocolate

- Dip each raspberry into the tempered chocolate with a long-pronged fork.
- Put the dipped raspberries on a sheet of parchment paper.
- Leave in a cool, dry place for 30 minutes and then repeat the operation.
- When dry, store in an airtight container.

Freeze-dried strawberry slices with white chocolate

For the yogurt sugar

60 g Pral yogurt powder
35 g dextrose
5 g powdered citric acid

- Mix all the ingredients in a bowl and store in an airtight container in a cool, dry place.

For the freeze-dried strawberry slices dipped in white chocolate and yogurt sugar

10 freeze-dried strawberry slices
Yogurt sugar (previously prepared)
250 g tempered white chocolate
Rose essential oil

- Put 50 g yogurt sugar in a container.
- Mix the tempered white chocolate with 1 drop of rose essential oil.
- Dip the strawberry slices one by one in the chocolate with a long-pronged fork and put on top of the yogurt sugar.
- Sprinkle the rest of the yogurt sugar over the dipped strawberries before the chocolate crystallises.
- Leave in a cool, dry place for 3 hours.
- Store in an airtight container in a cool, dry place.

Freeze-dried apricot chunks with white chocolate and mint

For the freeze-dried apricot chunks

2 x 75 g apricots

- Peel and halve the apricots.
- Cut each half into 3 chunks.
- Freeze on a tray lined with parchment paper.
- Put in the freeze-dryer for 48 hours.
- Once the freeze-drying process is complete, store in an airtight container in a cool, dry place.

For the dehydrated mint powder

10 fresh mint leaves

- Place in the dehydrator for 2 hours at 60 °C until completely crisp.
- Place in a bag and crush lightly by hand to produce a fine powder.
- Store in an airtight container in a cool, dry place.

1214

Fruit-LYO in chocolate

For the freeze-dried apricot chunks dipped in white chocolate

10 freeze-dried apricot chunks
(previously prepared)
400 g tempered white chocolate
Dehydrated mint powder (previously prepared)

- Dip each apricot chunk in the tempered white chocolate with a long-pronged fork.
- Put each dipped apricot chunk on a sheet of parchment paper.
- Before the chocolate crystallises, sprinkle each chunk with a little dehydrated mint powder.
- Leave in a cool, dry place for 3 hours.
- Store in an airtight container.

Freeze-dried peach chunks with milk chocolate and lemon verbena

For the freeze-dried peach chunks

2 x 180 g peaches

- Peel and halve the peaches.
- Cut each half into 4 chunks.
- Freeze on a tray lined with parchment paper.
- Place in the freeze-dryer for 48 hours.
- Once the freeze-drying process is complete, store in an airtight container in a cool, dry place.

For the dehydrated lemon verbena powder

10 leaves of fresh lemon verbena

- Put in the dehydrator for 2 hours at 60 °C until completely crisp.
- Put in a bag and crush lightly by hand to create a fine powder.
- Store in an airtight container in a cool, dry place.

For the freeze-dried peach chunks dipped in milk chocolate

10 freeze-dried peach chunks
(previously prepared)
400 g tempered milk chocolate
Dehydrated lemon verbena powder
(previously prepared)

- Dip each peach chunk in the tempered milk chocolate using a long-pronged fork.
- Put each dipped peach chunk on a sheet of parchment paper.
- Before the chocolate crystallises, sprinkle each chunk with a little dehydrated lemon verbena powder.
- Leave in a cool, dry place for 3 hours.
- Store in an airtight container.

Finishing and presentation

- Serve in a suitable dish.

Cutlery

- None.

How to eat

- In a single mouthful.

  NB: *Freeze-dried apricot chunks with white chocolate and mint* are served in June, July and August. *Freeze-dried peach chunks with milk chocolate and lemon verbena* are served in June, July, August and September.

Phaidon Press Limited
Regent's Wharf
All Saints Street
London, N1 9PA

Phaidon Press Inc.
180 Varick Street
New York, NY 10014

www.phaidon.com

First published 2014
© 2014 Phaidon Press Limited

ISBN 978 0 7148 6548 5

A CIP catalogue record for this book is available from
the British Library

Commissioning Editor: Emilia Terragni
Project Editors: Daniel Hurst and
Lucy Garcia Barreiro
Manufacturing Manager: Paul McGuinness

Designed by William Hall
Page layout by Oscar Germade,
Carles Rodrigo and Ana Minguez
Photography by Francesc Guillamet
Texts coordinated by Josep Maria Pinto

Printed in China

Notes on the recipes

All recipes serve four people unless otherwise stated.

A number of the recipes require advanced
techniques, specialist equipment and professional
experience to achieve good results.

Cooking times are for guidance only. If using a fan
(convection) oven, follow the manufacturer's
instructions concerning the oven temperatures.

Eggs are medium (US large) size, unless specified.
Some recipes include lightly cooked eggs, meat and
fish. These should be avoided by the elderly, infants,
pregnant women, convalescents and anyone with an
impaired immune system.

Exercise a very high level of caution when following
recipes involving any potentially hazardous activity,
including the use of high temperatures, open flames
and when deep-frying. In particular, when deep frying
add food carefully to avoid splashing, wear long
sleeves and never leave the pan unattended. Liquid
nitrogen is a dangerous substance and should not be
handled without training in how to use it safely.

All herbs, mosses and lichens should be thoroughly
washed before use.

Mushrooms should be wiped clean.

All spoon measurements are level.
1 teaspoon = 5ml. 1 tablespoon = 15ml.
Australian standard tablespoons are 20ml; Australian
readers are advised to use 3 teaspoons in place of 1
tablespoon.